The Terrorism Spectacle

The Terrorism Spectacle

Steven Livingston

Westview Press

BOULDER • SAN FRANCISCO • OXFORD

Copyright © 1994 by Westview Press, Inc.

Published in 1994 in the United States of America by Westview Press, Inc., 5500 Central Avenue, Boulder, Colorado 80301-2877, and in the United Kingdom by Westview Press, 36 Lonsdale Road, Summertown, Oxford OX2 7EW

Library of Congress Cataloging-in-Publication Data
Livingston, Steven.
    The terrorism spectacle / by Steven Livingston.
        p.   cm.
    Includes bibliographical references and index.
    ISBN 0-8133-8776-0 (HC)
    1. Terrorism—Political aspects.   2. Terrorism in the mass media—
United States.   3. United States—Foreign relations.   I. Title.
HV6431.L578   1993
070.4'49303625'0973—dc20   93-32042
                                                                                                      CIP

Printed and bound in the United States of America

 The paper used in this publication meets the requirements of the American National Standard for Permanence of Paper for Printed Library Materials Z39.48-1984.

10   9   8   7   6   5   4   3   2   1

To Cathy

Contents

Tables

Preface

While this is a book about terrorism, it is also intended to address other more general concerns not specific to terrorism. I am most interested in how various components of the policy process—officials and other political actors, the news media, and the public—interact. There are a number of issues besides terrorism which would make the same or similar points. They include, among others, the politics of race, poverty, crime, the war on drugs (as an example I use in chapter one suggests), and the images which have surrounded the more recent conventional wars the United States has found itself involved in.

Here are the points I wish to make in the book: First, to understand the policy process requires an awareness of how issues are first defined in public debate. This may even involve the exclusion of some issues and issue interpretations from public debate altogether. What the public takes to be important, whimsical, sad, celebratory, threatening, reassuring, and to some extent even real in the world outside of personal experience are constructs, which are usually found in news accounts and are often a part of a strategy to encourage the adoption of a particular set of policy options.

In the particular case of terrorism, I will argue that public perception of terrorism and counterterrorism has had more to do with the desired objectives of policy makers and far less to do with any clearly identified and assiduously adhered to counterterrorism policy. Sustained, though incomplete, official and media attention to terrorist violence around the world has created a public climate and public arousal, which has invited a more assertive foreign policy abroad and politically motivated investigations of political, religious, and civic groups at home. Terrorism—or at least the official view of terrorism—has invited and justified particular policy responses.

This is certainly not to say that terrorism has not been a serious problem. Quite the contrary, there has been a tragic surfeit of terrorist violence in recent years. In fact, there were far more acts of terrorism than American politicians, officials, and the news media generally recognized in the 1980s and early 1990s. In the case of the Reagan and Bush administrations, there was a limited recognition of terrorism, one based more upon consideration of the policy implications involved in any given terrorism designation.

Outline of the Book

Chapter one introduces the reader to the idea that terrorism is often understood to have a special or symbiotic relationship with the news media. Terrorists benefit from the free publicity given to them in news coverage while news organizations benefit from the drama of terrorism. A more complete understanding, I propose, must also take into account political power, which is understood as issue management and official interaction with the news media.

Chapter two reviews the Reagan and Bush administrations' counterterrorism policies toward Iraq from February 1982 to its invasion of Kuwait in August 1990. This review is based largely on interviews of several counterterrorism and Middle East policy makers in both administrations. Iraq's involvement in the sponsorship of international terrorism was excluded from consideration by the Reagan and Bush administrations in their pursuit of desired Middle East policy goals. This is merely illustrative of a more general trend.

Chapter three offers two additional examples of the administrations' failure to recognize the terrorist activities of strategic allies: the anti-Soviet rebels in Afghanistan and the UNITA rebels in Angola. News coverage of these conflicts is compared to official reports on terrorism regarding Angola and Afghanistan.

Chapter four presents a summary of the results of an extensive analysis of *New York Times* stories about political violence.

Chapter five examines features of the news media and government policy that help explain the results described in chapters three and four. The news is understood as the product of a "transactional" relationship between the mainstream news media and government officials. This relationship is itself the result of the economics of news production, news routines, and government news management techniques.

Chapter six takes this argument one step further by presenting evidence which suggests a "news repair" process occurs in instances where the credibility of official sources is seriously threatened.

Chapter seven examines the foreign policy implications of the particular terrorist-problem construction most evident in the results presented in previous chapters. The point made is really quite straightforward: The selective treatment of political violence created an environment which helped legitimize the foreign policy and defense objectives of the Reagan and Bush administrations. Chapter eight makes the same point, though this time regarding domestic policy.

Chapter nine summarizes the findings and offers concluding remarks concerning the theoretical and practical implications of those findings. Several possible solutions are also discussed.

Steven Livingston

Acknowledgments

I am very grateful for the generous contributions made to this project by so many talented people. First and foremost, I wish to thank Lance Bennett. My gratitude goes well beyond any words I might offer here. I trust that he knows this.

I also owe special thanks to several extraordinary teachers, colleagues, and friends at the University of Washington, only some of whom may be mentioned here. David Olson and Don McCrone's support over the years made this book possible. Michael McCann, Don Matthews, Ruth Horowitz, Jim Larson, Gladys Engel Lang, and Kurt Lang have been important sources of insight and inspiration from the very start of my academic career.

Glenda Pearson of the University of Washington's Suzzallo Library was an enormous help to me. Her professionalism and good cheer actually made the many days of reviewing microfilm pleasurable. (Glenda, I probably won't get the circulation Ivan Doig does, but I want you to know that my thanks to you and your staff stretches from here to Gros Ventre).

I have also benefited from stimulating discussions with many outstanding students in Seattle and Washington, D.C.: Pat Matteson, Dean Frits, Saul Kelner, and Sean Smith, to mention but a few. My colleagues at The George Washington University's National Center for Communication Studies have also been a great source of insight and encouragement. Jarol Manheim, Philip Robbins, Charles Puffenbarger, and Jean Folkerts have been particularly helpful. Rama Odeh and Ghassan Alkhoja of the Computer Information and Resource Center have been reliable sources of assistance in the completion of this book. And for his friendship and invaluable example of what it takes to do meaningful scholarship and teaching, I want to thank David Satterwhite.

Jennifer Knerr, Eric Wright, and Julie Seko of Westview Press have deftly seen the manuscript to print. Thanks also to Sandra Rush for her production assistance. Alan Henney, Maria Hartwell, William Dorman, and the anonymous reviewers who offered valuable suggestions also deserve a lot of the credit for getting the book ready for publication.

Two people deserve special recognition: Catherine Curran Livingston and Christopher Livingston. Without Cathy's encouragement, sacrifice, and patience with an all-too-often preoccupied husband, this book would never have been possible. And Christopher's love and youthful innocence have been constant reminders to me of why it is all worth it.

Responsibility for any shortcomings of this book rest with me alone. Without the counsel, support, and encouragement given to me by so many friends and colleagues, including many not mentioned here by name, this book would have never been written. I sincerely thank them all.

S.L.

1

Political Power, Violence, and the News Media

In confronting the challenge of international terrorism, the first step is to call things by their proper names, to see clearly and say plainly who the terrorists are, what goals they seek, and which governments support them.[1]
—William Casey,
Director of the Central Intelligence Agency

A central function of some public administrative agencies is the publicizing of narratives about threats remote from daily experience, for these narratives create the rationale for intelligence organizations, national police agencies, and departments of defense.[2]
—Murray Edelman,
Constructing the Political Spectacle

On one of the most extraordinary days in American political history, citizens watched the simultaneous release of U.S. embassy personnel held hostage in Iran and the inauguration of Ronald Reagan. After the 444 days of humiliation, Americans were ready to strike back at terrorists. The feeling could only intensify in the years to follow as one terrorist event after another filled the news. It is little wonder that when respondents were asked by a 1986 New York Times-CBS poll to list the most important problems facing the United States, mentions of terrorism led all other responses.[3]

The 1980s also saw a substantial increase in news coverage of terrorism. For example, between 1981 and 1985 the number of *New York Times* stories concerning terrorism increased by more than 60 percent.[4] On average, by 1986 the *Times* was running nearly four terrorism stories per day. Meanwhile, the number of American deaths and overall terrorist incidents showed more modest increases.[5]

For over two decades terrorism has been a horrible presence in the life of the nation. Yet, if we stand back for a moment and reconsider the terrorist phenomenon, interesting questions and contradictions begin to emerge. For instance, from the standpoint of cold statistics it could reasonably be argued that a great deal of public attention and anxiety has been directed at a comparatively minor problem. After all, statistically, one had a greater chance of choking to death on one's lunch than of dying in a terrorist attack.[6] According to the Department of State's Bureau of Diplomatic Security relatively few Americans have been killed in terrorist attacks. From 1973 to 1987, 447 Americans lost their lives overseas in 162 terrorist attacks.[7]

Of course, the death of a single American, much less hundreds at the hands of terrorists is unacceptable. This is no doubt the case. But these numbers also raise other questions. At a time when an average of twenty thousand lives per year were taken by handguns in the United States, when the numbers of the homeless were expanding, and when tens of thousands of innocent civilians around the world died at the hands of their own superpower-supplied armies, terrorism became one of the dominant concerns of the American news media and public.

How can this be?

The standard explanation is that terrorists are very adept at using the news media. In capturing media attention terrorists are able to generate awareness of themselves far beyond what their numbers—or the number of casualties they cause—otherwise warrants.[8] Much of the explanation of the "success" of terrorism hinges on a description of how the news media operate. Journalists are attracted to drama, and few political spectacles offer greater dramatic appeal than violence.[9] Terrorists know this and use it to their advantage. As terrorism expert Walter Laqueur remarked:

> The success of a terrorist operation depends almost entirely on the amount of publicity it receives. This is one of the main reasons for the shift from rural guerrilla to urban terror in the 1960s; for in the cities the terrorist could always count on the presence of journalists and TV cameras and consequently a large audience.[10]

Terrorism, in short, is a media spectacle calculated for specific political ends.

Generating awareness may be only the half of it. The *very existence* of terrorism is also said to be closely tied to the news media.[11] Cherif M. Bassiouni, for instance, implied this when he stated there is a "symbiotic relationship" between the news media hungry for violent drama and terrorists who desire publicity. A symbiotic relationship is one of mutual dependence for survival. Bassiouni explained his idea this way:

The correlation between the escalation of global terror-violence in the past twenty years and the innovations in media technology that facilitate rapid dissemination of information to large audiences is more than mere coincidence. In essence, this correlation illustrates the symbiotic relationship between 'terrorism' and the media: the *terrorists rely on the media to further their terror-inspiring goals, the media utilize the terrorists' acts as necessary or rewarding news items.*[12]

David E. Long made the same point in his 1990 book *The Anatomy of Terrorism*: "The media's mission to cover the news and the terrorist's ability to 'create' news have led to a symbiotic relationship between the two, one in which the media not only convey the news but help the terrorists create it."[13] Terrorist attacks, Long continued, are often "carefully planned theatrical events" which "virtually guarantee evocative, emotional treatment by the media." Brian Jenkins and Gabriel Weimann also used the metaphor of theater to explain terrorism.[14] In this view, the violent act is intended to produce effects beyond any immediate physical damage. The immediate victims of violence serve merely as attention getting devices. Terrorist violence, in this sense, is aimed at the people watching, not at the actual physical victims of the violence.

Serious political consequences are thought to result from news coverage of terrorism. Most importantly, it has been suggested that terrorist violence undermines the legitimacy of the state by creating the impression that it is failing in its essential function of providing for the security of its citizens.[15] Michael Kelly and Thomas H. Mitchell, for instance, argued that "The ultimate objective of the terrorist group is to undermine to legitimacy of established governments by revealing them to be either brutally repressive or simply incapable of maintaining order and public safety."[16] Likewise, Brazilian revolutionary Carlos Marighella stated in his *Minimanual of the Urban Guerrilla*:

The war of nerves or psychological war is an aggressive technique, based on the direct or indirect use of communication and news transmitted orally in order to demoralize the government. In psychological warfare, the government is always at a disadvantage since it imposes censorship on the mass media and winds up in a defensive position by not allowing anything against it to filter through. At this point it becomes desperate, is involved in greater contradictions and loses time and energy in an exhausting effort at control which is subject to being taken at any minute.[17]

The state is caught on the horns of a dilemma. Should it do nothing it risks looking weak and ineffective; if, on the other hand, the state reacts (or overreacts) it runs the risk of infringing on the civil liberties and democratic rights of its citizens.[18] In either instance, the state suffers a crisis of legitimacy.

This is the most serious of the alleged consequences of terrorism. Furthermore, as the quotes above indicate, it receives support from scholars and revolutionary theorists alike. The question of whether terrorism conventionally understood can lead *only* to the delegitimation of the state, including its policy initiatives, is a central concern of this book.

Before we embrace this understanding of terrorism and the news media yet once again, it would be wise to examine its assumptions. Are there alternative ways to conceptualize the relationship between terrorism, the news media, and political outcomes?

An Alternative Model

Whereas the central feature of the understanding of terrorism just outlined is the mutually beneficial relationship between terrorists and the news media, the central feature of the alternative outlined below, referred to here as the legitimation model, is the relationship between the news media and officials. The alternative conclusion is this: *The state is capable of achieving greater latitude in implementing favored but divisive foreign and domestic policies when the problem of terrorism can be delimited to key 'enemies' and their alleged agents at home and abroad.* Because the United States is a democracy, public opinion must be taken into account by policy makers, even in foreign affairs. This in turn means news management is an essential part of policy making. The place to begin sketching the outlines of the alternative model proposed here is with the difficulty experienced in reaching agreement on a generally acceptable definition of terrorism.

Definitions

One of the fundamental, though usually tacit assumptions made in the understanding of terrorism outlined in the beginning of this chapter is that terrorism is an unambiguous problem. Yet, as nearly every serious work on terrorism can attest, one of the most salient features of the debate on terrorism is the lack of agreement as to what it is. As one prominent scholar of terrorism put it: "Agreement on a definition, alas, does not exist, and there is no reason to assume that it will in the near future."[19] In 1981 Alex Schmid offered a list of 109 different definitions of terrorism provided between 1936 and 1981, and no doubt more have been produced in the time since.[20] J. Bower Bell summarized the situation by noting that there exists "no common academic consensus as to the essence of terror and no common language with which to shape a model acceptable to political scientists or social psychologists." "Terror," said Bell, "appears to be a condition known implicitly to most men, but which is somehow beyond rigorous examination.[21] Government analysts of terrorism in the State Department and the Central Intelligence Agency also acknowledge the ambiguous nature of terrorism. One analyst recently confided that "there is a lot of gray area in what I do."[22]

One of the more sincere responses to the problematic nature of terrorism's definition has been the attempt to devise typologies based upon more precise, value free language. Nearly all of these typologies are based on a ruler-ruled or rebel-regime dichotomy. Brian Crozier, for instance, attempted to distinguish "terror," violence used by insurgents, from "counter-terror," solely responsive violence used by the state and its security forces against the anti-state forces.[23] Though commonly used, such a dichotomy is overly simplistic for, as Thomas Perry Thornton noted of Crozier's early work, "It is by no means inevitable that the insurgents will initiate terrorism; in some instances, they may be reacting to the terror of the incumbent's."[24] His solution was to attempt to distinguish "enforcement terror" from "agitational terror." In the same way, W. F. May referred to "regime of terror" versus "siege of terror," Edward Herman referred to "wholesale terror" versus "retail terror," and Richard Falk referred to "functionary" terror and "revolutionary" terror.[25]

Though Thornton, May, and Falk, respectively, were more even-handed than Crozier in their conceptualizations of terrorism—recognizing as they did that the term may just as well be applied to state agents as to insurgents—gross categorizations such as these have also been criticized for lacking the precision necessary for "more sophisticated conceptual analyses."[26] Paul Wilkinson's highly regarded theoretical work, with refinements by Grant Wardlaw, have sought even greater precision in terms.

Wilkinson distinguishes between four major types of terrorism, criminal, psychic, war, and political. Political terrorism is subdivided into revolutionary, sub-revolutionary, and repressive terrorism. Revolutionary terrorism itself has seven further sub-types; sub-revolutionary is further divided into "Vengeance, assassination, dynastic assassination, 'sultanism', and several others; and repressive has subdivisions such as "Systems of state terror, colonial terror, police terror, martial terror, . . . prison and prison-camp terror, ideological and thought terror, and counter-insurgency terror."[27]

These attempts to clarify and distinguish terrorism from other types of violence become bogged-down in their own complexity. Wilkinson, for example, failed to adequately specify the boundaries between each of his major subtypes of political terrorism. How are we to distinguish sub-revolutionary from revolutionary terrorism? Even major types are not clearly distinguished, such as is the case with war versus political terrorism.[28] Such an unwieldy and complex array of terrorism types and sub-types is not likely to offer much assistance in our effort to gain a better understanding of terrorism. In fact it is likely to be a hindrance.

To a large extent, this good-faith effort to bridge the gap between language and violent practices account for the volume and range of definitions of terrorism formulated over the years. Yet greater specificity alone will not overcome the difficulties surrounding terrorism's definition. *The fundamental problem is found in the relationship between political language and values.* Use of the term implies a moral judgment. As Jenkins has pointed out, if one party can successfully attach the label 'terrorist' to its opponent, then it has indirectly persuaded others to adopt its moral viewpoint. Terrorism is, after all, what the bad guys do. More precise definitions alone cannot distinguish "terrorism," on the one hand, from the "heroic struggle of freedom fighters" on the other. Nor can a more refined definition distinguish between "enforcement terrorism" and the legitimate exercise of police power to insure public safety and law enforcement. The problem of defining terrorism may not necessarily rest with a failing of words but rather in a failing of will.

Yet, despite the ambiguity, news accounts commonly refer to "terrorist" violence, as do government reports. In the face of terrorism's definitional ambiguity, on the one hand, and its deep, mordacious emotional and moral meaning on the other, what are the patterns of use in the news media of the "terrorism" and "terrorist" labels and what seems to account for those patterns? What, for instance, separates the "terrorism" of the Irish Republican Army from the "freedom fighting" of the UNITA[29] guerrillas in Angola or the Mujahideen in Afghanistan? *These are political judgments influenced by the exercise of power, understood as the ability to define issue and issue content.*

Rather than attempting to plow through the conceptual ambiguity with yet another definition of terrorism, we will focus much of our attention on the ambiguity itself—and its political uses. It is not even necessary to generate another definition. The State Department's is quite acceptable: "Terrorism is premeditated, politically motivated violence perpetrated against noncombatant targets by subnational groups or clandestine state agents, usually intended to influence an audience."[30] The key is with this definition's application to the world.

The fundamental point of this book is that in the case of terrorism, ambiguity is resolved by officials interacting with the news media in ways which encourage the adoption or continued implementation of foreign and domestic policies, policies which fall under the general heading of "counterterrorism." What makes the study of terrorism interesting are the myriad policy implications which result from particular understandings of, to use Director Casey's words, "who the terrorists are, what goals they seek, and which governments support them."

Understood in this way, the analysis of terrorism and the news media can be appropriately placed in the context of a more far reaching debate regarding media-state relations and issue formation. This debate centers on an understanding of political power and the news media.

Social Problems and Political Power

A growing number of scholars have come to regard political power as the ability to concentrate public attention and anxiety on some issues and issue definitions or, conversely, draw public attention away from other issues and definitions. In approaching the study of politics and issues in this way, the relevant questions of political inquiry do not concern influence over decisions made in public councils but rather influence over the range and type of issues to be included on the public agenda in the first place.[31] Power is the ability to define and limit the questions to be asked, not just the ability to influence decisions.

Different kinds of questions are encouraged by this perspective. Working within the premise that social problems arise naturally, one might ask questions such as: How are we to respond to this problem? or: Who is likely to influence this decision? If, on the other hand, we assume issues of public concern are political constructs ultimately used for political purposes, we are led to questions such as: How did this particular issue become the focus of public concern at this time? or: Why has another issue—or underlying condition—failed to become a problem? Furthermore, why has the issue been framed in the particular way it has? What alternatives have been excluded? Political power, in short, is the ability to define the content of the issue agenda in the first place. This idea can be illustrated with a brief discussion of the problem of drug abuse and the "war on drugs."

The War on Drugs

While statistics from the U.S. Department of Health and Human Services indicate a complex array of trends regarding drug use in the United States, the overall indication is that at the time Ronald and Nancy Reagan began to promote it as a problem—just prior to the 1986 congressional elections—drug abuse was actually on the decline in the United States.[32] Of course, public anxiety over drug abuse, at any level, is understandable. But what is more puzzling, and for our purposes here more interesting, is how drug abuse and the "war on drugs" was defined in the first place.

Underplayed or excluded from the category were relatively acceptable drug addictions, such as the addiction to a poisonous alkaloid often used as an insecticide. Nicotine is responsible for an estimated 480,000 cancer deaths per year in the United States alone. This statistic does not include other smoking related deaths, such as death due to premature birth or low birth weight of full-term babies born to mothers who smoked during pregnancy. Though comprehensive annual statistics on cocaine-related deaths are not available, according to 1987 testimony given by former U.S. Surgeon General, Dr. C. Evert Koop, during the previous year approximately two thousand people died from cocaine use, or about 4 percent of the tobacco related deaths.[33]

Thinking of nicotine as a lethal addictive drug grown by American farmers as a major cash crop—much as coca leaves are in other nations—also places international drug trafficking in a different light. While we hear quite a lot about the Medellin drug cartel, far less is heard about the international trafficking of nicotine, particularly by Americans to Asian markets. The drug lords of this trade are known by the names R.J. Reynolds, Phillip Morris, Brown & Williamson, and British-American Tobacco. The governments which facilitate and share in the complicity of this drug trade are not Panamanian dictators or corrupt Colombian governments but the United States and British governments. As one commentator has remarked, "(C)igarette manufacturers won powerful U.S. Government backing in their fight for new markets. The threat of U.S. trade retaliation enabled U.S. and British cigarette manufacturers to enter the previously untapped monopoly markets of Japan, South Korea and Taiwan."[34] In 1992, the Agriculture Department awarded millions of dollars in grants to tobacco farmers in an effort to promote export of agricultural products overseas. For example, the Tobacco Associates, an association of tobacco farmers, was given $3.36 million by the Agriculture Department to promote cigarette sales to Turkey, Taiwan, South Korea, and other nations.[35]

The levels of overseas addiction and profit are staggering. Japan annually imports 300 billion American cigarettes worth $23 billion in sales. Of the male population in Japan, 61 percent smoke and are presumably addicted to nicotine. Furthermore, as with cocaine in the United States, young people are particularly vulnerable targets. About 90 percent of the Japanese who take-up the habit for the first time are adolescents.

But the brightest glow in the eyes of the American cigarette cartel is China where 1.5 trillion cigarettes, 30 percent of world consumption, go up in smoke each year. In an earlier era the British sent their fleets to keep China open for the opium trade. In the 1990s the marketing strategies for addictive substances to China are a bit more subtle. In the face of Chinese import restrictions, R. J. Reynolds began manufacturing cigarettes in China for its domestic market. As one tobacco executive put it, "Even a 1 percent share of that market would be something worth having."[36]

Also de-emphasized in the war on drugs is the addiction to a solvent used in a variety of ways, including as a thinner for varnishes, stains, and in antifreeze for automobiles. This solvent is ethanol, more commonly referred to by its generic label, alcohol. Among the health problems associated with ethanol abuse are brain and heart disease, gastritis, pancreatitis, depression of the immune system, nervous disorders, cirrhosis of the liver, and malnutrition. Fetal Alcohol Syndrome is also a leading cause of mental retardation.

The National Council on Alcoholism estimates that there are 10 million alcoholics in the United States and that at least 100,000 persons a year die from alcohol related disease or accidents. Furthermore, measured in terms of medical treatment and productivity losses to industry, alcoholism costs the United States $118 billion annually.[37] By 1990, at the on-set of an economic recession, alcohol abuse cost American society $136 billion. Yet the drugs safe for politicians and most news media to treat as a major problem were limited to cocaine, marijuana, and other less widely used substances.

The relative malleability of the drug problem becomes even more apparent when we consider that the particular drug or substance treated as a social problem changes with shifting ideologies and historical circumstances. During Prohibition in the United States, for instance, the use of alcohol was treated in ways similar to the use of other drugs today. In 1919, the Anti-Saloon League, the National Prohibition Party and the Women's Christian Temperance Union succeeded in pushing through the Eighteenth Amendment to the Constitution. As a result, some 200,000 saloons were destroyed and contraband alcohol confiscated and destroyed. While alcohol is no longer a prohibited substance, there is evidence that the use of nicotine in the United States has begun to be regarded as a problem, with subsequent restrictions on public use.[38]

The point here is not about drug abuse, per se. Rather the point is simply this: *What is considered a problem is in some measure malleable and the product of politics.* Social and political problems are not fixed and immutable but rather reflect the ideology and distribution of power at a given point and time. This is likely to be all the more true with a concept as poorly defined as terrorism.

A number of scholars have contributed to the development of this way of thinking about politics and issues. E.E. Schattschneider argued that political organizations develop a "mobilization of bias . . . in favor of exploitation of certain kinds of conflict and the suppression of others. . . . Some issues are organized into politics," said Schattschneider, "while others are organized out."[39] Likewise, Roger W. Cobb and Charles Elder argued that "pre-political" or "pre-decisional" processes often play the most critical role in "determining what issues and alternatives are to be considered by the polity and the probable (policy) choices that will be made."[40]

Simply put, power is the control of information and access to the channels of mass communication.[41] This notion recently received support from a series of experiments by Shanto Iyengar and Donald Kinder. They found that television news content had the capacity to influence what viewers regarded as important and pressing issues.[42]

Political power as issue management manifests itself in two ways: First, it is the ability to *exclude* issues from public attention and concern. Power is exercised when

> 'A' devotes his energies to creating or reinforcing social and political values and institutional practices that delimit the scope of the political process to public consideration of only those issues which are compara- tively innocuous to 'A'. [43]

In other instances, issues which are comparatively innocuous or even beneficial to 'A' are *given greater emphasis*, even becoming the objects of melodrama. In such instances, the public may be flooded with informa- tion by what might be referred to as "issue entrepreneurs." An issue entrepreneur is a group, administrative agency, or individual political actor—simply referred to above as 'A'—who encourages the adoption of a particular issue or issue definition rather than some other one. In doing so the entrepreneur distinguishes the problem's "causes," what the appropriate measures are for its resolution and who the relevant actors are in seeking solutions. The objective is the legitimation of a certain set of policies and actors. Who the entrepreneurs are is likely to vary with the issue. Yet as Edelman notes: "A central function of some public administrative agencies is the publicizing of narratives about threats remote from daily experience, for these narratives create the rationale for intelligence organizations, national police agencies, and departments of defense."[44]

With national security concerns, the primary issue entrepreneur is the executive branch of the national government. In the specific case of terrorism, the issue entrepreneurs are found in the Office of Counter-terrorism, Office of Public Diplomacy, and the Office of Diplomatic Security, all found in the State Department. The Central Intelligence Agency and the executive branch more generally are also involved in the creation of the terrorism spectacle. Various "think tanks," such as the Heritage Foundation, Hoover Institute, and Jonathan Institute, have also been involved in the defining of the terrorist threat in the 1980s and 90s. Finally, support also comes from key members of Congress, academia, and the press.[45]

The Policy Consequences of Power

How a problem is understood, how it is defined, noted Edelman, "involves alternative scenarios, each with its own facts, value judgments, and emotions." Human relations, identities, responsibilities, and *"what is necessary,"* are all established in the definition process.[46] This is what makes the analysis of power important. A particular problem definition redounds with practical political consequences for leaders in several ways:

1. *Simplification of the environment.* By focusing on specific problem origins other possible explanations and solutions are eliminated. Much of the ambiguity and complexity that is often endemic to politics is removed. Clarification such as this is evident in the annual reports on terrorism described in chapter four.
2. *Matching problem definitions to desired solutions.* Constructions or definitions of problems do not necessarily precede solutions.[47] Rather, problems are often constructed in ways which meet the requirements of desired solutions. Former Secretary of State Dean Rusk once commented that staff memoranda in government are often written backward. "Many, many times those who wrote such staff memoranda started with (recommendations) and then wrote the memorandum backwards. Sometimes the most strenuous arguments occurred over how to state the problem to fit what had already been written."[48]

   The task before those who favor some set of acts or policies over others, such as a more militaristic foreign policy, is to cast about for a widely feared problem which is then attached to the favored solution. I will argue in this book that at least two general policy areas benefited from the terrorism spectacle as constructed in the 1980s: The first was a foreign policy free of the legacy of Vietnam—an American public reluctant to see the United States involved in another war in the Third World; the second was to give the intelligence community freer rein in the conduct of domestic intelligence gathering. "Goals (such as overcoming the Vietnam syndrome) are carrots and problems are sticks; both are inducements to support measures people might otherwise find painful, unwise, or irrelevant to their lives."[49]

3. *Investment of authority.* Particular problem definitions invest authority in some and a variety of subordinate roles to others. "When we name and classify a problem, we unconsciously establish the status and roles of those involved with it, including their self-conceptions."[50] To treat drug addiction, for example, as criminal behavior invests authority in the police and judicial system. On the other hand, when treated as a disease, more common in the politically sensitive cases of alcohol and nicotine addiction, authority is invested in health care professionals. A third option, one not often raised, would be to understand drug addiction as a consequence of the social and economic conditions found in America's cities—that is, to treat it as systemic failure, not individual criminal pathology. To do so would be to encourage the investment of authority in social and economic reformers and not in law enforcement and judicial authorities.

The same can be said of other endemic conditions. To regard terrorism as apolitical criminality or psychopathology, and not as a political act in response to grievances, establishes the authority of the military over the diplomat and the counterterrorism unit over the relief agency. Likewise, to single out an airstrike from a continuing series of violence and label it "counterterrorism" is to assign moral justification to this violence and deny it to the initial violence. In this way problem definitions simultaneously define relative status of political groups and individuals.

Enemy threats to security such as these are perhaps most significant. Security is the primal political symbol, for threats "engage people intensely in news of public affairs."[51] This is evident with terrorism. It does not matter that relatively few Americans die at the hands of insurgent terrorists for

> enemies need not do or (or even) threaten harm. Instead, *the uses of all such terms in specific situations are strategies, deliberate or unrecognized, for strengthening or undermining support for specific courses of action and for particular ideologies.*[52]

If particular problem definitions serve to rationalize and justify desired solutions, images of enemies serve to focus anxiety on a single dreaded object. To facilitate hate and exterminationist tendencies, enemies are often dehumanized: To the Nazi the Jew was a rat. To the American during World War II the Japanese were often depicted as monkeys. When the commandant of Treblinka, Franz Stangl, was asked why such extraordinary measures were taken to humiliate and dehumanize the Jews before they were killed, he replied, "To condition those who actually had to carry out the policies. To make it possible for them to do what they did."[53]

Summary

The legitimation model presented above understands political power as the management of information and public dialog regarding issues and issue definitions. As we will discuss in chapter five, this usually takes the form of news content management. As Jarol B. Manheim has remarked: "The key to understanding why strategic political communication," his term for power-laden issue agenda management, "works so effectively is to realize that words and pictures generate images that do shape popular perceptions of reality. That is why politicians and others are able to use them to create and exercise political power."[54]

In the chapters to follow I will argue that what is understood as terrorism in the mainstream American press is largely, though certainly not entirely, a reflection of official exercise of political power. I will argue that terrorism in and of itself was not taken very seriously by the Reagan and Bush administrations. Both tended to exclude from consideration the terrorism conducted or supported by strategic allies. What was regarded as "terrorism" often had more to do with the geopolitical calculations of the moment and far less to do with any assiduously followed conceptualization of terrorism.

Here, then, are the questions we will seek to eventually address in the examination of terrorism and the news media to follow:

1. Which violence was regarded by the Reagan and Bush administrations and the news media as terrorism? (Chapters two, three, and four.)
2. What features of news media operation account for these findings? (Chapter five.)
3. What were the political consequences of the particular understanding of terrorism most evident in the news and official documents? (Chapters seven and eight.)

We will begin to address these questions with a review of U.S. policy responses to Iraqi sponsorship of terrorism throughout the 1980s. The point here is that the fight against terrorism, at best, was half-hearted, a mere secondary concern to the Reagan and Bush administrations. In chapters to follow I will show that the same could be said regarding the administrations' view of terrorism in other parts of the world. The primary purpose of these reviews goes back to the questions raised above: If U.S. counterterrorism policy was, as I will suggest, only half-hearted and not seriously pursued, *what were the purposes of all the attention paid to terrorism and counterterrorism by these two administrations?* These questions will be addressed in the second half of the book.

Notes

1. William Casey in Uri Ra'anan, Robert L. Pfaltzgraff, Jr., Richard H. Shultz, Ernst Halprin, and Igor Lukes, eds., *Hydra of Carnage: the International Linkages of Terrorism and Other Low-Intensity Operations* (Lexington, Mass.: Lexington Books, 1986), p. 5.

2. Murray Edelman, *Constructing the Political Spectacle* (Chicago: University of Chicago Press, 1989), p. 30.

3. Unsigned, "Terror Issue Cited in Poll," *The New York Times*, April 12, 1986, p. A4. Twenty-one percent of the respondents listed terrorism as the number one problem facing the United States. The next most frequently listed response was the economy at 11 percent.

4. *The New York Times* foreign desk stories regarding terrorism stood at 878 in 1981 and held steady for the next three years. By 1985 the number of such stories passed the one-thousand mark (1,054) for the first time. *The Times* published 1,416 stories in some way about terrorism in 1986.

5. Eight Americans died in terrorist attacks in 1981, while nine more died in the next year. In 1983 the figure rose precipitously to 271. Subsequent years saw a high of 41 American deaths in 1985 and a low of seven deaths in 1987 (*Lethal Terrorist Actions Against Americans: 1973-1986*, Bureau of Diplomatic Security, U.S. Department of State, 1987).

6. Barbara Ehrenreich and Todd Gitlin, "Panic Gluttons," *The Washington Post*, March 7, 1993, p. C1.

7. This figure was obtained by adding the deaths reported in the State Department's annual terrorism reports for 1987 to 1991 to the totals reported between 1973 and 1986 in *Lethal Terrorist Actions Against Americans: 1973-1986* issued by the Bureau of Diplomatic Security in 1987. The downing of Pan Am flight 103 caused the totals to skyrocket for 1988. Casualty totals have decrease to low levels in subsequent years.

8. According to this understanding of terrorism, several objectives are achieved by the terrorists in gaining publicity. Coverage, for instance, may enhance the "power image" of what is otherwise a small and relatively weak and unpopular group. This would result from what Lazarsfeld and Merton call

"the status conferral function" of the media: "The audience of mass media apparently subscribe to the circular belief that if you really matter, you will be the focus of mass attention and if you are the focus then surely you really matter" ("Mass Communication, Popular Taste and Organized Social Action." In Lyman Bryson [ed.] *The Communication of Ideas*, 1948, p. 95-118). Krattenmaker and Powe remark that since the mass media have the capability to "confer status upon an individual or an event merely by presenting them," the prospect of media exposure is an irresistible lure to terrorists ("Television Violence: First Amendment Principles and Social Science Theory," Virginia Law Review 64 [1978], p. 1123-1134).

An alternative hypothesis holds that exposure to media violence has just the opposite effect, that is, media coverage of violence has a cathartic effect on potentially violent persons. If the purpose of terrorism is to generate publicity, then media coverage of some event or social grievance may actually dampen other's motivations to violence (Cherif M. Bassiouni, "Problems of Media Coverage of Nonstate-Sponsored Terror-Violence Incidents" in L. Z. Freedman and Y. Alexander, eds., *Perspectives on Terrorism* [Wilmington, DE.: Scholarly Resources, 1983], p. 186).

9. On the idea that the news media is attracted to drama see Herbert Gans, *Deciding What's News: A Case Study of CBS Evening News, NBC Nightly News, Newsweek and Time* (New York: Vintage, 1979); David L. Paletz and Robert M. Entman, *Media Power Politics* (Lexington, Mass.: Heath, 1981); W. Lance Bennett, *News: The Politics of Illusion* (New York: Longman Press, Second Edition, 1988).

10. Walter Laqueur, *Terrorism* (Boston-Toronto: Little, Brown and Company, 1977), p. 109.

11. See also Dan D. Nimmorg and James E. Combs, *Nightly Horrors: Crisis Coverage by Television Network News* (Knoxville, TN.: University of Tennessee Press, 1985); Alex P. Schmid and Janny F. A. De Graaf, *Insurgent Terrorism and the Western News Media: An Exploratory Analysis with a Dutch Case Study* (Leiden: 1980); Yonah Alexander, "Terrorism and the Media in the Middle East," in Yonah Alexander and S. M. Finger, eds., *Terrorism: Interdisciplinary Perspectives* (New York: John Jay Press, 1977), pp. 166-208; Yonah Alexander, "Communications Aspects of International terrorism," *International Problems* 16 Spring 1977, pp. 55-60; Yonah Alexander, "Terrorism, the Media and the Police," *Journal of International Affairs*, 32:1, 1978, pp. 101-113; Yonah Alexander, "Terrorism and the Media: Some Considerations," in Y. Alexander, D. Carlton and P. Wilkinson, eds., *Terrorism: Theory and Practice* (Boulder, CO.: Westview Press, 1979), pp. 159-174; Yonah Alexander, "Terrorism and the Mass Media" in D. Carlton and C. Schaerf, eds., *Contemporary Terrorism* (London: Macmillan, 1981) pp. 50-65; J. Bower Bell, "Terrorist Scripts and Live-Action Spectaculars," *Columbia Journalism Review*, Vol. 17, May 1978, pp. 47-50; Lord Chalfont, "Political Violence and the Role of the Media: Some Perspectives," *Political Communication and Persuasion*, Vol. 1:1, 1980, pp. 79-99; Robert Cox, "Comments: The Media as a Weapon," *Political Communication and Persuasion*, Vol. 1:3, 1981, pp. 297-300; Russell F. Farnen, "Terrorism and the Mass Media: A Systemic Analysis of a Symbiotic Process," *Terrorism*, Vol. 13, pp. 99-143; George Gerbner, *Symbolic*

Functions of Violence and Terror (Boston: Terrorism and the News Media Research Project, Emerson College, July 1988); John L. Martin, "The Media's Role in International Terrorism," *Terrorism*, Vol. 8:2, 1985, pp. 127-146; John O'Sullivan, "Media Publicity Causes Terrorism," in *Terrorism*, David L. Bender and Bruno Leone, eds. (St. Paul, Minn.: Greenhaven Press, 1986), pp. 68-74.

12. Bassiouni, "Problems of Media Coverage of Nonstate-Sponsored Terror-Violence Incidents," pp. 177-200.

13. David E. Long, *The Anatomy of Terrorism* (New York: Maxwell Macmillian International, 1990), p. 119.

14. Brian M. Jenkins, "International Terrorism: Trends and Potentialities," *Journal of International Affairs*, Vol 1, No. 1, 1978; Brian M. Jenkins, *The Study of Terrorism: Definitional Problems*, RAND P-6563 (Santa Monica, CA.: RAND Corporation, 1980); Brian M. Jenkins, "The Study of Terrorism: Definitional Problems" in *Behavioral and Quantitative Perspectives on Terrorism*, Yonah Alexander and John M. Gleason, eds. (New York: Pergamon Press, 1981). Jonathon Institute, International Terrorism: The Soviet Connection (Jerusalem: Jonathon Institute, 1979). Gabriel Weimann, "The Theater of Terror: Effects of Press Coverage," *Journal of Communication*, Winter 1983, pp. 38-45.

15. The term "state" will be used in this book interchangeably with "officials" or "government officials." I recognize that this leads to important questions regarding how one thinks of "the state." There is not, I would argue, a single state entity. Rather the state is comprised of hundreds, thousands of officials and agencies, none of whom are necessarily in agreement regarding policy objectives. As Entman (1990) notes, the degree of consensus amongst these officials is of direct relevance to the boundaries of debate. The greater the consensus, the more restricted will be the debate, as reflected in news coverage. In foreign affairs coverage, the bounds of legitimate, official dominated debate are usually quite narrow. This will be discussed more in chapter five.

16. Michael J. Kelly and Thomas H. Mitchell, "Transnational Terrorism and the Western Elite Press," *Political Communication and Persuasion*, 1:3, 1981, p. 271.

17. Carlos Marighella, *Minimanual of the Urban Guerrilla*, (Chapel Hill, N.C.: Documentary Publications, 1985), unpaginated.

18. For a highly regarded presentation of this dilemma, see Paul Wilkinson, *Terrorism and the Liberal State* (London: Macmillian, 1977).

19, Walter Laqueur, "Reflections on Terrorism," *Foreign Affairs*, Fall 1986, p. 88.

20. Alex Peter Schmid and A. J. Jongman, *Political Terrorism: A Research Guide to Concepts, Theories, Data Bases and Literature*, 2nd ed. (Amsterdam: SWIDOC, 1986).

21. J. Bower Bell, *Transnational Terror*. AEI-Hoover Institute Studies, No, 51 (Stanford, CA.: Hoover Institute Press, 1975).

22. Interview in April 1992 with author at the State Department. This State Department official requested anonymity.

23. Brian Crozier, *The Rebels: A Study of Post-war Insurrections* (Boston: Beacon Press, 1960).

24. Thomas Perry Thornton, "Terror as a Weapon of Political Agitation" in

Internal War: Problems and Approaches, Harry Eckstein, ed. (New York: Free Press of Glencoe, 1964). p. 71.

25. W.F. May, "Terrorism as strategy and Ecstasy," *Social Research* 41, 1974, pp. 277-98; Richard Falk, *Revolutionaries and Functionaries: The Dual Faces of Terrorism* (New York: E. P. Dutton, 1988).

26. Grant Wardlaw, *Political Terrorism: Theory, Tactics, and Countermeasures* (New York: Cambridge University Press, 1982), p. 12.

27. Wilkinson, *Terrorism and the Liberal State*, p. 43.

28. Wardlaw, *Political Terrorism*, p. 13.

29. Union for the Total Independence of Angola.

30. *Patterns of Global Terrorism: 1986.* The same general definition has appeared in recent additions of this annual report. International terrorism has been usually defined by the State Department simply as terrorism (see definition) "involving the citizens or territory of more than one country."

31. Murray Edelman, *Political Language: Words that Succeed and Policies that Fail* (New York: Academic Press, 1977; Murray Edelman, *Constructing the Political Spectacle* (Chicago: The University of Chicago Press, 1988); Roger W. Cobb and Charles Elder, *Participation in American Politics* (Baltimore: Johns Hopkins University Press, 1972).

32. Telephone interview, National Institute of Health, Information Clearing House Press Office, October 20, 1988; see also *National Institute on Drug Abuse Statistics Series: Annual Data, 1987*, Series 1, #7.

33. Alexander Cockburn, "Getting Opium to the Masses: The Political Economy of Addition," *The Nation*, October 30, 1989, p. 482.

34. Carl Goldstein, "Drags to Riches," Far *Eastern Economic Review*, March 29, 1990, p. 62. Section 301 of the revised 1974 Trade Act permits the government of the United States to take punitive action against any nation it considers to be "unfair" or "discriminatory" in its trading practices.

35. Unsigned, "On Both Sides of the Leaf: U.S. Condemns Tobacco, Subsidizes Sales," *The Washington Post*, June 4, 1992.

36. Goldstein, "Drags to Riches," p. 63.

37. Telephone interview, National Council on Alcoholism, Washington, D.C., October 24, 1988.

38. In Singapore, even the considerable malleability of the drug problem was strained in 1992 when, according to *The Washington Post*, authorities "adopted the language of drug trafficking . . . to describe offenses related to gum pushing" (William Branigin, "No Chew Ways About It: Singapore's Ban on Gum a Sticky Subject," *The Washington Post*, February 4, 1992, p. D1.). Following the official ban on chewing gum in Singapore, fines for the sale of this substance ranged as high as $1,250. Travelers carrying even a few sticks of gum into Singapore, even for solely personal consumption, resulted in fines of $6, 250 or imprisonment for up to one year for first time offenders. Subsequent convictions resulted in fines of $12,500 and/or two years in prison.

39. E.E. Schattschneider, *The Semisoveign People* (Hinsdale, Illinois: The Dryden Press, 1960,) p. 30.

40. Roger W. Cobb and Charles Elder, *Participation in American Politics*

(Baltimore: Johns Hopkins University Press, 1972), p. 12. See also Peter Bachrach and Morton Baratz, "Decisions and Nondecisions: An Analytical Framework," *American Political Science Review* 57, 1963, pp. 632-42; Peter Bachrach, *The Theory of Democratic Elitism: A Critique* (London: University of London Press, 1969); John Gaventa, *Power and Powerlessness: Quiescence and Rebellion in an Appalachian Valley* (Urbana: University of Illinois Press, 1980); Lester Salamon and Stephan Van Evera, "Fear, Apathy and Discrimination: A Test of Three Explanations of Political Participation," *American Political Science Review*, 67, 1973, pp. 1288-1306.

41. Steven Lukes, *Power: A Radical View* (Macmillian, London, 1974), p. 23.

42. Shanto Iyengar and Donald R. Kinder, *News That Matters: Television and American Opinion* (Chicago: University of Chicago, 1987).

43. Bachrach and Baratz, "Decisions and Nondecisions," p. 948. Steven Lukes has taken this one step further by offering what he described as a "third dimension" to political power (Lukes, 1974). Gaventa in *Power and Powerlessness* summarizes Luke's point this way: "Not only might 'A' exercise power over 'B' by prevailing in the resolution of key issues (power dimension one) or by preventing 'B' from effectively raising those issues, (power dimension two) but also through affecting 'B's' concepts of the issues altogether (the third dimension of power)" (Lukes, *Power*, p. 15). In this sense, the means of power rest in the capacity to influence or otherwise determine B's conception of what is necessary, possible, or even desirable. The analysis of power so conceived would involve the study of political mythology, language and symbols, including how they are shaped or manipulated in power processes. Gaventa summarized the dynamics of power conceptualized in this way:

> It may involve, in short, locating the power process behind the social construction of meanings and patterns that serve to get 'B' to act and believe in a manner in which 'B' otherwise might not, to 'A's' benefit and 'B's detriment (p. 15).

This conceptualization of power is fascinating and potentially very fruitful. It does, however, take the analysis one step further than is necessary for the purposes at hand. Though I am of course interested in and indirectly making an argument about "thinkable thoughts," none of the data I will present addresses the question of what anyone thinks—only what they read.

44. Edelman, *Constructing the Political Spectacle*, p. 30.

45. Jarol B. Manheim has offered one of the more sophisticated and complete models of this process. His "agenda dynamics" model takes into account the multiplicity of competing and overlapping agendas of various political actors. (Jarol B. Manheim, *The Evolution of Influence: Strategic Public Diplomacy and American Foreign Policy*, [New York: Oxford University Press, forthcoming]. See also Manheim, "A Model of Agenda Dynamics," in Margaret L. McLaughlin, ed., *Communication Yearbook* 10. (Beverly Hills, CA: Sage, pp. 499-516)].

46. Edelman, *Political Language*, p. 26. Emphasis added.

47. Ibid., p. 21.

48. Quoted by Richard Neustadt and Ernest R. May, *Thinking in Time: The Uses of History for Decision Makers*. (New York: The Free Press, 1986), xvi.

49. Edelman, *Constructing the Political Spectacle*, p. 22.

50. Edelman, *Political Language*, p. 29.

51. Ibid., p. 5.

52. Edelman, *Constructing the Political Spectacle*, p. 11.

53. Sam Keen, *Faces of the Enemy: Reflections of the Hostile Imagination* (San Francisco: Harper & Row, 1986), p.61. For other vivid accounts of dehumanization and its consequences, particularly in war, see John W. Dower, *War Without Mercy: Race and Power in the Pacific War* (New York: Pantheon Books, 1986). Dower, 1986; Fussell, Paul, *Wartime: Understanding and Behavior in the Second World War* (Oxford: Oxford University Press, 1989).

54. Jarol B. Manheim, *All of the People All the Time: Strategic Communication and American Politics*, (Armonk, New York: M.E. Sharpe, Inc., 1991,) p. 10.

2

Counterterrorism in the
1980s and 1990s: The Case of Iraq

(D)etermining what state support for terrorism is and deciding which states qualify is an issue more political than definitional, particularly in the absence of an internationally acceptable set of criteria for what constitutes terrorism in the first place.[1]
—David E. Long,
The Anatomy of Terrorism

If a policy maker doesn't want to take intelligence that is contrary to his policy stance, then he's always going to find a way to explain it away.[2]
—Vincent Cannistraro,
Central Intelligence Agency

The first step in our effort to develop a more complete understanding of terrorism, news, and public policy is to undertake an honest appraisal of recent U.S. policy responses to terrorism. We will begin this appraisal with the American response to Iraqi supported terrorism prior to the August 2, 1990 invasion of Kuwait by Iraqi forces.

For foreign policy officials such as Peter Rodman, doing what we could for Iraq in its war against Iran simply made good policy sense. After all, the alternative was the preeminence of Iranian inspired Islamic fundamentalism throughout the oil-rich Gulf states. "We had to do what we could in the region." Doing what we could included ignoring Iraqi sponsored terrorism for a decade.

On February 26, 1982 the United States government quietly dropped Iraq from the State Department's list of terror sponsoring nations. This official action had very little to do with the reality of Iraqi sponsorship of international terrorism. It continued to provide sanctuary and support to some of the world's most dangerous and reprehensible terrorists; men such as Abu Nidal, Abu Abbas, and Abu Ibrahim. Instead, the decision was based on the geopolitical calculations of the moment.

Similarly, in 1990 when the balance of power calculations for the

Middle East changed, Iraq once again found itself on the list . On the eve of the Persian Gulf war, counterterrorism experts and newspaper columnists warned of Saddam Hussein's "ultimate fifth column" and that the United States government was fearful that Iraq was "cultivating terrorists ties," as if such ties were not in existence all along.[3] In response to this rekindled fear of Iraqi sponsored terrorism, the Bush administration warned Iraq that it faced serious consequences should it be found to sponsor terrorism.[4] Unstated was the fact that if in 1990 Iraq presented a terrorist threat to the United States, it was at least in part because the Reagan and Bush administrations ignored Iraqi sponsorship of terrorism in the 1980s.

Dropping Iraq from the State Department's list of terror sponsoring nations fits a pattern of playing politics with the fight against terrorism from the Middle East to Central America, from Southwest Asia to Africa. The Reagan and Bush administration's application of the emotionally loaded term "terrorist," and its repetition in the news media, had more to do with the political status of the violent actors and its relation to the foreign policy goals of the United States than it has had to do with adherence to any clearly conceptualized and assiduously adhered to counterterrorism policy. As David E. Long remarked:

> (D)etermining what state support for terrorism is and deciding which states qualify is an issue more political than definitional, particularly in the absence of an internationally acceptable set of criteria for what constitutes terrorism in the first place .[5]

This was as true in Angola, Afghanistan, and elsewhere around the world as it was in the Middle East. "Terrorism," in short, too often has been what the bad guys of the moment do. For policy makers, this meant the issue had to be managed: Some violence had to be highlighted while other violence and violent actors had to be ignored.

There is, of course, nothing new in pronouncing yet once again that one person's terrorist is another person's freedom fighter. That is cliché, not policy analysis. What this cliché lacks, among other possibilities, is insight into how the application of categories of meaning—particular and in some instances quite deliberately shaded understandings of a problem—profoundly impact policy outcomes. What we see does indeed determine what we do. But what we want to do affects what we see. In the process of rationalizing and articulating U.S. foreign policy goals to a sometimes fickle and often disinterested public, the contradictions of U.S. foreign policy in general and counterterrorism policy in particular went unrecognized while the less than admirable qualities of allies such as Saddam Hussein and Manuel Noriega were ignored, at least in public, until it was time to send in the troops.

The Refracted Images of the Terrorism Spectacle

Counterterrorism has not been taken seriously in the last several years. Former CIA counterterrorist Vincent Cannistraro put it this way:

> Terrorism is like one of those ugly members of the family, like one of those bad members of the family that we don't like to recognize. We find them an embarrassment. . . . That's the way terrorism is considered in the context of U.S. foreign policy. It's an irritant, its bad, (though) its a motherhood issue: everyone *says* its bad. Its not a question of anyone saying its okay. Its a question of how important is it in terms of our diplomatic relations with a particular country.
>
> Saddam Hussein is a good example, . . . We overlooked or undervalued the fact that there was continuing evidence of Iraqi support of terrorist over a prolonged period of time. . . . We didn't put Iraq back on the State department list of state supporters of terrorism until Iraq invaded Kuwait. Now all of a sudden, in a one month period we discovered 'Oh my gosh, he belonged on that list.' What had been going on for the previous seven years? What had been going on for the previous seven years was business as usual.[6]

But what does "business as usual" mean in policy terms? By refusing to publicly acknowledge Iraq as a sponsor of terrorism, the United States was able to lend vital assistance to Saddam Hussein in his effort to amass one of the largest and most well-equipped armies in the world. At the time this was intended to prevent Iraq's defeat in the war with Iran. But it also allowed Saddam Hussein to pursue a policy of genocide against Iraq's Kurdish population, and eventually invade Kuwait at the ultimate cost of ten of thousands of lives.

This was possible because, like the relative we would just as soon go away, the United States government under the Reagan and Bush administrations pursued a policy of willful ignorance regarding Iraqi support of terrorism. Because desired policy goals required it, Iraq's involvement in terrorism was simply defined away. And as we will see in subsequent chapters, when official Washington chooses to avoid the impolitic, the American news media generally follow suit. It was a case of the willfully blind leading the willfully blind. In the process, however, it was the American people who were left in the dark.

To fully grasp the complexity and contradictions found in United States counterterrorism policy, one must place it in the context of larger—or at least other—United States foreign policy objectives. The terrorism spectacle must be viewed from policymakers perspective.

The Prism

In discussions with current and former officials of the Reagan and Bush administration's foreign policy, intelligence, and counterterrorism communities, a metaphor frequently arose intended to describe the relationship between American counterterrorism policy, on the one hand, and foreign policy objectives more generally. How one perceived the terrorism spectacle depended on the "prism" through which one observed it. Howard Teicher, former National Security Council director for the Middle East and senior director for Political-Military Affairs, stated that "the prism (of U.S. foreign policy) changes shape and changes size and changes orientation."[7] Changes in the balance of power produced new calculations of national interest. With each new shape or calculation came a new variant on terrorism, new terrorist enemies, and new campaigns to "fight terrorism."

In 1982 the desired vision in the Middle East was to see Saddam Hussein as a "moderate," out of the terrorism business. "There was a fundamental tilt," explained Teicher, "an attitude in most people's mind in Washington that Iraq was going to be the pillar of U.S. security in the Gulf." Just as the Shah had served as the proxy for the Americans in the Gulf region during the 1960s and 1970s, Saddam Hussein was to fill that role in the 1990s. In 1989, secret State Department cables to American embassies in NATO alliance countries spelled out U.S. strategic planning in the Persian Gulf region and Saddam's role in it.[8]

> The U.S. has vital interests in the Persian Gulf. Access to oil at reasonable rates and blunting Soviet advances are strategic requirements. Trade, finance, and development policies, as well as the political orientation of each of the Gulf states is important to us.

These general objectives (cheap oil and blunting Soviet advances) were to be achieved through the advancement of a long cherished goal of U.S. foreign policy: Stability. One cable put it this way:

> Our increasing dependence on Gulf oil and our desire to slow Soviet political advancement argue the need for continued stability in the GCC (Gulf Cooperation Council) states, a moderate orientation for post-war Iraq and a degree of political coherence in Iran which will ensure that traditional centrifugal forces not overwhelm central authority.

Ironically, in the view of intelligence and foreign affairs specialists in Washington, Saddam Hussein was the key to maintaining stability and the integrity of "central authority" in the Persian Gulf region. "Iraq's interest in development, modernity and regional influence will compel it in our direction," explained the document. "We should welcome and encourage the interest and respond accordingly."

One of the policy makers who saw Iraq as a new moderating force in the Middle East was Peter Rodman, former head of the State Department's Policy Planning Staff and a member of the National Security Council during Reagan's two terms in office. He also served in the same capacity during the first two years of the Bush administration. According to Rodman, "It was totally against his (Saddam Hussein's) policy to be posing this kind of a (terrorist) threat in this period. He is a murdering thug, he always was a murdering thug. (But) the point is, we were trying to conduct a Middle East policy, and the balance of forces between the moderates and the radicals in the Arab world is one of the decisive determinants not only of peace negotiations but the whole American strategic position."[9]

Balance of power calculations took precedence over other considerations, including terrorism. After all, said Rodman, in the 1980s "Iraq was doing a lot of things that were strategically very positive for us." Richard Murphy, a former ambassador to Saudi Arabia and a key player in formulating U.S. Middle East policy in the 1980s, summed it up succinctly when he said "We were convinced that Iraq was changing."[10] This, of course, proved not to be the case.

As the American vision of Iraq and its involvement in terrorism passed through the prism of U.S. foreign policy desires, evidence of Iraqi gassing of entire Kurdish villages, or its continued support of terrorism, could simply be ignored. "It is quite clear to me," said Teicher, "that American policy makers generally had no desire to believe that Iraq was as bad as it was." Vincent Cannistraro put the same thought this way: "If a policy maker doesn't want to take intelligence that is contrary to his policy stance, then he's always going to find a way to explain it away."[11]

Ignoring impolitic information was but one measure, and perhaps one of last resort. More typical, perhaps, was the failure to collect contradicting information in the first place. Without the desire to believe, there was little desire to collect evidence to the contrary. Cannistraro remarked that throughout the period that Iraq was off the State Department's official list of terror sponsoring nations, there was little interest in collecting information which would call into question the wisdom of that action.

Terrorism was being sponsored, organized, and deployed by the Iraqi government. There was information on that but it was not a focus of our concern. And when U.S. foreign policy concern is in one area and (the) resources to develop information are in another area, they don't follow. In other words, I'm suggesting that intelligence resources to collect information about the Iraqi government, outside the narrow area of its war effort (against Iran), weren't there. . . . There was no allocation of resources, no effort, no energy being devoted in collecting intelligence on what the Iraqi's were doing outside that particular arena.

While the intelligence efforts may have been less than complete, the case cannot be made that the United States was unaware of Iraq's continued support of terrorism. State Department documents make it quite clear that privately, in the backstage world of secret cables and policy planning meetings, the United States was well aware of Iraqi involvement in international terrorism. A secret 1989 State Department document made this clear when it stated that "Even though it was removed from the terrorism list six years ago, (Iraq) had provided sanctuary to known terrorists, including Abu Abbas of Achille Lauro fame."[12]

In the face of a growing list of congressional investigations, on June 5, 1992, the State Department declassified several documents relating to Iraq's continued ties to international terrorism throughout the 1980s. Among the released documents was a 1986 memorandum to then Secretary of State George Shultz from the department's top intelligence officer. It surveyed the history of U.S. policy regarding Iraqi sponsorship of terrorism, concluding that though it was an overall success, it had many "blemishes." The memorandum detailed Iraq's "painfully slow" retreat from terror sponsorship in the 1980s.

For example, contrary to Iraqi promises to expel terrorist organizations following its removal from the list, the Abu Nidal organization remained in Iraq while it "struck repeatedly at Israeli and Jewish targets in Europe."[13] A 1985 memorandum stated that "two bomb-toting individuals arrested in Rome (were) linked to the May 15 group." The same memorandum also stated what the 1989 State Department document quoted above stated, that "(Abu) Abbas seems to have been permitted to take refuge in Iraq following the Achille Lauro hijacking." "The documents," wrote R. Jeffrey Smith of *The Washington Post*, "state that Abu Nidal, Abul Abbas and May 15 terrorist organizations were allowed to operate from Iraq or maintain headquarters there despite repeated protests by the Reagan and Bush administrations."[14] The Reagan and Bush administrations were quite well aware of continued Iraqi sponsorship of terrorism throughout the period, though other U.S. foreign policy objectives demanded public representations to the contrary.

Government intelligence was but one of several sources of information available to policy makers. Human rights groups such as Amnesty International and Middle East Watch attempted to raise concerns regarding Iraq's use of poison gas and its abysmal human rights record well before Saddam Hussein became a "little Hitler," rather than the preserver of regional stability. Yet, according to Teicher, reports from such groups had minimal impact on policy makers. "Certainly (human rights reports) wouldn't have made it to a principal, let alone a deputy assistant secretary. That's the nature of the system. I think that people on the outside who think that they have influence on insiders are doing themselves a disservice." If the "insiders" do not want to see it, the prism of desired visions will cast the information aside.

Noel Koch, a deputy assistant secretary of defense and head of the Pentagon's counterterrorism forces from 1981 to 1986, described the "very silly arrangement" in which U.S. policy toward Iraq continually shuffled about unwanted information in an effort to maintain the illusion that Iraq was no longer involved in the sponsorship of terrorism. Koch's metaphor was a cluttered house, one full of terrorists. "'Okay, so that we can deal with you (Iraq) let's move all this stuff over here into the back bedroom and we can say that the front room is clean . . . ' Then we want to go to bed so we'll have to move all this stuff over to the dining room. Then we can represent there are no terrorists in there. This is just shit-for-the-birds. Its all the same house. If you're serious about getting rid of terrorist you arrest them."[15] Neither Iraq or the United States was very serious about actually getting rid of terrorists, not as long as doing so would get in the way of other foreign policy objectives.

When the geopolitical calculations dictated, sponsorship of terrorism around the world simply did not count and, as we will see, was literally not counted by the State Department and other agencies of the United States government. After all, as Peter Rodman retorted, there is a foreign policy to be conducted: "I mean, it is absurd to think that because of some of these sins, that he (Saddam) is undoubtable guilty of, that we were wrong to do what we did. I mean, we are trying to conduct a Middle East policy and I think we did it right." "No government," continued Rodman, "is going to isolate one aspect of its policy. Its going to have to take all of these factors into consideration and decide where, on balance, its strategic interest comes out." In the process, counterterrorism was regarded as merely one factor in the "bigger picture of things."

On the other hand, while CIA counterterrorist Cannistraro agreed that this accurately characterized the process, he thought is was mistaken: "In the past and in large measure in the present, we keep terrorism off as a separate item. We bring it up after we've gone through our diplomatic agenda and (then) we say—kind of out of the corner of our mouths—'You know, it would be nice if you got rid of this guy, he's done a lot of terrorism there.' But you don't let that subject interfere with your bilateral relations."

This is not the image of U.S. counterterrorism policy that comes across in public pronouncements from government officials. There, terrorism was and remains an untoward evil unto which the United States gives no quarter. In *Patterns of Global Terrorism: 1991*, for instance, the State Department insisted that it has been the firm policy of the United States to stand-fast against terror-sponsoring nations. "A central part of U.S. Government counterterrorism policy is to press countries that sponsor terrorism to cease such support. This is what the international community did last year with the great success against Iraq . . ."[16] These words in 1992 echo the statements made in 1986 by then Vice President Bush in the *Public Report of the Vice President's Task Force on Combatting Terrorism*. " The U.S. policy and program to combat terrorism is tough and resolute. We firmly oppose terrorism in all forms and wherever it takes place. . . . We will make no concessions to terrorists." While this may well have been the public line on U.S. counterterrorism policy, the Reagan and Bush administrations made a practice of making deals with terrorist groups and terror sponsoring nations (beyond the well-known deals with Iran during Iran-Contragate), including Iraq, when doing so suited their perceived policy goals. A brief review of several incidents makes the point.

Turning a Blind Eye

A brief outline of several terrorist incidents makes the point that Iraq never suspended its support for international terrorism, official United States policy not withstanding.

The first incident occurred approximately four months after Iraq was dropped from the State Department's list of terror sponsoring nations. On June 3, 1982, Israel's ambassador to Great Britain, Shlomo Argov, was mortally wounded as he stood at the steps of the Dorchester Hotel in London. The incident was the spark which led to the Israeli invasion of Lebanon on June 5. According to investigative journalist Kenneth R. Timmerman, this was exactly what Saddam Hussein had hoped would happen.[17]

In May 1982, with Iraq's war with Iran looking bleaker by the day, Saddam Hussein approached the Ayatollah Khomeini with a peace proposal. When his offer was rejected, Saddam became desperate. He needed a diversion, a way of drawing his enemy's attention away from

Iraq and to another common enemy: Israel. Ambassador Argov's assassination was the result. Intelligence intercepts of Iraqi communications to embassies around the world revealed that Baghdad had instructed its officers in Mukhabarat, the notorious Iraqi intelligence organization, to find a suitable Israeli target.[18] The police investigation in London eventually determined that the weapon used in Argov's assassination was supplied by a Mukhabarat officer from the Iraqi embassy in London. "Iraqi agents had planned and financed the operation, which was carried out by a hired assassin from the Abu Nidal Organization, then based in Baghdad."[19]

According to Richard Murphy, after Iraq's complicity in the assassination became known, "There was never any discussion at State to put Iraq back on the terrorism list. The subject simply never came up."[20] Yet, the procedure at the State Department for determining whether a state should be added to the terror sponsor list, according to Frank Moss, director of policy and public affairs in the Office of Counterterrorism, is quite fixed.[21] The list is "reviewed at least annually. It has to be recertified—a formal, annual recertification. In addition, any time during the year that evidence arises about a state engaging in sponsorship, they can be added to the list." Iraq, however, was not added to the list following the assassination of the Israeli ambassador in London, despite its horrendous consequences.

The Abu Nidal Organization was but one of the terrorist groups which continued to operate out of Iraq during this time. Abu Ibrahim's May 15 Organization also conducted its business out of Baghdad with the blessing and support of Saddam Hussein. On August 11, 1982, Mohammed Rashid, a leading May 15 Organization operative, concealed a bomb under a seat on Pan Am flight 002 bound for Hawaii from Tokyo. Just outside of Honolulu, the bomb exploded instantly killing one fourteen-year-old boy. Twenty-six other passengers, including the boy's parents, were injured in the blast, many seriously. In the next several days, two additional bombs would be found on board planes, though this time before they had a chance to explode. After several months of painstaking work, investigators determined all three bombs had been made by the same bomb maker, Hussein Mohammed al-Umari, better known as Abu Ibrahim, a master bomb maker who got his start in terrorism years before with Waddi Haddad's Palestinian Front for the Liberation of Palestine—Special Operations Group. Following the death of Haddad in 1978, Abu Ibrahim formed the May 15 Organization in Baghdad.

On April 2, 1986, a bomb exploded on board a TWA flight from Rome as it approached Athens. Four people—all Americans—were killed when the explosion ripped a large hole in the side of the plane.

The rapid decompression of the passenger cabin following the explosion sucked them out of the aircraft.

Though the initial suspects for the bombing were members of an Abu Nidal splinter group, it was eventually determined that Abdullah Labib's Hawari Apparatus was responsible for the blast. This group, however, was little more than the May 15 Organization renamed. "In reality it was the May 15 Organization operating under another name," said FBI counterterrorism expert Denny Kline.[22]

Three months later, in October 1985, Abu Abbas's Palestinian Liberation Front hijacked the Italian cruise ship Achille Lauro with eighty passengers on board (hundreds of other passengers had disembarked earlier to see Cairo and the Pyramids). The world watched as the standoff played itself out over the next several days. After an elderly wheelchair-bound American named Leon Klinghoffer was murdered by the hijackers, the leader of the Palestinian Liberation Front, Abu Abbas, arrived on the scene to negotiate a deal with Egypt. The plan was to free the passengers in exchange for free passage to Iraq, which had agreed to provide the hijackers sanctuary. When American jets forced the Egyptian airliner carrying the hijackers to freedom in Iraq to instead land in Italy, all of the terrorists were arrested, including Abu Abbas. Abbas, however, was released and eventually made his way to Baghdad where he continued to enjoy safe haven. Yet, once again, despite the presence of Abu Abbas, Iraq was not returned to the list of terror sponsoring nations.

Why, despite all the evidence to the contrary, was Iraq taken and kept off the list of terror sponsoring nations? Acknowledgment of Iraq's participation in terrorism had to be ignored because policy goals required it.

The Policy Consequences

When Iraq was dropped from the State Department's list of terror sponsoring nations, more than the mere opprobrium of association with international terrorism was lifted from Saddam Hussein's shoulders. It opened for him a vast network of arms merchants and intelligence mavens with whom he was able to consort for the next eight years, right up to when the first Iraqi tank rolled into Kuwait on August 2, 1990. The list, established by Congress in 1979 under Section six of the Export Administration Act, requires the State Department to formulate an annual accounting of "countries that have repeatedly provided support for international terrorism."[23]

After input from the State Department's Intelligence and Research office, the Central Intelligence Agency, and other members of the intelligence community, the State Department's Office for Counterterrorism is responsible for making the recommendation to the Secretary of State. "The final decision," according to one State Department official involved with the process, "clearly rests with the Secretary of State."[24]

As long as Iraq was on the list, it was subject to restrictions which made "even the most innocuous commercial exchanges difficult" and entirely denied it access to American military hardware and sensitive technology.[25] These restrictions proved a hindrance to executive branch foreign policy makers as early as the summer of 1980.

After the fall of the Shah of Iran in February 1979, revolutionary Iran began to threaten the stability of conservative oil sheikdoms in the region. To make matters worse, there was also growing alarm at the rise of Soviet influence in the Persian Gulf region. It appeared to President Carter's national security advisor, Zbigniew Brzezinski, that the Soviets were on the verge of undermining the delicate balance of power in the region.

It was at about this time that Saddam Hussein began to emerge as a good candidate to replace the Shah as the fulcrum of whatever leverage the United States had in the region. On March 25, 1980, Saddam signed an agreement with Saudi Arabia to assist North Yemen in its struggle against Soviet-backed rebels from South Yemen. Saddam pledged to "liberate South Yemen from communist agents and their masters."[26] Saddam, Brzezinski concluded, might make an effective counterweight to not only the Soviets but also the Iranian Islamic militants under Ayatollah Khomeini.

While the United States wanted a counterweight to the Soviets and revolutionary Iran, Saddam Hussein wanted access to the same American weapons and weapons technology that had made Israel the regional superpower. When the Iraq's purchased four frigates from Italy they insisted that the ships be outfitted with General Electric engines. While the eight engines were cleared for export by the Commerce Department, members of the U.S. Senate eventually blocked the deal. Iraq, they pointed out, was on the State Department's list of terror sponsoring nations and therefore was barred from receiving the engines. Though the State Department eventually managed to reverse the Senate's enforcement of the provisions of the 1979 Export Administration Act, the restriction would continue to hinder military and technical exports to Iraq. Dropping Iraq from the terrorism list changed all this. If it could not be stopped, ignoring it would have to do.

According to Timmerman, the argument for dropping Iraq from the list came from State Department officials, specifically Nicholas Veliotes, assistant secretary of state in charge of Middle East policy and Michael Armacost, Undersecretary of State. According to Teicher, the former

NSC director for the Middle East, the actual decision was made by former Secretary of State Alexander Haig and CIA director William Casey. "I'm convinced that at the most senior level, Bill Casey was the prime motivator for doing something about this so that he could tell the Saudis he was doing something to help Iraq." Teicher explained that Haig and Casey were under pressure from the Saudis, who were themselves under "great pressure from the Arabs generally having to do with collapsing Iraqi military position. There was absolutely no way we could do anything to help them, even secretly, covertly, as long as they were on the list of countries that supported terrorism." Dropping them from the list meant the United States could do something for Iraq; in fact, doing so opened the flood gates.

By 1983 Iraq had depleted its $35 billion reserve of foreign currency and was therefore unable to feed its people and, more importantly in Saddam's view, its army. By 1984, Iraq was spending some 60 percent of its gross domestic product on weapons and weapons related technology.[27] To finance these expenditures required outside help, someone to feed the Iraqi people and army while Saddam spent his oil revenue on weapons. Such help came from the Reagan and Bush administrations. Most of the American aid was in the form of credits and loan guarantees. In the eight years following Iraq's removal from the terrorism list, some $5 billion in American economic aid was provided to Iraq.[28] In 1988 alone, the United States government provided Iraq with $1.1 billion in agricultural loan guarantees.[29] The agricultural loans were just one form of aid made possible by the exclusion of Iraq from the terror sponsor list.

Another area of extensive American assistance to Iraq was an intelligence sharing agreement worked out by CIA director Casey on a trip to Amman, Jordan in 1982. This trip occurred at about the same time Iraq was dropped from the terror list.[30] Peter Rodman, the former NSC official, remarked that such intelligence sharing was "very sensible." "It would help them resist the Iranian onslaught but yet would be a sort of perishable nature." The CIA continued to provide Saddam Hussein with intelligence reports until August 2, 1990; the day of the invasion of Kuwait.[31]

It was not until September 1, 1990, one day short of the one-month anniversary of Iraq's invasion of Kuwait, that then Under Secretary of State Lawrence Eagleburger declared that "Iraq is a country which has repeatedly provided support for acts of international terrorism."[32] By this time the Bush administration was pressing its new found distaste for Saddam Hussein, equating him with Adolf Hitler. Shortly thereafter the American public was met with a barrage of news accounts detailing the Iraqi terror threat, Saddam Hussein's "ultimate fifth column," and how the United States government was fearful that Iraq was "cultivating terrorists ties."

It is beyond the scope of this book to offer a detailed recounting of the intricate and close relationship between Saddam Hussein, the U.S. government and business communities.[33] *The point is that such a relationship existed and that it was possible due only to the construction of a terrorism spectacle which hinged on the ability to ignore Iraqi participation in the sponsorship of international terrorism.* Commercial deals could be made and military and intelligence agreements reached only after Iraq was removed from the list of terror sponsoring nations and the national security export controls were lifted. To accomplish this, public dialog regarding Iraqi involvement in terrorism had to be managed, which in this case meant simply ignoring the evidence. Once that was accomplished, desired policy outcomes followed throughout the 1980s and right up to August 2, 1990. Similarly, in 1990 when the Bush administration determined Iraq had become a strategic liability in the Middle East, Iraq's sponsorship of terrorism was prominently acknowledged, becoming an important component in the effort to define Saddam Hussein in new terms. The outlines of the terrorism spectacle were defined through a process of exclusion, exclusion of information which would hinder the adoption of favored policies. Once those policies changed, so too did the outlines of the terrorism spectacle.

At about the same time Iraq's continued involvement in international terrorism reemerged as an acknowledged concern of United States foreign policy, observers both inside and outside of government became concerned that the President Bush was making the same mistake with Syria as he and his predecessor had with Iraq. Syrian complicity in international terrorism was brushed aside in the pursuit of policy objectives. Much of this concern centered on developments in the investigation of the bombing of Pan Am flight 103.

Pan Am 103

On December 21, 1988, Pan American flight 103 blew apart over Lockerbie, Scotland killing all 259 people on board. Eleven more residents of Lockerbie died when debris from the plane landed on their homes. The bombing of Pan Am flight 103 accounted for approximately half the overall total of American deaths due to terrorism in the last several years. A bomb had been concealed in a radio/cassette player, packed in a suitcase, and somehow smuggled into the forward luggage compartment of the giant Boeing 747. After thousands of investigator man-hours, fourteen thousand interviews in fifty-three countries, millions of dollars, and an equal number of words in scores of books and articles, the fog of mystery and suspicion surrounding the Lockerbie bombing remained.

As with any crime story, the basic elements in the Pan Am 103 story involved motive and means. Who had the motive and who had the means of actually carrying out the crime? Until November, 1990, the prime suspect in the bombing was the Syrian-backed Popular Front for the Liberation of Palestine - General Command (PFLP-GC).[34] While Syria was the PFLP-GC's chief patron, it was also concluded that Iran actually bankrolled the bombing of flight 103. American intelligence agents even managed to trace an Iranian transfer of several million dollars to a PFLP-GC bank account in Vienna.[35] The motive was simple. Iran sought to avenge the deaths of the 298 killed that previous July when an Iranian Airbus was shot down by the U.S.S. Vincennes. The plane had been mistaken for an attacking Iranian fighter-bomber.

Then in June 1990, investigators discovered a tiny fragment of the bomb's timer embedded in the side of baggage container which had held the bomb. The timer was identified as one manufactured by Meister et Bollier (MEBO) of Zurich, Switzerland. MEBO was the sole manufacturer of a total of twenty such timers, all delivered to Libya in the late 1985. The existence of this evidence was crucial to the Bush administration's new case.[36]

That Libya was involved in the bombing of flight 103 seemed highly likely in the early summer of 1992. What professional intelligence and counterterrorism experts found more difficult to believe was the Bush administration's claim that Libya was *solely* responsible for the bombing and that somehow Syria and Iran were not involved. "A lot of people thought it was the Syrians," remarked President Bush in November, 1991. "The Syrians," he continued, "took a bum rap on this."[37] It was the Bush administration's official—that is, public—view that there were two independent operations conducted simultaneously, though without coordination and without collaboration, both targeting an American air carrier. "The activities in fall 1988 by those Libyans directly responsible for the December 1988 Pan Am bombing indicate that Libya was planning an aircraft bombing at the same time as the PFLP-GC cell was building its bombs in Germany"[38]

For some in the counterterrorism and intelligence communities, the timer evidence was not very convincing. Instead, they concluded that the Bush administration simply decided to ignore Syrian involvement in the 103 incident as a part of a quid-pro-quo for Syrian participation in the alliance against Iraq during the Gulf war and because Syria's cooperation was needed in Middle East peace negotiations. Neil Livingstone, director of the Washington-based Institute on Terrorism, has stated "The State Department indicated to the Syrians that if they would play a constructive role not only with the coalition but in reducing their support for international terrorism and come to the peace table and have direct, face-to-face negotiations with the Israelis, that the administration would make every effort to remove them from the list."[39]

In the minds of many analysts, Syria had not been absolved of responsibility for past acts of terrorism, such as the bombing of Pan Am flight 103. Former Pentagon counterterrorism chief Moel Koch, for instance, remarked: "I don't think they have solved it. I think Syria's in it up to Assad's ears (Syrian President Hafez al-Assad). . . . Its very difficult for me to believe that this was exclusively and entirely a Libyan operation. It wasn't."[40] "There is a tolerance for Syria's activities," remarked CIA counterterrorist Cannistraro, "that is remarkably close to the tolerance that we showed for Saddam Hussein in the 80s."

The administration has been "willfully blind in determining that this is all Libya," remarked Koch. "The players involved in this thing aren't that stupid." But it is official policy, Koch continued, to now say that Syria was given a bum rap and that Libya is responsible, "just the way it was official policy from at least 1982 to the second week in August of 1990 that Saddam Hussein was a swell guy." Former NSC Middle East expert Howard Teicher agreed: "The President made a conscious decision to dis-indict the Syrians for political reasons. . . . There is no doubt in my mind that the operation was Iranian instigated, Syrian managed, and handed-off to the Libyans."[41]

Mid-level officials in the State Department who were involved in the Pan Am 103 investigation responded cautiously when pressed on the bombing investigation. When asked if they ever felt political pressure from higher-ups regarding the specification of linkages between terrorism, one official remarked: "I think, basically, we are allowed to call them as we see them." But when pressed further this same official remarked that in assessing foreign involvement in terrorism "No one wins all the battles." Was Syria given a bum rap, as President Bush claimed? "I think the President regretted those words shortly after he said them. Clearly the PFLP-GC in the fall of 1988 was trying to blow-up aircraft. Syria has the GC penetrated, it is headquartered in Damascus. Jibril is a former Syrian army officer. I think it is fair to say the Syrians had to know something of what the GC was up to."

Just as Iraq was rewarded in February, 1982 for thwarting Iranian-based Islamic fundamentalism, Syria was being rewarded for its support of the American-led coalition against Iraq. Ignoring Syrian and Iranian involvement in terrorism—if not in the actually bombing of Pan Am flight 103, than their involvement with PFLP-GC's attempts to blow-up civilian airliners in the fall of 1988—parallels the dropping of Iraq from the State Department's list of terror sponsoring nations.

It also fit a pattern of playing politics with the fight against terrorism. The Reagan and Bush administration's application of the term "terrorist," and the largely uncritical repetition of such applications in the news media, had more to do with the political status of the violent actors in relation to administration foreign policy goals than it had to do with any clearly defined counterterrorism policy. This was true of Reagan administration policies toward Iraq in the 1980s, and it may have been true of Bush administration policies toward Syria in the early 1990s. Yet, *this was not unique to Iraq or Syria*. Instead, it is a consistent pattern found in the use and application of the terrorism designation in United States foreign policy. When it suited the interests of policy objectives, enemies were discovered to be terrorists or the supporters of terrorism. When such an acknowledgment undermined policy objectives, officials turned a blind eye to the terrorist activities of strategically important allies. Two more cases of strategic exclusion are presented in the next chapter.

Notes

1. David E. Long, *The Anatomy of Terrorism* (New York: Maxwell Macmillian International, 1990), p. 109.

2. Vincent Cannistraro was interviewed in McLean, Virginia on March 30 and Washington, D.C. on April 14, 1992.

3. See Bruce Hoffman, "Saddam Hussein's Ultimate Fifth Column—Terrorists," *The Los Angeles Times*, August 26, 1990, p. 2; Ronald J. Ostrow and Robin Wright, "U.S. Fears Iraq is Cultivating Terrorists Ties," *The Los Angeles Times*, September 2, 1990, p. 1.

4. Peter Grier, "U.S. Subtly warns Iraq on Terrorism," *The Christian Science Monitor*, October 15, 1990, p. 1.

5. Long, *The Anatomy of Terrorism*, p. 109.

6. Vincent Cannistraro retired from the Central Intelligence Agency in September 1990. From late 1984 to February, 1987 Cannistraro was assigned to the National Security Council as director of intelligence programs. In 1988 he was chief of counterterrorism and analysis for the CIA's Counterterrorism Center.

7. Howard Teicher served on the National Security Council from March 1982 to March 1987. He previously worked in the Bureau of Politico-Military Affairs at the State Department and as a policy analyst at the Department of Defense. During his tenure on the National Security Council he was responsible for collecting information on terrorist activities and helping develop counterterrorism policy. Teicher was interviewed in Washington, D.C. on April 1, 1992.

8. Obtained by the author.

9. Peter Rodman served as a senior aid to Secretary of State George Shultz from 1983 to 1986. In that capacity Rodman wrote several of Secretary Shultz's statements regarding terrorism and developed counterterrorism policy. In

March 1986 he went back to the National Security Council as Deputy Assistant to the President where he remained until September 1990. Before his tenure with the Reagan and Bush administrations, Mr. Rodman accompanied Henry Kissinger in his famed Middle East shuttle diplomacy. Rodman was interviewed in Washington, D.C. on April 1, 1992.

10. Kenneth R. Timmerman, The *Death Lobby: How the West Armed Iraq* (Boston: Houghton Mifflin Company, 1991) p. 193.

11. This even included the ability to explain away evidence of Iraqi efforts to build nuclear weapons. In April 1989, mid-level officials of the Energy Department wanted the opportunity to inform Energy Secretary James D. Watkins of their concerns that Iraq was conducting an all-out effort to purchase the materials and technology needed to complete its nuclear weapons program. The officials hoped that Watkins would inform the Secretary of the State of these efforts. Their request, however, was turned aside by ranking intelligence officials in the Department of Energy. As R. Jeffrey Smith of *The Washington Post* wrote in 1992, the mid-level officials' "assessment that Iraq's nuclear effort was both immense and fairly advanced conflicted with the intelligence community's consensus at that time that Iraq probably would not produce its first nuclear weapon for at least a decade" (*The Washington Post*, "DOE Official Discounted '89 Warning on Iraq's Nuclear Program," April 21, 1992, p. A15). Because their informed warnings put into question the accuracy of the official script of the intelligence community regarding Iraq, the evidence was ignored.

12. State Department cable obtained by the author in April, 1992.

13. R. Jeffrey Smith, "U.S. Aware of Terrorism: Documents Undercut U.S. Prewar stance on Baghdad's Record," *The Washington Post*, June 6, 1992, p. 1.

14. Ibid.

15. Noel Koch was interviewed in Potomac, Maryland on May 13, 1992.

16. *Patterns of Global Terrorism: 1991.* Issued April 1992, p. iii.

17. Timmerman, p. 114.

18. Emerson and Del Sesto, 1991, p. 115.

19. Timmerman, p. 114.

20. Quoted by Timmerman, p. 114.

21. Interviewed at the State Department on May 5, 1992.

22. Emerson and Del Sesto, 1991, p. 156.

23. *Patterns of Global Terrorism: 1990*: p. iv.

24. May 5, 1992 interview of a senior State Department official at the State Department who asked to remain anonymous. The official was directly involved in the United States counterterrorism effort. Between March and June, 1992, I spoke with several U.S. government officials of various ranks and from various agencies who were directly involved in the analysis and policy making process regarding counterterrorism.

25. Timmerman, 1992, p. 113.

26. Quoted in Timmerman, p. 74

27. Glenn Frankel, "How Saddam Built His War Machine: West Provided Much of the Necessary Technological Expertise," *The Washington Post*, September 17, 1990, p. 1.

28. By 1992 Iraq had defaulted on some $2 billion of the total debt, leaving it to the American taxpayer's to foot the bill (Douglas Frantz and Murray Waas, "Secret Effort by Bush Helped Hussein Build Military Might," *The Los Angeles Times,* February 23, 1992, p. 1).

29. Much of U.S. aid came in the form of Commodity Credit Corporation (CCC) authorizations funneled through the Atlanta branch of the scandal-ridden Banco Nazionale del Lavoro (BNL), Italy's largest bank. Between 1984 and 1989, BNL's Atlanta office became Iraq's chief source of credit. The chairman of the House Banking Committee, Rep. Henry Gonzalez (D-Tex.), remarked "The CCC program for Iraq was the cornerstone of U.S.-Iraq relations. In turn, BNL was the largest participant in the CCC program for Iraq" (George Lardner, Jr., "Bush Aides' Ethics Questioned Over Loans to Iraq," *The Washington Post,* April 29, 1992, p. A6).

On paper, this was not suppose to be the function of the CCC program. Instead, it was intended to help U.S. grain dealers find overseas markets for American grain. Under the Reagan and Bush administrations, however, the program became a tool of U.S. foreign policy.

30. Timmerman, p. 242.

31. See George Lardner Jr. and R. Jeffrey Smith, "CIA Shared Data With Iraq Until Kuwait Invasion," *The Washington Post,* April 28, 1992, p. 6.

32. R. Jeffrey Smith, "U.S. Aware of Terrorism: Documents Undercut U.S. Prewar stance on Baghdad's Record," *The Washington Post,* June 6, 1992, p. 1.

33. See Kenneth R. Timmerman, *The Death Lobby: How the West Armed Iraq* (New York: Houghton Mifflin Company, 1991). See also testimony given before the House Banking Committee in March and April, 1992.

34. The PFLP-GC is led by Ahmed Jibril, a former Syrian army officer, and is headquartered in Damascus. It also has a training facilities just outside the Syrian capital.

35. *Time,* April 27, 1992, p. 27.

36. The two Libyans charged with carrying out the attack were Abd al-Basit al-Maqrahi, a senior Libyan intelligence officer, and Lamin Fhimah, the former manager of the Libyan Arab Airline in Malta. It was alleged that Fhimah and al-Maqrahi flew to Malta on December 20 where Fhimah secured Air Malta baggage tags and attached them to a brown, hard-sided Samsonite suitcase containing the bomb. The tags circumvented security measures while directing the suitcase to a Pan Am feeder flight to Frankfurt and then on to Heathrow airport in London. The timer was set to detonate the bomb approximately one hour after leaving Heathrow. On April 15, 1992, acting on these allegations, the United Nations imposed sanctions on Libya after it failed to hand over al-Maqrahi and Fhimah to British and American officials.

37. David Johnson, "Plane Blast Still an Open Case, Says U.S." *The New York Times,* November 26, 1991, p. A12.

38. Fact Sheet, U.S. Department of State Bureau of Public Affairs, November 15, 1991.

39. National Public Radio, "All Things Considered," January 20, 1992.

40. Nor was former CIA counterterrorism chief Vincent Cannistraro convinced. "Finding traces of a Libyan timer doesn't necessarily make the case. They could have sold it, traded it, they could have done anything with it."

41. Interview April 1, 1992.

3

"Quality" and "Marginalized" Violence: The Non-Terrorism of American-Backed Guerrilla Groups

Miss Tutwiler (State Department spokeswomen) said the crash (of a CIA plane carrying weapons to UNITA rebels, killing at least four Americans) would not deter Mr. Bush from protesting Soviet arms shipments. Asked whether she saw any similarity between American involvement in Angola and Soviet involvement in Central America, Miss Tutwiler said, "We don't do comparisons."[1]

This book examines the exercise of political power, power understood as the management of information and symbols. Such a consideration of political power is important because of the policy implications inherent in any given interpretation of reality.

In the last chapter we saw that when policy objectives required it, the Reagan and Bush administrations tended to ignore Iraq's support of terrorism. Then, when a new set of policy goals required it, Iraq was once again tied to a menacing, world-wide terrorist network, according to U.S. officials and press reports. Meanwhile, to preserve the fragile Arab coalition against Iraq, the Bush administration downplayed Syrian support of terrorism. Whether a nation was involved in terrorism seemed to have as much to do with the larger foreign policy objectives of the United States as it did actual association with terrorist violence.

In this chapter we explore similar circumstances. We will find that in the case of American-backed rebel groups, their "terrorist-like" violence was ignored or underplayed in both U.S. government reports on terrorism and in press coverage of political violence, much as Iraqi and then Syrian support of terrorism was ignored.

But what, one may ask, is "terrorist-like" violence? What distinguishes terrorism from other violence? Let us begin to flesh out a more complete understanding of what might constitute terrorism.

Terrorism as "Extranormal" Violence

Terrorism may be understood as qualitatively different from other forms of political violence. Thornton, for example, regarded terrorism as not just violence, but violence of an "extranormal" quality.

> Terror occupies the upper reaches of the spectrum of political agitation, immediately above other types of political violence. Terror may be distinguished from these other types by its extranormal quality; that is, terror lies beyond the norms of violent political agitation that are accepted by a given society .[2]

In stating this, he failed to explain what exactly constitutes "other types of political violence" and "extranormal violence." It is simply somehow different.

Though more carefully, Brian Jenkins has taken a similar approach. He stated that the perception of terrorism has more to do with the quality of violence than with the quantity of violent events. "Public perceptions of the level of terrorism in the world appear to be determined . . . not by the level of violence but rather by the quality of the incidents, the location, and the degree of media coverage."[3] It is ultimately, argued Jenkins, "a matter of communication"[4] The quality of the terrorist event is determined by three factors.

First, the type of incident is an important consideration. Immediate death, for instance, is less likely to be the subject of intense coverage than, say, a hostage situation. Potential violence and death has greater news value than does conclusive death. Secondly, the location of the incident is important in determining the quality of the news coverage. Incidents in developed, urban areas are more likely to be covered than incidents occurring in remote, rural areas.[5] It is simply easier to communicate news from North America, Western Europe, and Japan, or any major metropolitan location, than it is from less well developed areas of the globe.

Finally, what Jenkins called timing, or what might better be referred to as context, is important. Terrorist violence as a distinct form of political violence is easily submerged in the higher levels of violence found in war or war-like situations. High quality news is not likely in such cases, argued Jenkins.[6] Besides considerations of location, context, and action type, what other factors may help explain the coverage of political violence?

Certainly there are instances when we would simply expect news coverage of violence, such as when a prominent public figure is targeted. The kidnapping and assassination of Italian politician Aldo Moro by the Red Brigades is but one example. As analysts point out, terrorists often select victims such as Moro specifically for their media value.

But not all victims of terrorism are well-known public figures; indeed, many, if not most, are anonymous civilians. What differentiates quality political violence stories from less well publicized events, other things being equal?

Edward Herman and Noam Chomsky have argued that the news media will give selective attention to victims of political violence according to the ideological needs of what they call the "propaganda system."[7] As this phrase implies, they tend to regard the news media and the state as a single entity. Whereas Jenkins understands the independent variables of "quality violence" to be location, timing (context), and violent action type, Herman and Chomsky understand the ideological needs of the state and the media to be the most important variable in determining what violence will and will not be given extensive coverage.

How the victims of violence are treated in the news is a key indicator of the operation of the propaganda system.

> A propaganda system will consistently portray people abused in enemy states as worthy victims, whereas those treated with equal or greater severity by its own government or clients will be unworthy. The evidence of worth may be read from the extent and character of (media) attention and indignation.[8]

Herman and Chomsky offer evidence which indicates media attention to the victims of violence tends to correlate with ideological factors. While the casualties of enemy violence is accorded extensive and sometimes even histrionic news coverage, the same cannot be said of the coverage given the victims of U.S. or U.S. ally violence. For example, American news media gave more coverage to the murder of a single dissident Catholic priest by Polish police in October, 1981 than was given to the murders of one hundred Latin American dissident religious workers by American allies in Central America.

Father Jerzy Popieluszko was abducted, brutally tortured and killed by Polish police officers after he refused to end his outspoken support for the Solidarity trade union movement. In a comparative analysis of the news coverage devoted to Father Popieluszko's murder with that devoted to the politically inspired murders of one hundred Latin America church worker, Herman and Chomsky found that *The New York Times*, *Time* and *Newsweek* magazines, and the CBS Evening News coverage of the Polish priest's murder far exceeded the *combined* coverage given to the murder of all one hundred Latin America priests, nuns, and lay workers.[9] This included coverage of the murder by a Salvadoran army death squad of Archbishop Oscar Romero in 1980.[10] According to Herman and Chomsky's findings, whereas Father Popieluszko murder received over one thousand column inches of coverage in ten page-one stories, the murder of Bishop Romero received a little over two hundred column inches in four page one stories. Together, the Latin America one hundred received six hundred column inches of coverage in eight page one stories in *The New York Times*. There is a similar imbalance in editorial content, too. *The Times* ran three editorials condemning the Polish priest's murder. No editorials appeared condemning the murder of the religious workers in Latin America. Similar proportions of coverage was found in *Time, Newsweek,* and on CBS.[11]

Furthermore, unlike the Latin American one hundred, the brutality of the Polish priest's torture and murder was given greater emphasis in the news accounts. Coverage was replete with explicit descriptions of the physical damage done the Polish priest during torture. The sense of shock and indignation was also stressed. According to Herman and Chomsky, the difference in coverage resulted from the workings of ideology in the news. The mainstream news media shared with their policy maker counterparts an ideological perspective which discounted the significance of some victims while it elevated other victims to hero-victim status.

It seems highly likely that Jenkins's variables play an important role in determining the extent and nature of news coverage, and therefore of the "quality" of the violence. We must, however, also take into account ideological factors. According to the legitimation model, we would expect casualties resulting from U.S.-backed guerrilla violence to be ignored, much as were the stories of the Latin American religious workers, and generally not treated as terrorism. At the same time, we would expect casualties resulting from enemy violence to receive more extensive coverage, and more likely to be understood as terrorism. This would be true in both news media accounts and government statistics regarding terrorism.

Are terror-like violent incidents of American allies treated any differently in the U.S. press? In the remainder of this chapter we review terrorist-like violence done by *friendly*—from the perspective of the foreign policy of the United States—political agents and compare it to similar violence by U.S. foreign policy adversaries.[12] *The New York Times* coverage of two guerrilla factions supported by the United States for much of the 1980s is examined: the Union for the Total Independence of Angola (UNITA) and the Afghan Mujahideen.

The stories examined here were not randomly selected, as were the stories in the study reported in the next chapter. Rather, the examination of news coverage of these two guerrilla groups are case studies which should be treated with the same caution as, for instance, the numerous terrorism case studies of TWA flight 847.[13] But just as these case studies have provided us with important insights regarding the features of "quality violence" and news media, case studies may also tell us something about less well known "marginalized" acts of terrorist-like violence.

The Case of the Afghan Mujahideen

On December 24, 1979 the Soviet Union invaded Afghanistan. As John Prados has remarked, it was less a blitzkrieg invasion than a creeping intervention into a quagmire.[14] After a steady year-long build-up of Soviet troop strength in and around Kabul, the Soviets brokered a coup in 1979 which brought to power a new communist faction headed by Babrak Karmal.[15] For the first time the Soviets had extended the Brezhnev Doctrine—the policy of seeking to insulate the Soviet Union behind a buffer of Soviet-controlled states—to Asia.[16]

The Carter administration quickly responded to the invasion with a covert action program which enlisted the aid of several countries, including Egypt, China, and Pakistan. As President Carter's national security advisor, Zbigniew Brzezinski, remarked, the United States wanted "to make sure that the Soviets paid some price for their invasion."[17] Once in office, the Reagan administration substantially expanded what the Carter administration had only started.

By 1985, the Reagan administration was requesting at least $280 million in covert aid to the rebels, double the amount thought to have been given in 1984. According to several published reports, by 1992 the United States had given some $2 billion in military aid since the Soviet invasion. This is the known aid. How much more was sent through third country transfers or other means is impossible to say. What was clear was Washington's determination to "make sure the Soviets paid a price" by arming the Afghan rebels.

This included doing something to counter the Soviet's air superiority in the conflict. As the Americans had done against guerrilla strongholds in Vietnam, the Soviets conducted devastating bombing campaigns on villages thought to be rebel strongholds. The pain and destruction visited upon the villages was barbarous. Villagers and rebels alike soon began seeking respite from the bombing in refugee camps along the border in Pakistan. As early as 1982, nearly one-sixth of the population, nearly 3 million people, had fled Afghanistan and were living in 339 refugee camps in Pakistan. Another two million would be added before the war's end. Realizing these camps served as recruiting grounds, training facilities, arms depots, and way stations for the guerrillas, the Soviets soon began shelling and conducting airstrikes against them, too.[18]

To counter these attacks, in the spring of 1986 the Reagan administration provided Stinger anti-aircraft missiles to the Afghan rebels, much to the consternation of those who feared these lethal weapons, capable of downing civilian aircraft, would make their way to terrorist organizations elsewhere in the world.[19] In 1989, *The Washington Post* estimated that a total of nine hundred to one thousand Stingers had been supplied to the rebels, with approximately 340 having been fired.[20] What happened to the remaining seven hundred or so missiles was not clear. What was know was that in 1992, as the former Soviet-backed Afghan government fell, Washington was trying to find a way to regaining control of the missiles. As before, the fear was, as *The Washington Post* put it at the time, "the shoulder-fired antiaircraft missiles could fall into the hands of terrorist groups . . . posing potential danger for civil as well as military aircraft."[21] Never considered was the possibility the Muhajideen themselves would use these weapons for purposes of terrorism. We will explore this possibility in a moment.

The State Department's Accounting
of Terrorist Incidents in the Afghan Conflict

Soviet bombing attacks on Afghan refugee camps in Pakistan by agents of the Afghanistan intelligence ministry (WAD) accounted for a significant portion of the international terrorist incidents reported by the Department of State's annual *Patterns of Global Terrorism* .[22] The annual report, required by Congress, claimed to meet the legislative requirements calling for all relevant information about previous year's "activities of individuals, terrorist groups, or umbrella groups under which such terrorist groups fall," plus "any other international terrorist groups that the Secretary of State determines should be included in this report."[23] What constitutes relevant information and the guidelines the Secretary of State might use in determining whether a group should be added is not specified.

The very first paragraph of the 1988 report stated:

> The level of international terrorist activity worldwide in 1987 rose by more than 7 percent over 1986, . . . This increase resulted from a wave of high-casualty bombings in Pakistan carried out by agents of the Soviet-trained and organized Afghan intelligence service known as WAD.[24]

Terrorist attacks sponsored by the then Soviet-backed Afghanistan government, according to the report, rose from 29 in 1986 to 127 in 1987—an increase of 338 percent.[25] In fact, for all of Asia—the report does not offer figures for individual countries in this category—casualty figures increased significantly from the previous year, from 104 to 240. This increase is attributed in the report to the bombings in Pakistan by WAD agents. Indeed, as the report itself stated, "When the Pakistani numbers are subtracted, the number of incidents in the rest of the world decline by almost 10 percent from the 1986 statistics."[26]

Was WAD alone in its activities? Was there ever acknowledgment of rebel terrorism? The closest the 1988 State Department report came to acknowledging that U.S.-backed Afghan rebel conducted terrorist attacks was when it stated the following:

> In their insurgency against the Kabul regime, Mujahideen guerrillas generally eschew acts of violence that put civilians in jeopardy. Some bombs were detonated in Kabul, however, in areas where the likelihood of causing civilian casualties was high.[27]

In a non sequitur which followed, the report noted that the United States registered "strong concerns" with the Soviet Union and with the Kabul government. In the annual reports for 1987-1989, the Mujahideen were not mentioned at all. In short, according to the United States government, in the passive language of the 1988 report, on occasion the Mujahideen merely became lax in its vigilance against causing civilian casualties when "some bombs were detonated" in Kabul.

When asked about the absence of Mujahideen violence from the State Department's catalog of terrorist violence, a U.S. government terrorism analyst involved in the evaluation of data for the annual report responded that it was probably not included because it was a case of Afghanis killing other Afghanis. But so too was it a case of Afghanis (WAD agents) killing other Afghanis which accounted for the more than 7 percent rise in the level of international terrorist activity worldwide in 1987, according to *Patterns of Global Terrorism: 1988* .[28] When it was suggested to Middle East expert and former National Security Council member Howard Teicher that perhaps the absence of the Mujahideen from the annual report on terrorism had more to do with political considerations than actual rebel conduct, he responded emphatically, "You're getting the picture. They were our guys. Though we do not admit to it in public, terrorism is what the bad guys do." Teicher added, "What am I saying here? What I am saying here is that politics is in command."

The New York Times Coverage of Mujahideen Violence

It may not be surprising to find that a State Department publication emphasized the terrorism of ideological enemies while it de-emphasized or even ignored altogether the terrorist-like violence of an American proxy army. What *was* surprising, however, was the degree to which a world class newspaper like *The New York Times* was capable of doing the same thing. Even more surprising still was the degree to which *The Times* was capable of ignoring its own stories.

As a kind of metaphor for the entire body of *New York Times* coverage of Muhajideen violence, it is interesting to note that in reporting the release of the State Department's report on terrorism in 1987, the *Times* simply reiterated, nearly word for word, the State Department's own language concerning terrorism: The number of international terrorist incidents were up "mainly because of bombings in Pakistan by agents of the Afghan intelligence service." It even excluded the State Department's own cautious reference to Mujahideen bombings of civilian areas.[29] This exclusion is entirely in keeping with *Times* coverage for the previous seven years.

It becomes evident to anyone who reviews the annual *New York Times Index* that Mujahideen attacks on noncombatant targets were common throughout the 1980s. Table 3.1 is a summary of *New York Times* articles as identified by the *Index*. The table lists reported cases of indiscriminate violence directed at *noncombatant* targets between 1981 and 1987. It should be recalled that the victim's noncombatant status is one of the key features of the State Department's definition of terrorism.[30]

Afghan rebel stories are characterized by their obscurity, with stories averaging less than five paragraphs in length (approximately two column inches) and consistently found on the back pages of *The New York Times*. Furthermore, the incidents listed in Table 3.1 are analytically conservative examples of politically motivated violence directed at noncombatants, a reasonable basis for regarding them as examples of terrorism. Scores of other attacks found in the *Index* were excluded to avoid the inclusion of military or paramilitary casualties, despite the precedence established by the Department of State when it included the October 1983 bombing of the marines barracks in Lebanon as noncombatant casualties of a terrorist attack.[31]

In only one article is the violence characterized as terrorism, the very first article in 1981 reporting several assassinations. No names are mentioned. Furthermore, to date (March 1993), of the 1,273 *New York Times* articles or columns about the Afghan rebels, no more than four referred to Afghan rebel "terrorism," and none of those were direct references.[32] Yet, as Table 3.1 indicates, there are scores of events which, had they

TABLE 3.1   Summary of Violence Directed Against Non-combatant Targets by the Afghan Mujahideen as Reported by *The Times*: 1981-1987.

1. July 16, 1981: Authorities in Afghanistan are trying to "curb rebel terrorism" after three backers of President Babrak-Karmal were killed. Length: four paragraphs, page five.

2. July 17, 1981: Rebels kill twenty-seven senior members of the National Fatherland Front, Babrak-Karmal's party. The Front is composed of civilians who represent tribes and provinces. Length: three paragraphs, page five.

3. April 7, 1982: A high school principal and a popular religious leader in Kabul were assassinated by the "insurgents." Rebels also fired rockets at the Chekel Setoun Palace and at the ruling party headquarters. Length: four paragraphs, page six.

4. June 23, 1982: An "Afghan rebel success," according to the *Times*, is reported in the ambush of a convey of trucks carrying one thousand party members. "Several hundred" apparently unarmed "activists" were slain. Length: five paragraphs, page five.

5. August 25, 1982: A Kabul political rally is attacked by the rebels. "Several hundred" were killed. Length: three paragraphs, page five.

6. February 23, 1983: Three people were killed and ten were wounded when two bombs exploded on (or near) a bus in Kabul. Length: one paragraph, page four.

7. February 28, 1983: Three bombs explode in a crowded area of Kabul in an effort by the "guerrillas" to "incite the population against Soviet forces." Length: four paragraphs, page four.

8. July 6, 1983: Rebels attack Kabul airport, civilian aircraft damaged. Length: four paragraphs, page five.

9. July 16, 1983: *The New York Times Index* summarizes an article concerning two bomb explosions in Kabul. Available microfilm of *The New York Times* late city edition does not carry this article. Length: ?, page ?.

10. March 28, 1984: "At least 15 Afghan Communist Party officials" were slain in the previous ten days in a series of assassinations by the rebels. Length: two paragraphs, page seven.

11. September 1, 1984: "Several women and children" died in a bomb blast at Kabul airport. (In a report on the next day the number of dead was reported to be at least thirty with one hundred wounded. An October 5, 1984 *Times* article reported that fifteen rebels were sentence to death for, as best as can be determined, this bombing. This article put the figures at thirteen dead and 207 wounded. Length: (first article) three paragraphs, page four.

12. November 11, 1984: Several hotels and a theater are bombed by the rebels. Length: three paragraphs, page eleven.

13. June 17, 1985: A rebel bomb destroys a building in Nazar-i-Sharif killing "about 140." Length: two paragraphs, page six.

14. September 26, 1984: An Afghan civilian jet is forced to make an emergency landing after being hit by rebel machine gun and/or rocket fire. This is reported to be the third such attack on a civilian airliner in a week. Length: four paragraphs, page nine.

(continues)

TABLE 3.1 (*continued*)

15. October 28, 1985: The main mosque in Herat is hit by a rebel missile, killing 14 and wounding 78. It was fired at the time for afternoon prayer. Length: three paragraphs, page five.
16. April 7, 1986: "Guerrillas" set off a car bomb near a hotel in Kabul, wounding 22. Length: one paragraph, page five.
17. February 2, 1987: Bomb explodes near elementary school and Indian embassy. Four are killed, including two children. The bomb exploded as classes at the school were dismissed. Length: four paragraphs, page six.
18. June 12, 1987: Guerrillas using American-supplied Stinger anti- aircraft missiles shot down passenger jet killing fifty-three of fifty- five people onboard. Among the victims were sixteen children and ten women. Length: fifteen paragraphs, page eight.
19. October 10, 1987: Car bomb explodes near mosque in Kabul killing twenty-seven and wounding thirty-five. Length: ten paragraphs, page six.

taken place in a different context (with worthy victims or done by unworthy assailants), they most likely would have been heralded as "a grave new threat to civilization itself," as Secretary of State Shultz once characterized terrorism. There are other incidents worth considering.

On September 5, 1985, *The New York Times* ran a one column inch, page eleven account of several bombing attacks in Kabul. The lead was as follows: "Afghan rebels said today that they had bombed three hotels and a movie theater in Kabul, in addition to the previously reported blast at the Kabul airport, and they warned of more such attacks in the capital." The guerrilla source went on to say that the rebels had "turned to urban warfare in their struggle."[33]

In the article, the bombing of three hotels and a movie theater on the same day by the Mujahideen is described by anonymous Western diplomats not as terrorism but rather as "part of a new strategy." They also reported that twenty-eight people were killed and 350 wounded in the airport bombing. These bombings were further described by anonymous guerrilla sources as "urban warfare." One should recall that the State Department report describes such activities as "detonating bombs in places where the likelihood of civilian casualties was high."

This sort of violence is pervasive. Yet terrorism by the American-back Mujahideen in Afghanistan, according to *The New York Times*, was all but non-existent. On June 12, 1987 *The Times* carried an *Associated Press* dispatch telling of the downing of an Afghan passenger jet with a Stinger anti-aircraft missile. The attack killed 53 of 55 passengers, many of whom were reported to be women and children. As noted above, the

Reagan administration had provided these advanced portable anti-aircraft missiles to the rebels just the previous year. Despite the significant loss of life at the hands of a guerrilla movement armed by the United States, no mention of terrorism was made, nor was there follow-up coverage.

This was not the first time the Afghan rebels had fired on at a civilian airliner. In September 1984 an Afghan DC-10 passenger jet carrying 308 people was hit by rebel fire and forced to make an emergency landing. Furthermore, this particular attack was, according to the *Times*, the third on an Afghan civilian airliner that week.[34]

It is instructive to compare these attacks on civilian aircraft to any one of several "terrorist" attacks (as identified by the use of the term in news accounts) on civilian airliners in recent years. One of the biggest stories of the entire period under study was the April, 1986 attempt to down a TWA passenger jet while in-flight between Rome and Athens.[35] This incident precipitated the eventual American airstrike again Libya, killing over one hundred Libyans. The attack on the TWA flight and the administration's retaliation against Libya, who it said was behind the bombing,[36] resulted in over 220 articles in the *Times* over several weeks.

It is also instructive to recall the *Times* editorial response when another civilian passenger jet was blown out of the sky with a high-tech anti-aircraft missile. When the Soviets downed Korean Airline fight 007, the first sentence of a *New York Times* editorial the next day (9-2-83) exclaimed "There is no conceivable excuse for any nation shooting down a harmless airliner." The editorial was entitled "Murder in the Skies."[37] No similar sentiments appeared when the Afghan passenger jet was hit by an American made and supplied anti-aircraft missile.

By the end of 1989, Afghan rebel terrorism was difficult for the American press to ignore. On November 11, 1989 *The New York Times* reported a rocket attack on business and residential districts of Kabul which left at least thirty-eight people dead. Tallies of such attacks put the number of missiles which had struck Kabul since the Soviet withdrawal from Afghanistan at close to two thousand. The Afghan foreign ministry put the death toll at one thousand, while independent Western observers with the U.N. and other agencies put the number at six hundred. At least 90 percent of the dead were civilians. One attack included a direct hit on a school killing thirteen boys, the oldest of whom was twelve years old. The missiles were supplied by the United States and its ally, Saudi Arabia.

Reflecting upon this fact, Afghan Foreign Ministry spokesman, Mohammed Nabi Amani, remarked that the Bush administration should have explained how the killing of civilians accorded with

American concern for human rights. "(H)ow can the United States justify a policy that amounts to the encouragement of terrorism?"[38]

The New York Times' reporting of political violence, both in terms of attention and treatment of otherwise similar types of violence, seems to have paralleled the ideological preferences of the Reagan and Bush administration's geopolitical calculations of the moment. Events of an extraordinary nature were not sufficient for quality coverage. An implicit definition of terrorism was employed by the State Department and *The New York Times*, a definition which tended to exclude the terrorist-like violence of the Afghan rebels. This same trend was also found in the reporting of the Angolan civil war.

The Case of the Union for the
Total Independence of Angola

Besides the Contras in Nicaragua and the rebels in Afghanistan, the other major U.S.-backed insurgency campaign in the world was found in Angola. Angola gained its independence from Portugal in November 1975. Under an agreement brokered by the Portuguese, the three main rebel groups vying for control of Angola, the Popular Movement for the Liberation of Angola (MPLA), the National Front for the Liberation of Angola (FNLA), and the Union for the Total Independence of Angola (UNITA), were to form a coalition government until elections could be held. The coalition never succeeded.

Almost immediately after independence the situation in Angola degenerated to civil war. The United States Central Intelligence Agency (CIA) began "Operation Feature" at the direction of Henry Kissinger's 40 Committee. Besides transferring tons of weapons to the Angolan rebels (the FNLA and UNITA), the CIA coordinated its efforts with the South African Defense Force (SADF) and the South African Bureau of State Security (BOSS). Besides the sharing of intelligence, the CIA is known to have supplied SADF with the resources needed to move armored cars to UNITA placements.[39]

These measures on the part of the Americans and white South Africans were met by Moscow when it increased its support for its ally, the MPLA. Another MPLA ally, Cuba, began sending troops to the new MPLA government, with approximately fifteen thousand troops in Angola by the spring of 1976.

Reports, however, soon surfaced in the United States of SADF troops fighting along side American-backed UNITA rebels. Once word of American involvement with South Africa began to filter back to Congress, the chair of the African Affairs subcommittee of the Senate Foreign Relations committee, Senator Dick Clark of Iowa, held hearings which eventually produced a ban on further military aid to the Angolan guerrillas, what came to be know as the "Clark Amendment." It prohibited expenditure of CIA funds in Angola (except for intelligence gathering) and prohibited the Pentagon from funding Operation Feature.

Though the administration had tried earlier to have the ban lifted, it was not until July, 1985 that the House voted to repeal the Clark amendment. The Senate soon followed suit. It is interesting to note that 1985 was also the last year—until 1990 when American support for UNITA began to weaken—that *Patterns of Global Terrorism* mentioned UNITA attacks on civilian targets. By November 1986, President Reagan was calling for covert aid to UNITA. The CIA acknowledged in February, 1986 that it was once again conducting the same type of activities once barred by the Clark amendment.[40] The United States provided UNITA with at least $30 million worth of military aid in 1986-87. As in Afghanistan, this also included advanced Stinger anti-aircraft missiles.[41]

Meanwhile, the previous September South Africa admitted aiding UNITA, just as it had before. In fact, South Africa had actually expanded its military and financial support for UNITA during the 1980s. As early as 1985 there were reports of up to ten thousand South African troops in Angola fighting along side UNITA guerrillas. South Africans were also reported to be flying combat missions during major UNITA offenses. In short, the political conditions in Angola which had earlier given rise to the Clark amendment remained virtually unchanged. Yet, in 1988, one of the first official acts of the Bush administration was a letter from President Bush to UNITA leader Jonas Savimbi promising "all appropriate and effective assistance."[42]

By 1992 the Bush administration had begun to entertain second thoughts concerning continued U.S. backing of UNITA guerrillas, even as elections in Angola neared. Reports filtered out of Angola that Savimbi had ordered the assassination of two respected UNITA officials, Pedro "Tito" Chingunji and Wilson dos Santos, both well-connected UNITA leaders who were highly respected in the west.[43] Ironically, it was Chingunji who persuaded the Reagan administration and Congress to supply Stringer antiaircraft missiles to UNITA guerrillas.

By the end of the year Angola was plunged into near anarchy. After losing the elections in September 1992, Savimbi resumed the civil war, gaining in battle what he had failed to gain at the ballot boxes. By December, Huambo, the political capital of Angola's central highlands and its second most populous city, along with three other provincial capitals, had fallen to UNITA forces.[44] The battle for Huambo alone was reported to have cost ten thousand lives. In January 1993, Savimbi's guerrillas kidnapped twenty foreigners who worked in the northern oil center of Soyo, the center of several Western oil operations.[45]

The New York Times Coverage of UNITA

Between January 20, 1981 and March 1993, *The New York Times* published 662 articles and columns which made reference to the UNITA guerrillas. Of those 662, six made reference to UNITA terrorism, three were news accounts and three were columns or other op-ed pieces.[46]

The reported kidnapping of oil workers in Soyo would not surprise anyone familiar with UNITA conduct during the war. Kidnapping was the most frequently reported terrorist-like activity carried out by the UNITA insurgents throughout the 1980s. As was true of Afghan rebel violence, as best as can be determined, all of the incidents described below were directed at noncombatant targets. For instance, sixty-four Czechoslovakians and twenty Portuguese were, according to the *Times*, "captured" in 1983 and held for ransom.[47] They were released fifteen months later after a six hundred mile forced march across Angola. In September 1983, twenty-seven Spaniards, Brazilians and Portuguese were taken hostage; in November, five British and twelve more Portuguese were captured. In 1984, seventy-seven Portuguese, Filipinos, and British civilians were, again as *The New York Times* reported it, "captured." *The Times* reported more captured foreigners in April, though how many was not clear. In June 1984 Americans were among eleven more foreigners taken captive.

To be captured by UNITA, however, may have been to be included among the more fortunate. In a small page seven article on March 28, 1984, *The Times* reported that eighty-six foreigners were killed when UNITA insurgents raided an Angolan town.[48] This was the only article to appear on this incident. The identity of the victims was not made clear beyond their designation as "foreigners."

In 1985, twenty-two more foreigners were kidnapped, including two Americans.[49] Also in 1985, one priest was killed and another disappeared after their car was attacked by UNITA insurgents.[50] Despite these reported violations of human rights and international law, less than two months later the House of Representatives voted to repeal the Clark Amendment.[51] By February 1986 the Central Intelligence Agency acknowledged it was supplying aid to UNITA, including advanced Stinger anti-aircraft missiles.[52] In total, at least 238 foreigners were kidnapped by UNITA insurgents between 1982 and 1985. Like the Czechs, some of these hostages were released at different times. How many and who is not clear. Amnesty International's annual report for 1985 stated "UNITA released about thirty foreign workers" but

"Amnesty International had no information about other prisoners held by UNITA."[53]

Here again, it is instructive to compare this to the level of press and government attention paid to the captivity of other foreigners, this time in Lebanon. While the captives of UNITA in Angola were largely ignored, the hostages in Lebanon were the object of long exposes and, one might say, countless articles and columns. One, however, *can* count them. *The New York Times* made reference to the Americans held hostage in Lebanon in 2,604 articles and columns.[54] Nevertheless, while the American and other hostages in Lebanon were provided a public "identity" in extensive press accounts: Names, faces, career, and worried relatives back home, the American and other hostages in Angola were largely ignored.

This served to maintain the legitimacy of the UNITA guerrillas, or at least American public indifference to a situation they knew practically nothing about. The very existence of hostages in Angola was known to few, and remembered by fewer still.

It would be impolitic for the State Department and other administration officials to wax hysterical about hostages held by the very "freedom fighters" for whom military aid was sought. And because the officials upon whom the media relied ignored these hostages, the news media, too, ignored them. This was true even in instances of violence most commonly associated with terrorism.

Car Bombings

The type of violence may have an important role to play in determining the overall perceived "quality" of the event, as Jenkins suggested. But it seems also to be the case that ideological factors are also at work. For instance, *The New York Times* reported on April 23, 1984 that a jeep loaded with dynamite exploded in the Angolan city of Huambo, killing thirty soldiers and wounding seventy others. An undetermined number of people were also killed later when a nearby building collapsed after having been weakened in the blast. In taking responsibility for the explosion, the UNITA guerrillas claimed that contrary to official Angolan estimates, over two hundred soldiers were killed in the blast.[55]

Whether thirty or two hundred deaths, the obvious comparison is between this bombing and the one which took place exactly five months earlier, the October 23, 1983 bombing of the American military barracks in Beirut. There, too, over two hundred soldiers were killed. Yet whereas that story continued for weeks in *The Times*, there was only one report concerning the UNITA barracks bombing.

Table 3.2 is a simple accounting of *The New York Times'* coverage of the October 1983 marine headquarters building bombing in Beirut. As it indicates, extensive coverage was provided, as one would of course expect. Between October 23 and November 26 *The New York Times* carried 141 articles on the bombing. There were one hundred stories in just the first week alone.

What is more interesting is that while the Department of State regarded the marines in Lebanon as noncombatant casualties of terrorism, it failed to include or even mention the Huambo, Angola car bombing. Like the Mujahideen, according to the implicit definitions of terrorism used both the Department of State and *The New York Times*, UNITA violence was not terrorism and, therefore, UNITA was never referred to as a terrorist organization.

TABLE 3.2   Total Volume of *New York Times* Coverage of 1983 Bombing of Marine Headquarters Building in Lebanon

Date		Number of Paragraphs	Number of Stories
Oct.	23	25	1
	24	336	21
	25	386	30
	26	232	15 *
	27	419	14
	28	200	9
	29	65	7
	30	164	9
	31	10	3
Nov.	1	17	1
	2	60	3
	3	56	3
	4	43	4 **
	5	191	8
	6	51	2
	17	27	2
	18	46	3
	21	29	1
	23	25	1
	24	15	2
	25	21	1
	26	7	1
Totals		2,425	141

* Grenada invasion
** Israelis bombed

It is certainly not surprising or inappropriate for *The New York Times* to devote so much attention to the tragic loss of so many young American lives. That is not the point. The point rather is that as a result, and as a result of ignoring other tragic incidents of an exact or similar nature, *The New York Times* replicated, amplified, and reinforced the State Department's apparent attempt to present a limited and carefully shaded terrorism spectacle, one which tended to include only the terrorism of enemies and not allies. This lent support to certain policy outcomes desired by the Reagan and Bush administrations.

Targeting Passenger Jets

The UNITA rebels were involved, by their own admission, in a rather noteworthy incident which appeared in *The Times* on November 11, 1983.[56] A page five story described actions taken by UNITA "special commandos." "Pro-western insurgents" claimed to have shot down an Angolan civilian airliner killing all 126 passengers on board the plane. Denying this, Angolan officials claimed the plane crashed due to technical failings. The reader was left to wonder which was the case. No attempt was made to clarify the incident. For instance, there were no aviation or terrorism experts ruminating as to whether the plane crashed due to mechanical failure or as a result of "terrorist attack."

Again, comparison with other incidents of a similar nature is most revealing. On June 23, 1985, Air India flight 182 crashed off the coast of Ireland killing all 329 people on board.[57] As with the downing of the Angolan airliner, there was considerable uncertainty surrounding the circumstances of the crash. The lead paragraph of the very first *Times* story quoted an Indian official who speculated the cause of the crash was an explosion caused by a terrorist bomb. The primary suspects were Sikhs who desire an independent homeland in India. Speculation regarding the cause of the crash remained the major theme of subsequent coverage.

The search for the flight data recorder, typically referred to as the black box, was regarded as the tantalizing clue which would solve the mystery. The mystery, however, would remain unsolved. On July 1, a *Times* article stated "Investigators said today that nothing in the examination of the wreckage recovered so far from the Air-India jetliner . . . has confirmed the initial suspicion that the plane went down because of a bomb explosion." Furthermore, it was stated "there is no evidence of damage to the bodies such as burns or shrapnel that would support the bomb theory."[58]

Despite the inconclusiveness regarding the cause of the crash of Air-India flight 182, U.S. government terrorism statisticians once again included it when compiling their statistics for terrorist events in 1985. In fact, half the total terrorism related deaths of Americans for that year (nineteen of thirty-eight) resulted from this one incident.[59] On the other hand, as already indicated, the State Department statistics for terrorist incidents in 1983 *did not* include the crash of the Angolan airliner. The Angolan airliner incident was simply forgotten, as if it had never happened. And unless one was able to find in the first place, and then recall a three paragraph article tucked away in the interior pages of *The New York Times* in November 1983, for all practical purposes it never did happen. The silence of officials was mirrored by the relative silence of *The New York Times*.

The crash of the Angolan airliner in 1983 was not the only marginalized violence to be found in *Times* coverage of UNITA.[60] For instance, a little over a year prior to the airliner incident the *Times* carried a single Angolan press agency report which claimed UNITA guerrillas had killed three hundred and wounded 140, apparently all civilians, in an attack on a village in Angola. Who specifically the dead were or what the circumstances of the attack were was not made clear.[61] There was no shortage of UNITA violence directed at civilians and other noncombatants. What was missing, as one would have expected with the legitimation model outlined in chapter one, was extensive coverage and the use of the condensation symbol "terrorism" in connection with the American-backed UNITA guerrillas.

Summary

It should be emphasized that the purpose of this chapter is to demonstrate the exercise of power understood as the ability to manage information and thereby encourage the pursuit and maintenance of desired policy options. The legitimation model argues that violence done by ideological or foreign policy allies is treated much differently than violence done by enemies. In the latter case, "points will be scored" against enemy regimes or threatening ideas when the opportunity arises.[62] This is done by way of publicity campaigns designed to focus public attention on enemy transgressions. Media attention and appropriate terms of reference—such as "terrorist"—are cued by dominant government sources in their interaction with the press. On the other hand, similar transgressions by friendly regimes or clients are ignored or marginalized.

The examination of *The New York Times* coverage of UNITA and the Mujahideen reveals such a pattern of ignored violence. Little of the violence perpetrated by American-backed groups received more than a single report. Much of the reporting was comprised of a single article, approximately four paragraphs long, buried in the back pages of *The New York Times*. The next chapter examines these press tendencies in greater depth.

Notes

1. Robert Pear, "C.I.A. Crash Called Problem in Angola," *The New York Times*, December 1, 1989, p. A9.

2. Thomas Perry Thornton, "Terror as a Weapon," pp. 75, 76.

3. Brian Jenkins, "The Study of Terrorism: Definitional Problems" in *Behavioral and Quantitative Perspectives on Terrorism*, Yonah Alexander and John M. Gleason, eds.. (New York: Pergamon Press, 1981), p. 8.

4. Ibid., p. 9.

5. Ibid., p. 9.

6. Each of Jenkins points are appealing but also in need of some qualification. Intuitively, it makes sense to consider that some kinds of violence are more likely to produce media attention than are others. The denouement of a news story about death is embedded in the story itself. Death simply lacks the dramatic appeal that potential or impending death carries. Yet, according to the findings reported in chapter four, this doesn't appear to be the case. Whereas most hostage situations did not receive follow-up coverage, high casualty violent action types, such as car bombings, bombings, and shootings, were the three leading categories of follow-up coverage. Only about 13 percent of the car bombings, 18 percent of the shootings, and none of the hijackings or kidnappings were referred to as terrorism in the sample. It is not clear whether the type of action has any bearing on the quality and nature of news coverage.

Jenkins may also be missing an important point regarding timing or context. The reported deaths of undifferentiated casualties, it is true, does not invite the reader's empathy. They remain nameless and faceless. Yet, even in the midst of war some deaths take on tremendous symbolic significance. They are given identities in the form of personal histories, careers, and grieving family and friends. Symbolically significant victims can and do arise from the ashes of mass murder. Anne Frank symbolizes the death of millions of Jews and other victims of Nazi barbarities. Likewise, Solzhenitsyn's *A Day in the Life of Ivan Denisovich* presents a fictional character who symbolizes the brutality visited upon the victims of Stalin's repressive rule. Haing Ngor, the Cambodian portrayed in the film "The Killing Fields," represents for many the victimization of millions at the hands of Pol Pot and the Khmer Rouge.

7. Edward S. Herman and Noam Chomsky, *Manufacturing Consent: The Political Economy of the Mass Media* (New York: Pantheon Books, 1988), V.

8. Ibid., p. 37.

9. Herman and Chomsky limit their analysis to media coverage found within an eighteen-month period from the time of the first report of the victim's death or disappearance.

10. United Nations Salvador "Truth Commission" summary report, March 15, 1993, p. 4.

11. Father Popieluszko's murder received a combined total of sixteen stories (313 column inches) in *Time* and *Newsweek*. The one hundred Latin American victims were given coverage in ten articles (248 column inches). CBS Evening News devoted twenty-three stories to the Polish priest, sixteen total for the Latin American one hundred.

12. Adversary and ally assignments were made with the assistance of the Department of Defense's *Defense Almanac*, "International Security Relationships."

13. See Gabriel Weimann, "The Theater of Terror: Effects of Press Coverage," *Journal of Communication*, Winter 1983, pp. 38-45; Tony Atwater, "Network Evening News Coverage of the TWA Hostage Crisis," *Journalism Quarterly*, 64, 1987, pp. 520-525; "News Format in Network Evening News Coverage of the TWA Hijacking," *Journal of Broadcasting & Electronic Media*, 33, 1989, pp. 293-304; Wendy M. O'Donnell and Sarah W. Farnsworth, "Prime Time Hostages: A Case Study of Coverage During Captivity," *Political Communication and Persuasion*, Vol. 5, 1988, pp. 237-248.

14. John Prados, *President's Secret Wars: CIA and Pentagon Covert Operations From World War II Through Iranscam* (New York: Quill William Morrow, 1986), p. 358.

15. On April 27, 1978 the People's Democratic Party of Afghanistan seized power in a bloody coup. In response, the Soviets deployed several hundred military advisors to Afghanistan. In an ensuing power struggle, Marxist hardliner Hafizullah Amin took power in March 1979. The following December the Soviet full-force invasion took place. They install Babrak Karmal as president. In May 1986, Karmal was replaced by Najibullah, the chief of Afghanistan's secret police.

16. Nancy Peabody Newell and Richard S. Newell, *The Struggle for Afghanistan* (Ithaca: Cornell University Press, 1981), p. 108. On April 14, 1988 Afghanistan and Pakistan signed an accord clearing the way for the departure of Soviet troops. By February 15, 1989, the last of the Soviets pulled out of Afghanistan. Some fourteen years after the Soviet invasion, on April 17, 1992, Afghan President Najibullah fled the capital. Eight days later, on April 25 various rebel factions gained control of Kabul. Unfortunately, this did not bring to an end one of the longest civil wars in modern world history. In February 1993, upwards of a thousand people were killed in one week of fighting in Kabul.

17. John Prados, *President's Secret Wars: CIA and Pentagon Covert Operations From World War II Through Iranscam* (New York: Quill William Morrow, 1986).p. 360.

18. Prados, *President's Secret Wars*, p. 360.

19. Unsigned, "U.S. Ready to Send Missiles," *The New York Times*, March 30, 1986, p. A13.

20. Don Oberdorfer, "U.S. Asks Afghans to Return Missiles," *The Washington Post*, April 23, 1992, p. A36.

21. Ibid.

22. See in particular the annual reports for 1986-90.

23. *Patterns of Global Terrorism: 1988*, p. v. The report is mandated by the Foreign Relations Authorization Act and the Export Administration Act.

24. *Patterns of Global Terrorism: 1987*, p. 1.

25. Ibid., p. 4.

26. Ibid., p. 1.

27. Ibid., p. 35.

28. Ibid., p. 1.

29. Unsigned, "International Terrorism is Up 7%, Report Says," *The New York Times*, August 23, 1988, p. 3.

30. See *Annual Report*, 1988, p. v.

31. From an analytical perspective, the inclusion of the marine casualties in the annual State Department terrorism report is curious for it seems to violate the State Department's own definition of terrorism, a definition which limits terrorist violence to attacks *on non-combatant* targets. With the inclusion of the marines, approximately half the total number of casualties of terrorism in this time period hinge on the inferred non-combatant status of the two thousand man marine contingent sent to Lebanon in 1983. Is such an inferred status warranted in this case?

Certainly it is true that the U.S. service men killed in their barracks building in the early morning hours posed no immediate military threat to the Lebanese or anyone else. Yet, military historian Eric Hammel argued the combat role of the marines in Beirut was consistently underplayed by the Reagan administration for fear of raising American public opposition to the U.S. presence in war-torn Lebanon (Eric Hammel, *The Root: The Marines in Beirut, August 1982-February 1984* [San Diego: Harcourt Brace Jovanovich, Publishers, 1985]). The mission of the marines in Lebanon was never entirely clear. They first went there to help oversee the evacuation of the Palestinian Liberation Organization (PLO) following the June 1982 invasion of Lebanon by Israel. Following the September 14 assassination of Lebanese President Bashir Gemayel, a Christian Falangist, the marines found themselves slowly sinking in the complexities of Middle East politics. Rather than neutral arbitrator, they came to be identified with Israeli interests, and with the interests of Amin Gemayel, Bashir's successor to the presidency. Neither the Druze nor the Shi'ites regarded this Christian Falange leader to be the legitimate ruler of Lebanon, but rather only a puppet of the Israelis and Americans.

The Americans were also deeply involved in supporting Gemayel's army, pumping tons of weapons and training to his forces. In September, 1983 the marines even engaged in fire-fights with Druze forces while the Navy's big sixteen inch guns opened fire in support of Gemayel's army. If the marines were peace keeping forces, not everyone in Lebanon agreed with the terms.

32. The article and column count was achieved with the following Nexis command: "Afghan rebel or Afghan guerrilla or Mujahideen." The terrorism count was achieved with the same command but with the following modifier: "w/5 terror!." Nexis is a computer search service offered by Mead Data Central. Full text of most newspapers, journals, television news transcripts are available.

Besides the reference in Table 3.1, only three other articles approach making the reference to Afghan rebel terrorism, and two of those are quotes from the old Soviet official journalism outlets. Bill Keller, "Soviet Newspaper Rejects

Notion of Moscow Role in Death of Zia," *The New York Times*, August 23, 1988, p. A13; Leslie H. Gelb, "Administration Debating Antiterrorist Measures," *The New York Times*, June 6, 1984, p. A6; John F. Burns, "Moscow Indicates Unyielding Stand in Afghan Dispute," *The New York Times*, January 1, 1983, p. A3.

33. Unsigned, "Afghan Rebels Say They're Bombing Hotels," *The New York Times*, September 5, 1985, p. 11

34. Unsigned, "Afghan Airliner Lands After Rebel Fire Hits It," *The New York Times*, September 26, 1984, p. 9.

35. Terrorism story counts were obtained by directing Mead Data Central's Nexis system to identify all *New York Times* foreign desk stories in which the term terror, terrorist, or terrorism are present. The Nexis Research Service is able to scan the entire text of numerous publications almost instantaneously.

36. Though the initial suspects for the bombing were members of an Abu Nidal splinter group acting with the backing of Libya, Abdullah Labib's Hawari Apparatus—the Iraqi-supported May 15 Organization renamed—was later held responsible for the bombing (Emerson and Del Sesto, *Terrorist*, p. 156).

37. *Extra!* Newsletter of Fairness and Accuracy in Reporting, July/August, 1988.

38. John F. Burns, "Don't Give Rockets to Rebels, Kabul Tells U.S.," *The New York Times*, November 29, 1989, p. 11.

39. John Prados, *President's Secret Wars: CIA and Pentagon Covert Operations From World War II Through Iranscam* (New York: Quill William Morrow, 1986), p. 342.

40. Bernard Gwertzman, "President Decides to Send Weapons to Angolan Rebels," *The New York Times*, February 19, 1986, p. A1.

41. Of all the weapons sent to Angola, land mines left the most lethal legacy of this military aid. The human rights organization Africa Watch issued a report in February 1993 which quoted a land mine expert who said "The whole of Angola must be considered a mined area" (Dennis McAuliffe, Jr., "Rights Group Faults U.S., Others Over Land Mines in Angola," *The Washington Post*, February 28, 1993). Twenty million mines were planted during the sixteen year civil war (Angola is the size of Texas). Though some twelve countries supplied mines to either the government of UNITA rebels, the Africa Watch report singled out the United States, stated that it "has not accepted that it bears any responsibility for the large number of U.S.-manufactured mines in Angola."

42. Unsigned, "Bush to Continue Aid to Rebels in Angola," *The New York Times*, January 12, 1988.

43. See John M. Goshko, "Baker Seeks Answers From UNITA Leader," *The Washington Post*, March 30, 1992, p. A11 and David B. Ottaway, "After U.S. Questioning, Angolan Savimbi Denies Role in Ex-Aides' Death," *The Washington Post*, April 7, 1992, p. A21.

44. Karl Maier, "Angolan City Caught In Grip of Anarchy, *The New York Times*, December 5, 1992, p. A14.

45. Unsigned, "Government, Rebels Battle Across Angola," *The New York Times*, January 30, 1993, p. A22.

46. A Nexis search was done on March 25, 1993. It identified all *New York Times* references to UNITA (Nexis search command: "UNITA and date after 1-20-81" in the Nexis NYT library). A second search was modified to look for all *Times* articles or columns which referred to terrorism or terrorist within five words either side of UNITA (UNITA w/5 terror!).

Christopher Wren's October 21, 1988 article is an accounting of a UNITA rehabilitation camp in southern Angola. Much of the article is devoted to interviews and descriptions of the large number of rebels waiting to be fitted with artificial limbs. For balance in a story otherwise filled with accounts of alleged Angolan government gassing of rebels and the spreading of mines, Wren makes this statement, perhaps in an attempt at balance: "The Marxist government has asserted that the rebels plant the mines to terrorize civilians" ("Angolan Rebel Town Tries to Mend the Maimed," October 21, 1988, p. 8).

James Brooke January 22, 1985 article offers a long and generally sympathetic account of the non-military contingent of Cubans then working at various humanitarian undertakings in Angola. Brooke offers these two statements:

> Pro-Western guerrillas of the Union for the Total Independence of Angola, or Unita, have targeted Cuban workers for kidnapping and assassination. Last April a car bomb exploded outside the Cuban military headquarters in Huambo, killing 35 people.

A few paragraphs later, Brooke makes this statement: "Unita's terror campaign has left the Cubans edgy" ("The Cubans in Angola: They are Not All Soldiers," January 22, 1985, p. 2).

On April 1, 1984, *The Times* published a Reuters account of the Bulgarian government's charge that South Africa and the United States shared in the complicity of the UNITA rebel's kidnapping of two Bulgarian teachers, a doctor, and an unspecified number of Portuguese (Bulgarians Link U.S. To Angolan Rebel Raid," April 1, 1984, p. 3). The Bulgarian official is quoted as follows:

> Many facts show this action of Unita terrorists would have been impossible without support from the regime in Pretoria and of the American Government," the agency said, calling the rebel group by its acronym.

Three columns also use the language of terrorism in connection to UNITA. Senator Deconcini's (D-Arizona) April 30, 1986 op-ed piece raises objections to the provision of Stinger missiles to "resistance forces" around the world ("Sell Missiles to Kill Americans?" April 30, 1986, p. 31). His references to terrorism are directed at certain non-specific terrorists who may obtain stingers from the resistance forces. He does make this important assertion, though:

> The State Department has described some of the actions of Unita, the Angolan rebel force led by Jonas Savimbi, as bordering on terrorist activity. For example, Unita claims to have shot down at least three civilian Angolan aircraft.

The reference the Senator makes to the State Department's description of UNITA actions "bordering on terrorist activity" are not to be found in the public documentation. Secondly, there is only one *Times* account of UNITA actually downing civilian aircraft. It will be discussed below.

Two Anthony Lewis columns offered these nearly identical sentences: "He (Jonas Savimbi) uses terrorist methods, including the taking of hostages and the shooting down of civilian aircraft" ("Rhetoric and Reality," January 27, 1986, p. 27) and "Unita has used classic terrorist tactics, taking hostages and shooting down civilian planes"("Marching for Pretoria," October 31, 1985, p. 27). He goes on to ask if Savimbi's American supporters favor selective terrorism. Lewis's two columns offer the most forthright assertions regarding UNITA terrorism.

In total, out of 662 published pieces regarding UNITA, we have a handful of often carefully worded references to UNITA terrorism.

47. Unsigned, "Rebels in Angola Offer Prisoner Trade," *The New York Times*, March 15, 1983, p. 5.

48. Unsigned, "Angolan Rebels Claim a Provincial Capital," *The New York Times*, March 28, 1984, p. A7.

49. Unsigned, "Angola Rebels Taking Diamond Site," *The New York Times*, January 1, 1985, p. 3.

50. Unsigned, "Pretoria Denies Mission Against Oil Installations," *The New York Times*, May 30, 1985, p. 7.

51. John Fuerbringer, "House Acts to Allow Angolan Rebel Aid," *The New York Times*, July 11, 1985. p. 3.

52. Unsigned, "U.S. Said Ready to Send Missiles," *The New York Times*, March 30, 1986, p. A13.

53. *Amnesty International Report*, 1986, p. 19.

54. Nexis search ("American and hostages and Lebanon").

55. Unsigned, "Angolan Dynamite Blast Reportedly Kills 30," *The New York Times*, April 23, 1984.

56. Unsigned, "Pro-West Angola Rebels Say They Downed Plane," *The New York Times*, November 11, 1983, P. 5.

57. R.W. Apple, "329 Lost on Air-India Plane After Crashing Near Ireland; Bomb is Suspected as Cause," *The New York Times*, June 24, 1985, p. A1.

58. Unsigned, "No Firm Evidence Found in Air-India Jet Crash," *The New York Times*, July 1, 1985, p. 5.

59. *Patterns of Global Terrorism*, 1988.

60. Senator Deconcini's column ("Sell Missiles to Kill Americans?" April 30, 1986, p. 31) mentioned two other civilian Angolan airliners shot down by the UNITA rebels. No press reports could be found regarding the actual downing of additional aircraft.

61. Unsigned, "Angola Says Guerrillas Killed 300 in Village," *The New York Times*, Oct. 15, 1982, p. 5.

62. Edward S. Herman, "Diversity in the News: 'Marginalizing' the Opposition," *Journal of Communication*, Summer 1985, pp. 135–146.

4

Political Violence and the Official Designation of "Terrorism"

We have learned to call this propaganda. A group of men, who can prevent independent access to the event, arrange the news of it to suit their purpose.[1]
—Walter Lippmann

To this point we have focused most of our attention on questions of exclusion: Which violent acts tend *not* to be treated as terrorism in news accounts and in official summaries of terrorism? In this chapter we turn the question around and ask what *is* regarded as terrorism in the news. What are the defining features of such stories?

News and "Terrorism"

The analysis presented below is quite straightforward, centering on three basic questions.

1. What patterns, if any, emerge in the news regarding the use of descriptive terms such as terrorists, terrorism, guerrilla, and rebel?
2. Which violent acts are given extensive news coverage and which are ignored?
3. Is there any evident relationship between the label used to describe the violence and the overall extent of news coverage of that event?

This is what we will find. First, for at least one elite American newspaper, "terrorism" or "terrorist" are terms used with considerable care when reporters are speaking for themselves.

Secondly, we will find that events described in the news as "terrorism" or "terrorist" attacks tend to receive more coverage than do "nonterrorism" events *of an* exact or similar nature. Other factors, such as the numbers of people killed, the national identity of victims, the extent of destruction, or other indices of the nature of the violence itself, do not serve as viable explanations of coverage and descriptive terminology.

Thirdly and most importantly, the designation of violence as terrorism in news accounts often come from official sources quoted or paraphrased in the news story. As reported in the news, "terrorist violence" is most often distinguished from other violent acts by official sources. No other factor so clearly accounts for the distinction. Whereas enemy violence tends to be labeled by official sources in the news as "terrorism," the violence of the United States or its foreign surrogates and allies, such as Saddam Hussein in the 1980s, is labeled in a more benign fashion. Reporters are "cued" by dominant sources, such as friendly government officials, including those in the United States, as to what is and what is not "terrorism." In this way official versions of reality, and more importantly, *the selective legitimation and delegitimation of political actors and policies* is achieved.

The balance of this chapter is devoted as much as possible to a verbal description of the results of an extensive content analysis of *New York Times* stories about politically motivated violence: Assassinations, car bombings, and the like.

Data Source

The New York Times is the primary news outlet analyzed in this chapter. *The Times* was selected for several reasons. First, it offers what is arguably the most complete foreign affairs coverage of any American newspaper. Because the research design used in this project is as sensitive to what is *not* covered as it is to what is, *The Times '* reputation for thoroughness makes it the newspaper *least likely* to offer confirmation of the model's expectations.

Secondly, *The Times* reputation must be taken into consideration. Its alleged liberal bias, if true, makes confirmation of the legitimation model unlikely. If it is as critical and even biased against conservative policies and politics as is often claimed, *The New York Times* would seem *least likely* to accept the conservative Reagan and Bush administrations' line about terrorism.

A third reason for focusing on *The Times* is its leadership role in American journalism. Along with *The Washington Post*, *The Los Angeles Times* and more recently *Cable News Network*, *The New York Times* is often the newspaper other news media use to structure and prioritize their own news coverage. It is equally influential among the political elite, often serving as a kind of back-channel communication link between political players.

In short, while the sample used in this study is obviously not a random sample of U.S. news media coverage of political violence, a random sample of *The New York Times* is arguably better in the sense that it is the newspaper with the greatest number of resources and degree of independence.[2]

Research Design

The research design distinguished two general types of news stories: Initial and Follow-up. The *initial* news report is simply the very first *New York Times* account of some violent incident. As the term implies, *follow-up* coverage is any and all subsequent coverage of a violent incident *first covered* in one of the initial stories. Because of the common concern that terrorist are able to capture and hold the attention of journalists with violence, I was particularly interested to learn something about the dynamics and characteristics of those violent events which do indeed receive more extensive coverage.

To accomplish this sort of inquiry, initial news reports of political violence appearing in *The Times* on sample dates were found first.[3] Next, a search was made for all follow-up coverage for each initial story. In this way two groups of stories were eventually produced: Those initial stories which *were* followed-up and those which *were not.*

Secondly, patterns in the use of the terms "terrorist" and "terrorism" were noted for both those stories which were followed-up and those which were not.[4] In this way several questions were addressed: What seems to account for the difference in devotion of newspaper space to violence? Which violence is referred to as terrorism and why? What is the relationship between the use of the terror terms in news accounts of violence (terrorists, terrorism), the type of violence, and the extent of coverage? Are terror stories more likely to be prominently displayed in the news? And most importantly, what is the typical source of the use of the terror terms? Are reporters on their own using terror terms to describe some of the violence or are sources using these terms turned to by reporters? We will find that in the process of the use of these descriptive terms, "terrorism" is defined in news accounts of violence. Some violence is understood to be terrorism and/or done by terrorists while other violence is not.

Variables

The research design attempted to capture as much of the complexity of the news reports as possible. Information concerning twenty-one variables was recorded for each story. At the heart of the coding procedure was the collection of information regarding four central variables: "label," "action," "target," and "source." These variables may be put in the form of a question:

Who (label) did what (violent action) to whom (target of violent action) according to whom (source of these descriptive terms)?

"Source" is the person or agency specifically responsible for the violent action or label characterization of the actors or perpetrators of the violence specified in the article. In other words, *"source" is the specific origin of the characterization of the violence described in the article.* In some cases, reporters are themselves responsible for the use of the characterization. When sources were other than reporters, they could be either "hostile" or "friendly" according to their national or group origins. For the specific time period under review, hostile sources are sources from the Soviet Union and Eastern European nations, Sandinista controlled Nicaragua, Cuba, FMLN guerrillas in El Salvador, etc. These designations were made with the assistance of the Department of Defense's *Defense Almanac,* "International Security Relationships." The *Almanac* categorizes American security and defense relationships with other nations around the world.

As mentioned earlier, it was also noted whether the *initial* story received additional or follow-up coverage. Follow-up was any article mentioning, even if only in passing, the *specific* violent event reported in an initial report.[5] Taking approximately one year to complete, over one thousand days of *New York Times* coverage on microfilm was reviewed, often more than once, and photocopied in the search for follow-up coverage.

A simple "two day rule" was used to determine when the search for additional stories was to cease. If two consecutive days passed without any mention of the specific act of violence covered in the initial story, further searching was halted. If, however, the original violent act was mention, the search continued for at least two more days.[6] This rule was necessary due to the sheer volume of coverage under investigation. What did all of this coding find?

Results

Follow-up coverage is, according to the results of the content analysis, related to two factors, both associated with official sources. First, the very presence of U.S. officials in a news story is associated with total coverage. Secondly, when designated as terrorism, identical acts of political violence tend to receive greater amounts of coverage. More interestingly, though, the terror designation itself tends to originate with government officials appearing in the story. In other words, terrorism designations in the news are often, though certainly not always cued by government officials. *The New York Times* confronted the ambiguity of terrorism by allowing government sources to do the defining of terrorism for it. In the process, the political landscape, who the good-guys and bad-guys are, which actors are legitimate and which are not, is defined. Let's next take a look at several specific findings.

Violence News Which Was Not Followed-up

The first and perhaps most striking finding is the relative silence of *The New York Times* beyond its initial report of some act of violence. Of 325 cases of initial violence stories found in two hundred days of *Times* coverage, only twenty-nine violent incidents (9 percent of all initial stories) received follow-up coverage.[7]

As Table 4.1 indicates, reports of battles or exchanges of gunfire were by far the least likely type of stories to receive follow-up coverage, with some 97 percent of such stories reported but once in *The Times* sample. Likewise, almost three of every four car bombings and seven of every ten hijackings failed to receive more than a single news story.

Very few incidents of violence, even those types most commonly associated with terrorism, such as car bombings and hijackings, receive more than one news article in one of the most thorough newspapers in the country. Follow-up coverage was infrequent.

What was followed-up?

Part of the answer is provided by a multiple regression analysis of the attribution variables "Number of friendly foreign officials and the number of United States officials" with total frequency of paragraphs of

TABLE 4.1   Percentage Follow-up Versus No Follow-up for Different Violent Actions

Action	Percent Yes	Percent No	Totals
Bomb	12	88	(95)
Car Bomb	26	74	(23)
Shooting	5	95	(88)
Hijacking	33	67	(12)
Kidnapping	14	86	(07)
Other (gun battles, etc.)	3	97	(100)
Totals	(N=29)	(N=296)	

follow-up as the dependent variable. There is some indication that *as the number of attributions to U.S. officials increases, so too does the likelihood of additional coverage.* An attribution here refers to either quotations or simple references to those who speak in the article, both named and unnamed (Again, this should not be confused with "source").

Thirty-three percent of the variance in the amount of additional coverage is attributable to the presence of U.S. officials in the story. While it is possible that some third variable is in a position of demanding both additional coverage *and* U.S. official response, what that third variable might be is not readily apparent.

What additional variables might explain the variance?

To address this question requires that we shift gears for a moment and examine the use of descriptive terminology found in the sample stories.

The Use of "Terrorist" and "Terrorism" as Descriptive Labels

As stated earlier in this chapter, the evidence we are about to review indicates that "terrorism" stories—those which use "terrorism" or "terrorist" as descriptive terms—tend to receive more coverage than do any other violence story type. But we will soon see that a *terrorism* story is distinguished from a *non-terrorism* story by the presence of friendly government officials as news sources. No other variable, such as the type or location or victim of the violence so clearly differentiates the two. I turn next to describing this process.

What can be said of the descriptive terminology found in the sample stories? Table 4.2 compares actor labels used to describe the perpetrator

TABLE 4.2   Comparison of Initial and Follow-up Stories for Actors

Label for Actors	Initial		Follow-up	
Rebel, Guerrilla	37%	(101)	11%	(18)
Security Forces*	23	(63)	2	(3)
Gunman	12	(33)	1	(2)
Interactive**	12	(33)	0	(0)
Terrorist	11	(30)	48	(78)
Hijacker	2	(6)	5	(8)
Other***	3	(8)	33	(53)
Total	N=(274)		N=(162)	

*   Comprised of terms such as police, security forces, troops.
**   Two or more groups or persons "battling" one another.
***   In most cases this is the total absence of a label.

of violence in initial and follow-up stories.[8] As this table indicates, whereas a modest 11 percent of the actors were described as "terrorists" in the initial stories (30 of 274 initial stories), 48 percent (78 of 162 follow-up stories) of the actor references in follow-up stories use the "terrorist(s)" actor designation.[9] This suggests *The New York Times* tended to be more interested in "terrorism," just as one would expect given what is typically understood about the relationship between the news and terrorism. If it is a violent incident referred to as terrorism, *The Times* pays attention to it.

This leads us to the next question: Why is some violence reported in *The Times* understood to be about "terrorism" while violence of an exact or similar nature is treated differently? The nature of the violent act itself seems to have little to do with whether it is referred to as terrorism in any given article, as Table 4.3 indicates.

Note that in Table 4.3 even acts of violence most typically thought of as terrorism are generally not described by *The Times* as such. Of the shootings, 82 percent were not designated as terrorism. This reluctance to designate violence as terrorism even holds true for bombings and car bombings.

Reviewing a few examples taken from the sample might be helpful in gaining a clearer understanding of the phenomenon at hand. Among those car bombings *not treated* as terrorism, and given practically no coverage, were the following incidents: Two car bombs exploded in a Moslem low-income suburb in East Beirut killing at least ten. This occurred on February 27, 1982 and received three paragraphs of coverage.

On August 8, 1983 a car bomb blew up outside an open-air market in Baalbek, Lebanon. Thirty-three people were killed. Though this was a front-page story it was covered only once. No American sources

TABLE 4.3　　Action Type by Mention of Terrorism

	Terrorism Mentioned				
Action	*No*		*Yes*		*Total*
Other	94%	(94)	6%	(6)	(100)
Bomb	81%	(77)	19%	(18)	(95)
Shooting	82%	(72)	18%	(16)	(88)
Car Bomb	87%	(20)	13%	(3)	(23)
Hijacking	100%	(12)	0%	(0)	(12)
Kidnapping	100%	(7)	0%	(0)	(7)
Total	N=(282)		N=(43)		

were found commenting in any way in the story. A "psychopath" detonated a car bomb in front of a police station in Melbourne, Australia wounding twenty-three. Here an official was quoted as saying that this was specifically not a terrorist attack because the driver must have been a "psychopath, not a terrorist." It is interesting to note that one of the common explanations for terrorist motivations is psychopathology.[10] Finally, on October 10, 1987 the American-backed Afghan rebels exploded a car bomb outside a mosque killing twenty-seven people.

These are but a handful of car bombings not treated as terrorism and not given more than one news story in *The New York Times*. On their own, *Times* reporters tend to avoid the use of the terrorism terminology. What, then, determines the use of "terrorism" or "terrorist" as a descriptive label in *The New York Times*?

We can begin to clarify this by noting the distribution of sources between initial and follow-up coverage. Recall the variable "source" is simply the person or agency *specifically responsible for the actor or action designation coded for any given article.* It is the "according to whom" portion of the central research question "Who did what to whom *according to whom?*"

Table 4.4 displays the distribution of sources (the source of the descriptive term used to describe some violent act) for both initial and follow-up stories. Descriptive terms of violent actor and actions which originate with the reporter overwhelm all other possibilities for *initial* stories at 84 percent. This statistic indicates that with breaking stories about violence, reporters tend to rely on their own descriptions of events. Reporters show a tendency to avoid the use of the ambiguous yet emotionally charged labels terrorism and terrorist in initial stories and instead use more neutral terms like guerrilla or rebel.[11]

Yet, usage of the terms guerrilla and terrorist is essentially reversed as we go from initial to follow-up stories (see Table 4.2). At the same

TABLE 4.4   Sources Comparisons for Initial and Follow-up Stories

Source	Initial		Follow-up	
Reporter	84%	(244)	48%	(78)
Friendly Official	9%	(26)	20%	(33)
U.S. Officials	0%	(0)	18%	(30)
Hostile Officials	3%	(9)	4%	(7)
Police/Security Forces	1%	(4)	2%	(3)
Other	2%	(6)	7%	(12)
Total		(289)		(163)

time, reporters writing follow-up stories tend to be less self-reliant in their characterizations, though they still comprise nearly half of the sources for actor or action designations. As we move from initial to follow-up stories other sources also become apparent. United States government officials or spokespersons constitute 18 percent of the sources in the follow-up coverage, up from *zero* in the initial stories. United States and friendly foreign sources together account for 38 percent of all actor and action designations in the follow-up stories. This is second only to reporter designations. This is in marked contrast to their *total absence* in initial stories and is probably explained by the fact that follow-up stories, unlike the breaking story, reflects the engagement of news routines which encourage reporter reliance on official sources.[12] Though the origins and operations of these routines will be the subject of chapter five, a brief discussion of official-reporter interaction may be helpful at this point.

With the initial event the reporter is trying to meet the requirement of timeliness.[13] Getting the story out first is most important. But with follow-up coverage the reporter is more likely to utilize "normal" news routines. The business imperatives of efficiency and predictability of supply encourages reporters working for newspapers like *The New York Times* to utilize news routines or "beats" which insure contact with legitimate, credible, reliable and typically official sources. Sources such as these offer something generally understood as "newsworthy" on a scheduled bases.

The bureaucracies of government are the most ready (and willing) source for reliable, scheduled flows of information, often in prepackaged formats. For instance, one recent study found that just under 64 percent of all citations regarding national security reporting in five leading U.S. newspapers originated with but four government sources.[14] Likewise, Leon Sigal found news content in *The New York Times* and *The Washington Post* was comprised largely of "packaged" news.[15] Some 70 to 90 percent of the news, depending on how the stories are categorized, result from such reporter-source interaction.[16] Spontaneous events like those often found in the initial violence stories comprised only about 1 percent of the content analyzed by Sigal.[17] The vast majority of what constituted news in *The New York Times* and *The Washington Post* were planned, controlled interactions between officials and reporters. This constitutes the normal or more typical operation of the news. It has considerable significance for this study of terrorism news coverage.

Table 4.5 is a two-by-two crosstabulation of "source" by "terror" as an actor or action designation. In other words, this table counts how many times "terrorism" or "terrorist" was used and compares it to who is using the terms in the news article. We see that references to "terror" come from U.S. sources about a third of the time. (Recall that references to terrorism comprises about half of the follow-up coverage). When a non-U.S. source appeared in the news about violence, they were usually talking about something other than terrorism. On the other hand, *if a U.S. official talked about some violent event, he or she tended to refer to "terrorism" or "terrorists."*

This tendency is even more pronounced when U.S. and friendly foreign sources are combined and compared to other source categories, as they have been in Table 4.6. Another third of the references to "terrorists" or "terrorism" come from friendly foreign officials. The remaining third is largely comprised of reporter references, "other" in this case.

Taken together, *U.S. and friendly sources account for 67 percent of the references to terrorism in the follow-up coverage.* "Terrorism" is violence much like the rest of the violence reported in *The New York Times* except for the presence of U.S. officials and their allies. As a consequence of

TABLE 4.5   All Follow-up Stories Only
               Mentions of Terrorism by Source: U.S. versus Other

	Terrorism Mentioned					
Source	*Yes*		*No*		*Total*	
U.S. Source	86%	(25)	14%	(4)	100%	(29)
Other	40%	(53)	60%	(78)	100%	(131)
Total	N=(78)		N=(82)			

Chi-Square = 18.101, p less than .001

TABLE 4.6   All Follow-up Stories Only
               Mentions of Terrorism by Source: U.S. and Friends versus Other

	Terrorism Mentioned			
Source	*Yes*		*No*	
US or Friendly	84%	(52)	16%	(10)
	100%	(62)		
Other	27%	(26)	73%	(72)
	100%	(98)		
Total	N=(78)		N=(82)	

Chi-Square = 47.705, p less than .001

their position as dominant news sources, officials are in a position of encouraging select renderings of terrorism stories. *This replicates and reinforces the same sort of select renderings of terrorism found in official reports on terrorism produced by the State Department.*

If we turn the question around and ask whether hostile foreign sources (officials and offices of ideological and/or foreign policy adversaries of the United States) have the capacity to designate violence as terrorism, we find they do not. In fact, hostile sources are rarely heard, accounting for only 5 percent (four) of all terrorist references in the follow-up coverage. Ninety-five percent of the terrorist references originate with "non-hostile" sources.

The data also suggest that *once violence is labeled as terrorism*, it is more prominently displayed in the news. Follow-up stories about terrorism, for instance, tended to be longer than non-terrorism follow-up stories, with the former averaging 19.3 paragraphs as opposed to 12.5 paragraphs for non-terrorism follow-up stories. Measured in terms of total number of follow-up stories devoted to an act of violence, terrorism designated stories averaged eight articles whereas non-terrorism violence averaged over four articles.[18] And when measuring attention by paragraphs, stories without the terrorism designation tended to be considerably shorter than those with the designation.[19]

All in all, as politicians and counterterrorism officials often claim, "terrorism" stories do indeed tend to receive more prominent and extensive news attention. Yet, ironically, it would seem that it is these very officials who play a large role in designating some given act of violence as terrorism in the first place and, secondarily, encourage the extensive coverage.

This is not to say that officials interacting with reporters are solely responsible for the designation of violence as terrorism and the attention subsequently devoted to it in the news. This is obviously not the case. Well over half the designations came from reporters applying the terminology on their own. But even here it seems reasonable to consider the possibility that in some of these instances reporters are not entirely autonomous in their use of terminology. When reporters themselves are the sources of the terror designation it could be because the use of the terminology has already been sanctioned by official usage. In this context, reporters feel free to use the terror designation without attribution, something they are normally quite reluctant to do. This does not, however, mean they are using it autonomously; they are already cued.[20]

What the data presented above indicate are several things: First, we see a general reluctance on the part of *The New York Times* to devote resources to the coverage of most violent terrorist-like events beyond the initial story. This is contrary to the impression one would have from reading case studies of media coverage of "terrorism." Rather than extensive, even saturation coverage of politically motivated violence, it seems reasonable to conclude that most violent events, even kidnappings and hijackings, do not receive saturation coverage and that, indeed, such coverage is the exception rather than the rule.

Secondly, *The Times* also demonstrated something of a reluctance to apply the terms "terrorist" or "terrorism" independently from sources, usually friendly government officials. A good portion of the public dialog regarding "terrorism" was confined to the boundaries of official debate regarding political violence. As the previous chapter demonstrated, acts of terrorist-like violence, using the State Department's own definition, tended to be excluded from the public dialog regarding terrorism. Subsequent chapters will highlight the policy consequences of the particular and partial interpretation of terrorism.

Summary of Findings

What terrorism is, how it is best defined, remains the subject of intense debate. One of the common components of most definitions of terrorism, however, is the idea that terrorists attract an inordinate amount of media attention. Terrorists, it is usually explained, are very adept at using the news media to generate attention while the media tend to be particularly susceptible to being drawn into the terrorists designs.

The research findings described in this chapter add a new dimension to our understanding of the news media's role in political violence.

First, while it is no doubt true that drama, particularly violence, attracts media attention, the quality and duration of media attention is influenced by another set of factors: Journalists follow news routines which encourage the use of legitimate government sources. Friendly government sources, not "terrorists," influence the extent of coverage which any given act of violence receives. These same sources influence the determination of who are and who are not treated as "terrorists" in the first place. Bassiouni and others adherents to the idea that the news media are used solely by terrorists focus all their attention on the relationship between reporters and violent political actors while ignoring the more well documented relationship between reporters and officials.

Secondly, the findings presented in this chapter also reveal an interesting irony. On the one hand, journalists are often accused by government officials of playing into the hands of terrorists. On the other hand, those same officials often cue journalists as to what is to be understood as terrorism in the first place. Yet, something more than irony may be present here. To evoke the alleged symbiotic relationship between terrorism and the news media is to subtly imply that the press works in an environment free from constraint and external pressure (some would say management). It reinforces the free press ideal while it clouds the operations of power on the press. As we will see in chapter five, the press is not free from multiple sources of constraint and pressure in their operation.

Notes

1. Walter Lippmann, *Public Opinion* (New York: Free Press, 1949), p. 27.

2. In 1992, *The New York Times* preeminence in foreign affairs coverage was evident in its ability to gain access to Saudi Arabia when all other American news organizations found it impossible to do so due to difficulties in obtaining visas to that closed country. As *The Washington Post* reported on October 9, 1992: "Most major U.S. media organizations—including *The Washington Post, Los Angeles Times, Time* magazine, *Newsweek* and all major television networks—have tried in vain to obtain visas to Saudi Arabia in the last year. A major exception is *The New York Times*, whose reporter Youssef M. Ibrahim has covered the kingdom for years and has made several trips there since the war" (Caryle Murphy, "Saudis Spurn Reporters Seeking Access to Kingdom," *The Washington Post*, October 9, 1992, p. A29).

3. Finding the first report of violence was quite straightforward. All coders reported little trouble in their identification. First reports usually followed the violent event itself by one day. In instances where that wasn't the case, the news report put time signifiers in the story, such as "reports filtering out of _____ today told of _____". Another signifier was the anchoring of the source of the information in the present. An example would be "Government spokesmen today said . . ." The event reported may have taken place weeks or even months before, but the initial report itself was quite easy to spot.

4. Though it is rather common to see comparisons of terrorism news and chronologies of "terrorist" events, such a design in this study is unwarranted for a couple of reasons.

First, a given chronology is implicitly based on a definition of terrorism; that is, whatever definition was used in its construction. This is useful and interesting information, if for no other reason than it provides some indication of the variability in inclusion and exclusion of incidents according to varying definitions.

I am interested in another question: How do the news media, *The Times* in this case, handle the ambiguity of terrorism. If *The Times* is capable of setting a news agenda, the important question concerns how it treats various violent events in its coverage. What becomes terrorism and why?

5. Follow-up could also be anything relating to the violence covered in the lead article, even if it appeared on the same day. The same information collected for initial stories was collected for follow-up stories. The only exception to this was the addition of a variable called "case number." It merely reassigned the

initial story's SPSS-PC case number to all corresponding follow-up articles. Two variables intended to measure follow-up coverage were also added. One noted total coverage by counting the total number of individual articles devoted to some act of violence. A second method noted the total frequency of all paragraphs in any given series of follow-up stories.

6. It is likely some of the follow-up stories were missed, either because they were overlooked or because they appeared in the paper at some point beyond the two day limit imposed in the research protocol. Yet as far as can be determined, only two stories were affected by this rule: The bombing of a Greenpeace vessel in New Zealand by French intelligence agents in 1985 and the downing of an Air India passenger jet that same year. Both reappeared in the news after a lacuna of several weeks.

7. In the analysis reported here, the concern that a single coder would miss some of the follow-up coverage was met in this way. A second coder was given a thirty day subsample. The second coder did not try to locate all follow-up stories. Rather, coder number two searched for additional follow-up at the point where the first coder failed to find additional stories. Cost restraints required this approach. It is possible, therefore, that additional stories *within* the follow-up time frame may have been missed by the first coder and not looked for at all by the second coder. The second coder was unable to detect additional stories within the subsample. The first coder also re-examined scores of stories which appeared on the surface to warrant additional coverage but received none. This was actually done prior to the intercoder reliability test described above. This produced one additional follow-up story. In short, a thorough examination of the data was made over many months of painstaking review.

8. Note the total story number for initial stories equals 274 because not all initial reports identify an actor. An example would be a story which said only "A bomb exploded today outside a mosque".

9. Some care has to be given in interpreting these figures. They focus on the actor label used in 162 follow-up stories which were themselves the result of twenty-nine violent incidents. The range of follow-up per initial reports of a violent incident was one to thirty-three. The concern here regards a possible multiplier effect from one or two incidents producing most of the follow-up terrorism reports. Treating each story as a semi-isolated event, though, is well founded for at least two reasons: 1) No one series of stories about a violent incident is written by a single reporter. Different reporters are making independent judgments as to what to call the actors involved in the incident according to his or her interaction with officials. Secondly, and most compelling, further analysis will indicate the terrorist label is strongly associated with a particular source (the eighth variable on the codesheet), and not some other variable. "Terrorism" as a descriptive term tends to originate with specific sources, not specific incidents.

10. To characterize and treat as criminal the violence of those who claim political grievances is to remove that violence from the political arena, detaching it from consideration of historical, economic, and/or social conditions and is instead categorizing it as merely the result of pure criminal intent. For instance,

when 241 American servicemen died in the truck-bomb explosion in Beirut on October 23, 1983, President Reagan repeatedly characterized the bombing as criminal. "We must not allow international criminals and thugs such as these," said Reagan, "to undermine the peace in Lebanon." He went on to say that every effort would be made to "find the criminals responsible for this act." Finally, Reagan gave particular emphasis to the alleged apolitical criminal intent of the bombing by remarking that "The tragedy is coming not really from the warring forces. It is coming from little bands of individuals, literally criminal-minded, who now see in the disorder that's going on an opportunity to do what they want to do" (Francis X. Clines, "Reagan Declares Marines' Role 'Vital' to Counter Soviet's in Lebanon," *The New York Times*, October 25, 1983, p. 1).

A corollary to the common characterization of terrorism as criminal activity is to characterize it as a consequence of psychopathology (Philip Schlesinger, Graham Murdock, and Philip Elliot, *Televising 'Terrorism': Political Violence in Popular Culture* [London: Comedia Publishing Group, 1983], p. 5). The range of possibilities run from religious fanaticism to alleged sexual pathologies. The argument here is that because terrorists are psychopathic, they are predisposed to violence. Violence is in this way stripped of political content and is merely an outlet for antisocial or self-destructive tendencies.

At times categorizations such as these are very subtle, such as Reagan's "criminal-minded" remark above. On the other hand, it is often remarkably crude. Claire Sterling's analysis of Italian revolutionary Giangiacomo Feltrinelli's motivations offer an example:

> No layman could say how big a part emotional deformities played in drawing Feltrinelli toward political violence, . . . His troubles in that connection are all too plain. Fatherless and oppressively mothered, unbearably lonely and starved for affection, he was also born with a shriveled penis. Not for all the Feltrinelli money could he purchase the normal pleasures enjoyed, say, by his stepfather or the gardener (Claire Sterling, *The Terror Network* [New York: Holt, Rinehart and Winston, 1981], p. 31).

In this view it seems terrorism is the result of sexual frustrations, proclivities to violence correlated to penis size.

11. Robert G. Picard and Paul D. Adams also examined whether the most frequently used characterizations of violence in the news differed according to source. They found that reporters and witnesses to political violence generally used neutral terms like rebel or guerrilla, whereas government sources tended to use "words that are more judgmental, inflammatory, and sensationalistic" ("Characterizations of Acts and Perpetrators of Political Violence in Three Elite U.S. Daily Newspapers," *Political Communication and Persuasion*, Vol. 4, 1987, p. 6).

12. For a description of news routines, see among others Edward Jay Epstein, *News From Nowhere* (New York: Vintage, 1973); Mark Fishman, *Manufacturing the News* (Austin: University of Texas Press, 1980); Leon Sigal, *Reporters and Officials: the Organization and Politics of News Making* (Lexington, Mass.: Heath, 1973).

13. Robert Entman, *Democracy Without Citizens: Media and the Decay of American Politics* (New York: Oxford University Press, 1989); James F. Larson, *Television's Window on the World: International Affairs Coverage on the U.S. Networks* (Norwood, New Jersey: Ablex Publishing Corporation, 1984).

14. Danial Hallin, Robert Carl Manoff, and Weddle, "Sourcing Patterns of National Security Reporters," *Journalism Quarterly* (forthcoming). The four sources were the Department of Defense, Congress, government unspecified, and the State Department. The five newspapers were *The New York Times, The Washington Post, The Los Angeles Times, the Boston Globe, The Wall Street Journal, The Washington Times,* and *Chicago Tribune.*

15. Sigal, *Reporters and Officials*, p. 121.

16. Bennett, *News*, p. 95.

17. The exact figure was 1.2%.

18. The exact figure was 4.3 with a minimum of one and a maximum of thirty-three.

19. Stories without the terrorism designation have Manova cell means of .241, compared to nearly .4 where there is mention of terrorism.

20. I would like to thank an anonymous reviewer for suggesting this possibility.

5

Managing the News
and Setting the Agenda

They've got to write their story every day. You give them their story, they'll go away. As long as you come in there every day, hand them a well packaged, premasticated story in the format they want, they'll go away.[1]

—Leslie Janka,
Press officer for the
Nixon and Reagan administrations

The Reagan and Bush administrations were willfully blind to the full scope of the terrorism spectacle when to do otherwise threatened desired policy goals. On the other hand, when terrorist violence, particularly violence at the hands of enemy regimes or sub-national groups, served to encourage desired policy goals, the administrations' spokespersons were quite vocal in their denunciations. While it might be argued that it made political sense for the Reagan and Bush administrations to ignore the terrorism of strategic allies such as Iraq, UNITA in Angola, and the Afghan Mujahideen, it is strikingly less clear why the news media would do so as well. Why, for instance, were some acts of politically motivated violence extensively covered and understood as terrorism while others were generally ignored?

The difference, I have argued, was largely a function of political power understood as issue management. This argument presupposes considerable control over the content of information carried over channels of mass communication. The purpose of this chapter is to describe how the Reagan and Bush administrations managed news content, including news regarding political violence. The chapter begins with what is by now a rather familiar description of the corporate operating environment of the contemporary news media. Ben Bagdikian and James D. Squires, among others, have described the injurious consequences of the new business ethic in contemporary news media, one which undermines the importance of independent journalism.

The bulk of the chapter is devoted to a description of the Reagan administration's efforts to take advantage of these developments in the news business. An elaborate institutional structure was established in the administration to manage news and issue content to the administration's benefit.

The Corporate Milieu:
Money, Media, and News Management

Todd Gitlin has noted the sometimes confusing array of explanations of news content.[2] While some explanations are "journalist-centered," regarding news as the product of professional news judgments, others regard the news as the product of organizational factors.[3] Closely related to these are explanations of the news that focus on the pressures journalists bring to bear on one another, often referred to as "pack journalism."[4] Another variant on the organizational explanation is Tuchman's "phenomenological" approach. In this view the news is a "social construct" which both reflects and recreates power relations in society.[5]

Herbert Gans has sought to synthesize these various approaches. For Gans, news is

> information which is transmitted from sources to audiences, with journalists—who are both employees of bureaucratic commercial organizations and members of a profession—summarizing, refining and altering what becomes available to them from sources in order to make the information suitable for their audiences. Because news has consequences, however, journalists are susceptible to pressure from groups and individuals (including sources and audiences) with power to hurt them, their organizations, and their firms. . . . Sources, journalists, and audience coexist in a system, although it is closer to being a tug of war than a functionally interrelated organism.[6]

Gitlin argues these "tugs of war" are resolved through the operation of political power, a power understood as the management of audience perceptions of reality. Philip Schlesinger has similarly stated that news is "the exercise of power over the interpretation of reality."[7]

Though these expressions are similar to the descriptions of power offered in chapter one, we need to take the analysis of power and news to another level and ask how power manifests itself in the day-to-day operation of news organizations and in the working lives of journalists.

Our answers here focus on economics, news routines, ideology, and a variety of inducements used by officials to encourage reporter compliance.

Concentration of Media Ownership

Central to nearly all explanations of news content is consideration of the concentration of mass media ownership. When Ben Bagdikian first published his superb book, *The Media Monopoly* in 1983, fifty corporations controlled nearly all of the major media. By the time *The Media Monopoly* went to a second printing in 1987 the number had been reduced to twenty-nine. By 1989, with the takeover of Warner Communications by Time, Incorporated, the number of major media owners was reduced to twenty-five.[8] At the 1980s rate of media mergers, Bagdikian estimated that by the turn of the century most media in the United States will be owned by five to ten corporations.[9]

These were not just communication corporations buying other communication corporations.[10] Their reach extended to nearly every corner of American life. The same people who brought you the movies, Columbia Pictures, also sold Coca Cola. The defense industry giant General Electric (light bulbs, refrigerators, nuclear warheads, jet engines) also owned RCA and the National Broadcasting Corporation (NBC).

The concentration of ownership in the media is quite apparent. What is not so apparent is how political power is exercised through the corporate media. What are the links between corporate ownership of the media and the actual content of the news? There have been several responses to this question, each differing more in emphasis than in substance. While some have argued that there is a "chain of command" running from the owners to the reporter on the beat, others have put forward the argument that the imperatives of the business world alone are sufficient cause for banal, "safe" news.

According to the "chain of command" argument, reporters and editors must produce news that is in compliance with the ideological disposition of the owner or board of directors. In this view the news is not what happened, or even what reporters say happened, but rather what the owners and news executives decided to print or broadcast.[11] News, in short, must pass a political test. Critics of this view have argued that it is often too reductionist, lacking the flexibility needed to accommodate the complexity of politics, particularly political violence. It forces us to look for "smoking guns," evidence of directives given by owners to editors and reporters as to what is politically acceptable. Evidence of this sort is often difficult to find.

While not necessarily discounting the chain of command thesis, others speculate that corporate ownership of the news media asserts itself in more subtle ways.[12] This might be called the "market forces" argument. Doug Underwood, for instance, has noted that the concentration of media ownership has produced subtle but important changes in the way stories are written, even what stories are written.[13] The test of news worthiness employed by editors, in Underwood's estimation, is not a political test but rather an economic one. Editors consult marketing spreadsheets, not the publishers politics.[14] David Burgin, editor of the *Dallas Times Herald*, has noted that "The new power in the industry is the marketing director. I want to see more swashbuckling editors, like Ben Bradlee or Jim Bellows. But those days are dead. Now it's marketing and target marketing and more marketing."[15] James D. Squires, former editor at the *Chicago Tribune*, expressed the same idea this way: "Today, with few exceptions, the final responsibility for newspaper content rest with the business executive in charge of the company, not the editor."[16]

There are important political consequences to this development. When profit is the driving force behind the corporate news business, like any other business, news as a commodity—*above all other considerations*—will lack the consistent critical edge of news content produced by a truly adversarial press. In exchange for predictable news gathering routines and profitability, the press gives up a certain degree of independence. This is largely the result of the relationship between commercialism and "objectivity" as conventionally applied to the press.

Objectivity

The fact that the owners and managers of news organizations seek a return on investment is not a new development. But the degree to which this is *solely* the case, according to former editors such as Bagdikian and Squires, is new. This new focus, along with the greater concentration of media ownership, reinforces tendencies long a part of the commercial press.

News as a commodity must be treated like any other mass production item. Production costs, for instance, must be kept to a minimum to encourage profitability. The resulting marketing practices have generally been referred to as "objectivity."

Objectivity emerged in the wake of the formation of the *Associated Press* in 1848.[17] Selling stories to the widest possible audience required standardized stories stripped of all obvious political markings. The use of standardized formats—simply presenting the who, what, when, where, *and a credible source's version of why and how*—meant that the widest possible market share would be attracted to, or at least not offended by, the story content. A politically bland, standardized newspaper wrapped in market-tested stylishness sold to the widest possible mass market.

Because the reporter could not speak for him or her self and still remain "objective," nearly everything said in the story had to be attributable to some, often official, source. The more official, legitimate, and credible the source, the more efficient and marketable the story. It simply made better economic sense to take information from sources regarded as credible (noncontroversial and/or official). To do otherwise invited the additional expense of conducting special investigations to document the claims made by alternative sources (read nonofficial) who were likely to invite attack by politically powerful actors. In this way officials essentially subsidized news gathering by reducing the cost of information acquisition.[18] The point made by Bagdikian, Squires, and other critics of the contemporary corporate press is that the dynamic put into place with the formation of the Associated Press has gotten out of hand, and in the process has undermined cherished free press ideals.

The result of news commercialism has been a strong press predisposition to report what officials wanted reported, as they wanted it reported, and when they wanted it reported, particularly in foreign affairs. Objectivity forced the reporter to appear less intelligent than he or she actually was. Former *New York Times* reporter David Halberstram put it this way:

> Despite all the fine talk of objectivity, the only thing that mildly approaches objectivity was the form in which the reporter wrote the news, a technical style which required the journalist to appear much dumber and more innocent than in fact he was. So he wrote in a bland, uncritical way which gave greater credence to the utterances of public officials, no matter how mindless these utterances. . . . Thus the press voluntarily surrendered a vast amount of real independence; it treated the words and actions of the government of the United States with a credence that those words and actions did not necessarily merit.[19]

Every step of the journalistic process involves a value-laden decision. What of the infinite possibilities is to be covered and what is to be ignored? Which of the infinite observations confronting the reporter will be noted and which goes unnoticed? If noted, which will be prominently displayed on page one and which will be buried under a back-page fold? The point Squires, Bagdikian, and other critics have made in recent years is that these sort of questions are increasingly answered according to marketing decisions, and not according to some older tradition of civic responsibility. Underwood put it this way: "What worries us (veteran reporters) is whether the true value of the business—the craft of writing, the vigor of investigating, the sense of fairness and equity, the gut-level impulse to want to right wrongs—will survive in the new MBA-run, market-driven newsroom.[20]

There is some danger here of romanticizing "the good old days of journalism." The relatively wide distribution of news media ownership during the early years of the Vietnam war did not lend itself to more critical reporting.[21] Likewise, during World War II, as Paul Fussell has shown, the news sanitized and distorted the brutalities of war.[22] What is clear is that contemporary conditions undermine whatever critical independence previously existed in the press. Here are a few of the consequences of corporate journalism.

First, costly investigative journalism gives way to "fluff" pieces, what some drolly refer to as "News Lite." After studies in the 1970s indicated a declining readership and, even worse, that younger people were watching television news instead of reading newspapers, newspapers sought ways to reverse these trends. The American Society of Newspaper Editors hired marketing expert Ruth Clark to devise a strategy. She concluded newspapers should use more graphics, features, briefs, and "help-me-cope" pieces.[23] In the ensuing years, many newspapers followed this advice, with Gannett's *USA Today* the most notable example.

In this environment hard news suffers. With finite resources, newspapers which brim with food, weather, sports and how-to sections, do not devote the resources needed for independent investigative journalism. Besides, appearing too aggressive may be bad for business. Stories can backfire. It is much safer—and market tested—to run more features or rewrite government press releases. Controversial issues are simply too dangerous from a marketing perspective.

In the fiscally conservative milieu of the corporate media, the journalists discover the limits of controversy through a long socialization process. Veteran *New York Times* correspondent R. W. Apple described it this way:

> The way to the top really communicates its views to the rest of the paper is through the subordinate editors, and even more important than that through longtime discussions with and shaping of people who are going to be senior correspondents. You can't do a lot as an editor in New York to set the tone of a Moscow correspondent's dispatches; it's just too far away. So you send somebody to Moscow who is in tune with what you want the newspaper to be. You use your system of promotion and personnel assignment to see that that happens.[24]

Middle of the road to conservative journalism, tied to the official line is the result.

Secondly, besides the tendency to produce non-controversial "fluff" pieces, the very availability of news is affected by the worldwide distribution of correspondents and news bureaus which, in turn, reflects the economics of news gathering.[25] Critics of the current system of international news gathering note the typically sporadic coverage of the Third World. Natural disasters or political instability and violence may temporarily draw media attention, only to find it quickly fade. We saw this pattern in the data presented in the last chapter. Mort Rosenblum calls this the "coup and earthquake syndrome." It is also sometimes referred to as "parachute" journalism and international "pack" journalism.

The problem with pack or parachute journalism is that it focuses on dramatic political events rather often more staid processes. As a result, wars, famine, and other social and political upheavals seem to spring out of nowhere in places previously unheard in the news. Even during the pack's crisis reporting, historical circumstances and processes are often missing from the news.[26] Instead, events are put into context for the newly arrived journalist by the embassy and local elite. The consequences are the same: Official sources dominate the news.

The heavy reliance on official sources and the costs incurred for doing otherwise point to the ultimate consequence of the commercial news media: *The news media are left susceptible to being "managed" by dominant sources.* Managing the public's issue agenda by managing the news has become a major preoccupation of government officials. Though this seems no less true of the Clinton administration than of the Reagan and Bush administrations, I am particularly interested in developing a more complete understanding of the Reagan administration's news media management apparatus. The Reagan administration created a sophisticated media management apparatus to take advantage of and reinforce the news gathering tendencies of the corporate media. The purpose of this apparatus was to set the issue agenda of the press, and by extension, the American public. This apparatus and how it functioned is described next.

The White House and News Management

Mark Hertsgaard's *On Bended Knee: The Press and the Reagan Presidency* and John Anthony Maltese's *Spin Control: The White House Office of Communication and the Management of Presidential News* present detailed descriptions of the news management apparatus put into place in the White House in the 1980s and 1990s. Both authors interviewed scores of former officials of the Reagan and Bush White House, as well as reporters, editors, producers, and other network executives.

James Baker, David Gergen, and Michael Deaver were most directly responsible for media management during Ronald Reagan's first term.[27] All agreed on one thing; controlling news content was essential to governing, to making policy and implementing it. Former White House communications director, David Gergen, put it this way: "To govern successfully, the government has to set the agenda; it cannot let the press set the agenda for it."[28] Lou Gerig, former head of the Office of Media Liaison remarked that "We really tried to define the agenda every day."[29] President Reagan's last director of communication, Thomas C. Griscom told Maltese something quite similar: His job was "to help set, influence, determine public opinion." To that end, he told Maltese, the administration had to control and manage the agenda.[30]

This meant managing news content as much as possible. Leslie Janka, former deputy press secretary for the administration remarked that "The whole thing was PR. This was a PR outfit that became President and took over the country. . . . (T)heir first, last and overreaching activity was public relations."[31] To set the terms of debate about issues it wanted discussed, the administration established a sophisticated media management apparatus run out of the White House by Reagan's top aides. There were several components to this apparatus.

In 1981, Gergen established the "Blair House" or "Friday Group" meetings. The purpose of these meetings was to establish long-term media strategy. Those usually in attendance were David Gergen, Michael Deaver, Richard Wirthlin, Richard Darman and Frank Ursomarso. Ursomarso told Maltese that Gergen was constantly pushing long-term planning. "'Frank, you've gotta be focused on the future. You've gotta be out there.' And I'd say, 'Well, I'm out there thirty days.' And he'd say, 'That's not enough.' You've got to be out there six months.'"[32]

The Blair House meetings were, however, only the first layer of the Reagan White House issue management apparatus. The second layer consisted of the daily media management coordinating meetings. A meeting of the White House communications group took place every weekday morning at 8:30. This was where the specifics of publicity campaigns were determined and designed. Whereas the Blair House meetings "may see the smoke beginning, or the opportunity available down the road, at the communications meeting we talk about how we will sell our story." "What do we want the press to cover today, and how?," was how one former participant described the daily objective of the communications group meeting.[33] Deaver explained how the group operated:

We would take a theme, which we usually worked on for six weeks—say, the economy. The President would say the same thing, but we had a different visual for every one of those stops. They see the President out at the auto plant because imports are down and American cars are up. They see the President at a high-tech plant in Boston because high-tech means jobs. Pretty soon it begins to soak in, pretty soon the people begin to believe the economy is getting better.[34]

Repetition of the desired message was key. In order for the White House version of reality to overwhelm all competing messages, the President and his surrogates had to say the same thing over and over again. "It used to drive the President crazy," said Deaver, "because the repetition was so important. He'd get on that airplane and look at that speech and say, 'Mike, I'm not going to give this same speech on education again, am I?' I said, 'Yeah, trust me, it's going to work.' And it did."[35]

Prior to the communications group meeting was the "line of the day" meeting held at 8:15 and chaired by James Baker. Among those typically in attendance was Larry Speakes, deputy press spokesman, Richard Darman, the man who sat in the powerful position of managing the document flow into the Oval Office, and media advisors Michael Deaver and David Gergen. As Deaver described the purpose of the meeting, it was to "make sure we're all saying the same thing."[36]

By coordinating their responses, Reagan administration officials attempted to shape news content. Events and issues the administration wanted played up received a barrage of official statements employing nearly identical language, while questions regarding events and issues the administration wanted to remain obscure were met with stony silence. This calls to mind the study results described in chapters three and four. The predilection of the press to rely on official sources, and the extraordinary efforts of the administration to take advantage of this predilection, produced selective "publicity campaigns," to use Herman's term for describing the media and official denunciation of select (enemy) political violence. These publicity campaigns were highly orchestrated by the administration.

Once agreed upon, the line of the day was immediately made available to other senior administration officials through computer electronic mail messages. By simply calling it up on one's computer screen, an administration official could be sure to be abreast of the coordinated response to certain questions that might be asked during encounters with the press that day. Others in the bureaucracy were apprised of the day's planned responses with conference calls. The use of conference calls for foreign policy coordination was in place from the very start of the Reagan administration. Each morning, Ursomarso and Lyndon "Mort" Allin of the Press Office staff, held conference calls on secure lines with public affairs officers in the State Department, Defense Department, Central Intelligence Agency, and the National Security Council. During these calls the officials attempted to anticipate the questions that might come up that day and coordinate their responses.[37] According to one participant, the calls went something like this:

> It was like, 'Okay, what do we say about Lebanon today?' We'd go through the paper and see a story about South Africa, say, and figure out how we wanted to handle that. 'Well, no-comment it,' we'd decide, or 'That's a Pentagon story, we will shut up. State, you've got the lead on George Shultz's press conference in Brazil.' Now the White House may say, 'Look, the President's got a statement tomorrow, so shut up today, goddamnit, just shut up, don't pre-empt the President, (we'll) cut your nuts off if you leak anything out on this one,' that kind of guidance. Other times we would say, 'Here's what we're going to say, everybody just say it at once. I don't care if you're asked the question or not, everybody in the administration today praises Gemayel's leadership,' or Mubarak's leadership, or whatever it is."[38]

Howard Teicher of the NSC remarked that when he was at the National Security Council, each day began with a 7:30 A.M. staff meeting dealing with the press. "The first thing we did," Teicher explained, "was deal with the press, and often times we never got beyond that; just contingency talking points for whatever was in the media that day." Shaping that day's news was a top priority of the administration.

The communication group and line of the day meetings were only the start. Throughout the day the White House would continue in its efforts to control the news. Gergen, for instance, acknowledged that he frequently called reporters working on a story.

> I tried to call them back late in the afternoon, after they had their information and wanted to put in some kind of context. That's what everybody referred to as 'spin control,' but I thought it was important, if they were way off base, to draw them back, or if they had something to make sure . . . they had some sense of what the White House view on it was.[39]

Gergen routinely called all three of the major television networks just prior to the airing of the nightly news to find out what they were going with that night. The calls were often followed, said Gergen, by a "flurry around here trying to influence what they were doing." Michael Deaver, who effectively took over as communications director after Gergen was reassigned, said the practice of calling reporters and network executives was "absolutely necessary."

The Reagan White House efforts to manage the news did not even end there. Weekly seminars for the spokespersons from various federal agencies were another component of the administration news management apparatus. At these seminars, one in the morning given by Donald Regan on economic matters and the other on foreign policy given in the afternoon by Robert McFarland, spokespersons were coached on the issues they were to promote. Again, the idea was to coordinate language, to encourage those who spoke for the administration to speak with one voice.

Another component of the Reagan administration's agenda setting apparatus were the public opinion surveys conducted by Richard Wirthlin. Shaping and directing the content of the public issue agenda required extensive monitoring of public opinion. Wirthlin conducted over five hundred surveys in Reagan's eight years in office, all funded by the Republican National Committee. These monthly surveys "probed just about every aspect of public affairs on a scale unmatched in U.S. history."[40] According to *Advertising Age*, Wirthlin's polls were also unmatched in detail.[41]

Richard Beale of the White Communications Office worked with Wirthlin to determine issue priorities and content strategies for the administration. Frank Ursomarso explain the system this way: The Office of Communications "determined what issue would be top priority, second priority—what the visibilities would be for the various themes." Ursomarso used the example of an issue concerning the Justice Department. "Then I would have to get together with the fellow at Justice and say, 'Look, this is the priority that we're going to be working on, and this is what we're trying to do. Now, how can you help and what can we do together and what do you know?'" The idea was to *"somehow move that issue and keep the visibility up."*[42]

To keep track of the success of their campaigns, Ursomarso's office "would generate graphs from his computerized system showing the number of minutes devoted to various stories. We would use those graphs to determine, in part, how well we were doing."[43] Setting the tone and content of issue dialog in the news was the name of the game.

Putting It All Together

One example of how all this came together to structure the news occurred in 1982. Wirthlin's polls detected rising public resentment of Reagan administration policies that favored the wealthy while hurting the poor. The perception of Reagan as a friend of the rich was fueled by

Nancy Reagan's expensive tastes. As Michael Deaver put it, "We had all those negative stories on Nancy Reagan at that time. You take the budget cut stories and pair them with the stories about the new (White House) china and the refurbishing of the dresses and all that, and it was beginning to hurt. We could see it in our polls." The White House public relations apparatus began devoting its energies to planning media events designed to counter the emerging grassroots issue of administration coddling of the rich and powerful. It effectively had to be made a "non-issue."

The White House media experts hit upon the idea of an antidrug abuse campaign. Mrs. Reagan was soon making the tour of drug abuse centers and schools warning about the evils of drugs. Though certainly not a complete success, the strategy seemed to help her image problem. Lee Lescaze of *The Washington Post* remarked, "(I)t suddenly became clear to us that we were not to take swipes at Nancy Reagan."[44] The press simply did not have it in them to attack her on such a mission of mercy, even if it was understood by nearly everyone within the Washington press corp to be a cynical public relations ploy.

Deaver and company's handling of the administration image problem regarding education policy offers another example. In 1983 Wirthlin's surveys detected a two-to-one disapproval rating of Reagan's education policies, largely due to cutbacks in funding. It was decided by the Blair House group that this had to be countered. The themes of the campaign were merit pay for teachers and better discipline. Among other media events, the White House invited the "teacher of the year" to the White House. It also made a tough talking, baseball bat and megaphone wielding New Jersey principal something of a national hero as a part of the campaign. Reagan himself made twenty-five speeches during the campaign. More accurately stated, Reagan gave the same speech twenty-five times. As Saul Freedman, a Knight-Ridder correspondent, said, "They understood that to shift the fulcrum of the debate, you have to do it with repetition, which the President is very good at."[45] By the end of the campaign, without Reagan administration education policies changing the least, Wirthlin's surveys detected a two-to-one margin in support of Reagan administration education policies.

Staging the news even included staging deadly international armed conflict. The Reagan administration felt shackled by the apparent reluctance of most Americans to allow the U.S. to become involved in Third World conflicts. This reluctance is generally referred to as the "Vietnam syndrome." It will be discussed more in chapter seven. On August 19, 1981, the administration took its first crack at reversing the Vietnam syndrome when United States Navy jets encountered jets from

Libya over the Gulf of Sidra. In the ensuing air battle, U.S. fighter planes downed two Libyan jets.

The White House media crew had, as always, planned this encounter to the last detail. The confrontation was originally scheduled for July but was postponed by chief of staff Baker. He feared that it would draw too much media attention away from the administration's legislative victories. A sense of timing was crucial to good news management. Once underway, though, the White House was ready. That morning Reagan was taken to the USS Constellation off the Virginia coast in time for a photo opportunity. On the news that night the Commander-in-chief was on the bridge, in naval garb and binoculars in hand. It was surely one of Reagan's finest roles. (Kaddafi tried a similar media event with his own navy and was roundly ridiculed by the American press.) The pictures on the news that evening subliminally conveyed the impression that Reagan was there in the heat of battle in the Gulf of Sidra, and not as he actually was at the time of the encounter—in bed sound asleep and undisturbed by his staff.

This episode is telling the administration's policies regarding terrorism, including its media tactics, were not meant to end terrorism, at least not all terrorism. After all, the United States was a major supplier of weapons and training to various regimes and guerrilla groups which routinely utilized terror tactics. Rather, like the encounter in the Gulf of Sidra, the administration was in search of a means by which it could overcome the Vietnam Syndrome, among other objectives.

Bringing in the CIA

Despite these successes, perhaps because of the setbacks in Central America, the White House evidently came to the conclusion that it needed help in its news media and issue management efforts. According to Robert Parry and Peter Kornbluh, the White House brought on board senior covert operations specialists from the Central Intelligence Agency (CIA). They were assigned to the White House to create and manage a propaganda operation directed at members of Congress, the press, and the American public.[46] The principal players in this operation were CIA Director William Casey and Walter Raymond, Jr., described by Parry and Kornbluh as the CIA's leading propaganda expert.

Once assigned to the Department of State, and "retired" from the CIA (it would have been illegal for the CIA to be directly involved in such domestic propaganda activities), Raymond created the Office of Public Diplomacy for Latin America and the Caribbean (S/LPD). Though housed in the State Department, S/LPD was not directed by it. Rather, it was under the guidance of "RIG," the "Restricted Interagency group" comprised of National Security Council staffers Oliver North, CIA Central America Task Force chief Alan Fiers, and Assistant Secretary of State for Inter-American Affairs Elliot Abrams. One source quoted by Parry and Kornbluh acknowledged that S/LPD was closely modeled after CIA overseas propaganda operations. "They were trying to manipulate (U.S.) public opinion . . . using the tools of Walt Raymond's trade craft which he learned from his career in the CIA covert operations shop."[47] Another source reported by the *Miami Herald* described S/LPD's efforts as a "vast psychological warfare operation."

The specific purpose of the operation was to put pressure on Congress and the news media to support the administration's war effort in Central America. As Raymond himself described it in a July, 1986 memorandum, "In the specific case of Nica(ragua), concentrate on gluing black hats on the Sandinistas and White hats on UNO (the contras)."[48] This meant encouraging Sandinista atrocity stories while the more numerous Contra transgressions had to be ignored. This, of course, was the same technique apparently applied to "terrorism" reporting.

It also meant looking for new angles for selling desired policies to a reluctant Congress and American public. When, for instance, Wirthlin's opinion surveys in 1983 discovered that Americans were beginning to be alarmed by the influx of Latin American refugees, Reagan tapped this concern by suggesting that this "tidal wave" could be stopped only by crushing the leftist movements in Central America. In a June 1983 speech, Reagan warned that unless a tough stand was taken, these "feetpeople" would be "swarming into our country."[49]

Raymond's operation also turned into something of an American Ministry of Information. In its first year alone, S/LPD arranged 1,500 speaking engagements (these included radio and television, and editorial board interviews), distributed material to 1,600 college and university libraries, 520 political science faculty, 122 editorial writers, and 107 religious organizations.[50] It also published three booklets on Nicaragua. Furthermore, according to a February 8, 1985 S/LPD activities report to the NSC:

> Correspondents participating in programs such as the 'McLaughlin Group,' 'Agronsky and Company,' and 'This Week with David Brinkley' receive special materials such as the report on Nicaragua's Military Buildup expeditiously and have open invitations for personal briefings."[51]

At every available point of leverage the administration attempted to direct media toward those issues and issue interpretations it wanted covered, as it wanted them covered. At the same time, it sought to turn media attention away from those issues and events it wanted left untouched. The administration was capable of managing the news as it did in part due to the corporate induced docility of commercial journalism. As the data in previous chapters indicate, with regard to such activities as guerrilla wars in Angola and Afghanistan, Iraq's continued support of terrorism, and politically motivated violence more generally, the administration was often stunningly successful in this effort.

The press, though, is not monolithic, and neither are the politically powerful who tend to dominate the debate. There are real policy differences between liberals and conservatives, Democrats and Republicans, though the differences are often marginal. There are also instances of inadequate socialization of reporters in the field. At times, journalists do report highly critical stories. We shall see an example of this in chapter six. In short, despite the economic and political pressures described to this point, enforcement mechanisms are necessary to keep the mainstream press, such as *The New York Times,* in line. "In line" means reporting those prepackaged events without too much deviation. We next turn to a review of several enforcement mechanisms used to encourage a particular news content.

There are at least two major enforcement mechanisms intended to keep the news in check: Co-optation of key journalists—referred to here as fawning, and attacks by government officials and other powerful political actors against journalists who stray too far outside the bounds of acceptable controversy—referred to here as flak.

Co-opting the Press

Successful news management required more than just the docile inclinations of the corporate news media. By cultivating friendly but controlled relations with journalists, and severely punishing or threatening to punish those who did not cooperate, Reagan administration officials were able to enhance their media management capability.

Many of the components of the news management apparatus outlined above were not new. David Gergen, a former Nixon administration aide, had taken many of the techniques described above straight out of the Nixon White House. The line of the day meetings and the conference calls, for example, were features of the Nixon White House.[52] But unlike the Nixon administration, the Reagan administration, at least on the surface, also attempted to foster good relations with the press corp.

Charming the press often meant simply paying attention to the creature comforts of journalists. An attempt was made to provide the White House press corp with everything they could possibly need—except uncontrolled information. Deputy assistant to the President Joanna Bistany explained the White House philosophy this way:

> If you give somebody a comfortable place to work, good facilities, provide food because you know they can't take time to go to a restaurant ten miles away to eat, and in general provide the creature comforts, how then can someone turn around and bite the hand that feeds him? I had reporters (at the 1983 Western economic summit meeting) in Williamsburg tell me, 'Jesus Christ, how can I write a nasty story? Every time I need something, somebody is there to provide it for me. I've got two phones right in front of me, food over there, it's really hard to write a nasty story'."[53]

Reporters also had what was essentially unlimited prepackaged information from throughout the Executive branch, a strategy which has been referred to as "manipulation by inundation." This was the same technique used by the Committee on Public Information (CPI), established during World War I to coordinate propaganda.[54] The CPI "discovered in 1917-18 that one of the best means of controlling news was flooding news channels with 'facts,' or what amounted to official information."[55] Leslie Janka, a press officer in both the Nixon and Reagan administrations described the strategy this way:

> As opposed to Kissinger and Haldeman and that crowd, whose view was that you control the media by giving them bits and pieces (of information), the Reagan White House came to the totally opposite conclusion that the media will take what we feed them. They've got to write their story every day. You give them their story, they'll go away. As long as you come in there every day, hand them a well-packaged, premasticated story in the format they want, they'll go away. The phrase is 'manipulation by inundation.' You give them the line of the day, you give them the press briefings, you give them facts, access to the people who will speak on the record . . . . And you do that long enough, they're going to stop bringing their own stories, and stop being investigative reporters of any kind, even modestly so.[56]

Despite all of these enticements to simply go along, not all journalists passively rewrote administration press releases. This was particularly true of journalists who operated outside the White House and Executive branch beat system. In order for "manipulation by inundation" to be successful, the costs of going outside the daily authorized press feeds had to be raised to unacceptable levels. Herman and Chomsky have referred to these measures as "flak"—the sanctions politically powerful actors impose on individual journalists and even entire news organizations should either begin to take adversarial journalism too seriously. They outline how powerful actors, such as advertisers and conservative media watchdog groups, exert pressure on the press to conform. What is offered below is an elaboration on Herman and Chomsky's basic argument. We will begin with a review of the methods of "official flak."

Official Flak

Probably the most effective method of handling a recalcitrant reporter was to freeze him or her out of insider reporting opportunities. Operating in the highly competitive Washington, D.C. press environment, where much of the terrorism spectacle was created, meant journalist were always vulnerable to being locked out. For instance, *New York Times* national security affairs correspondent Leslie Gelb was barred for a time from future press briefings by the State Department's Politico-Military Affairs office. Gelb had written an article on U.S. contingency plans to deploy nuclear depth charges in the territorial waters of eight allied countries, none of which had been told of the plan. Even though Gelb based his article on information already published in the foreign press, the State Department did not like the article and barred him from press briefings.

Journalists are also careful of what they say or write, remarked Howard Teicher of the NSC, because "they don't want to burn their bridges. . . . We don't shoot-off knees in Washington, but if someone wrote that Richard Haas (formerly of the National Security Council) or anybody else was duplicitous,[57] they're not going to return his phone calls." Teicher continued: "The ultimate parasitic relationship in this town, particularly in foreign policy, . . . is the symbiotic, parasitic relationship between policy makers—and I'm not talking about desk officers here—(between) mid-to-senior level policy makers—and the press."[58]

With so few credible and "legitimate" sources from which to choose, especially on the White House beat, journalists simply could not afford to be too adversarial for fear of retaliation. Beyond being barred outright, retaliation for overzealous reporting might also come in the form of favoring one's competitor with the next hot inside tip. "Its hard to avoid the analogy of the White House press corp as a bunch of caged hamsters thoroughly dependent on their masters for their daily feeding," remarked former *Boston Globe* White House correspondent Walter Robinson.[59] This was particularly true of *The New York Times*, said Robinson. It was "shameless."

It's so important for *The Times* to be first that they throw their standards out the window. There's general resentment among other print reporters of *The Times* and *The Post* because of their access. It's so much easier for (second term chief of staff) Don Regan to drop something in there as a trial balloon, and then everybody else will pick it up.[60]

This later point is worth emphasizing. Controlling *The New York Times*, as well as *The Washington Post*, was crucial for the administration. If *The New York Times* ran a story, sometimes because an administration official wanted it printed, the rest of the news media would usually follow suit. If, on the other hand, the administration could hinder the reporting of *The New York Times*, other papers faced difficulties filling the breech. Controlling *Times'* reporters created a de facto control over much of the national news agenda. What happened to former *Times* correspondent Ray Bonner illustrates this.

Following the March, 1982 Constituent Assembly election in El Salvador, *New York Times* Central America correspondent Ray Bonner was pulled from El Salvador by *Times* editors and reassigned to the financial desk in New York. Unlike much of the reporting coming out of El Salvador following the election, Bonner had continued to write of the atrocities committed by the Salvadoran army, the suspension of the modest land reform program, and of the massive frauds that had occurred in the election itself.

In January 1982 Bonner and photojournalist Susan Meiselas were the first to investigate the massacre of nearly eight hundred people at El Mozote, El Salvador. *Washington Post* correspondent Alma Guillermoprieto was soon to follow with her own account. In his story, Bonner described "the charred skulls and bones of dozens of bodies burned under burned-out roofs, beams, and shattered tiles." The story came at a particularly bad time for the Reagan administration as it attempted to "certify," as required by Congress, that El Salvador was making progress in its human rights conduct.

Bonner was attacked almost immediately by the State Department, conservative media watchdog groups, and even by other news organizations (*Time* magazine and *The Wall Street Journal* accused Bonner of political bias). Thomas Enders, then assistant secretary of state for inter-American affairs, claimed before a congressional committee that "no evidence could be found to confirm that government forces systematically massacred civilians."[61] And the commander of the U.S. military advisors in El Salvador, Colonel John Waghelstein, was reported to have told one U.S. reporter, "I'd like to get (*Washington Post* reporter John) Dinges and Bonner up in a plane." This was an apparent reference to a torture technique used by the U.S. military in Vietnam.

Though he did not face Colonel Waghelstein in an airplane, Bonner was pulled from El Salvador. "That story," said Bonner, " was the beginning of the end of my career at *The New York Times.*"[62]

Was Bonner pulled for political reasons? Michael Massing has argued that he was. Bonner also believes this to be the case, something then *New York Times* executive editor, Abe Rosenthal, vehemently denied: "That's bullshit. There's no other way to put it. It's plain, old-fashion bullshit."[63] Bonner, instead, was reassigned, said Rosenthal, because he had proven himself and the *Times* had decided to bring him home to "train" him.[64]

Whatever the reason behind Bonner's reassignment, the results were the same. Correspondents believed they had to be "more careful," that is, less critical of the Salvadoran government, security forces, and the Reagan administration policies in El Salvador. As Massing quoted one reporter, "(Bonner's transfer) left us all aware that the embassy is quite capable of playing hardball. . . . If they can kick out the *Times* correspondent, you've got to be careful."[65] Bonner also raised the same point: "I've had other Central America reporters tell me that after I left they found it harder to get their stuff in." While "the *New York Times* reported this much," spreading his arms wide, "there was that much space," narrowing his arms, "for others to file similar stories. Several reporters told me that after I left, it left them with that much less space, since their stories weren't being legitimized by (their editors) seeing the same angle being reported in the *New York Times.*"[66]

And what of the reported massacre at Mozote? In October, 1992, a team of forensic archaeologists finally offered gruesome confirmation of Bonner's and Guillermoprieto story. *The New York Times* article described it this way:

> Nearly 11 years after American-trained soldiers were said to have torn through El Mozote and surrounding hamlets on a rampage in which at least 794 people were killed, the bones have emerged as stark evidence that the claims of peasant survivors and the reports of a couple American journalists were true.[67]

The former *Post* correspondent, Alma Guillermoprieto responded this way to the stories eleven years after the fact:

> Two journalist from leading newspapers, traveling independently of each other, provided the same evidence. There were photographic documents, credible sources."
>
> "It was very, very hard to fight the Reagan administration; it's very hard to fight any administration. . . . What we see is that administrations

are increasingly able to dictate the terms of coverage—in Panama, for example, in the Iraq war.[68]

In a 1993 interview on CBS's "60 Minutes," Guillermoprieto summed the episode up this way: "The Reagan administration didn't want to know, they didn't want it to get in the way of policy." As with Afghan and Angolan rebel and Iraqi government involvement with terrorism, if news interfered with policy objectives, the news was ignored, discredited and shunted aside.[69]

Bonner and Guillermoprieto are certainly not the only journalists to have experienced personal attacks from officials trying to manage issues. *Associated Press* reporter, Robert Parry, for example, was the subject of a smear campaign directed by Gregory Lagana, the press secretary for the Assistant Secretary of State Elliot Abrams. Lagana attempted to discredit Parry by referring to him as a "Sandinista sympathizer." After that, another Reagan administration official tried to convince Parry that his partner at the *Associated Press*, Brian Barry, was "politically suspect." Said Parry:

> And if you don't succumb to all that, you get the line from your editors that maybe they should take you off the story, since you seem to be pursuing a political agenda. When the government attacks you, even your colleagues begin to doubt your credibility, when it should be just the opposite.[70]

Personal attacks on reporters or pressure on news organizations from officials was only a small part of official flak. The Reagan administration pursued a profoundly more threatening course of action in its efforts to control the news and public issue agenda. This involved a host of measures to seal off all uncontrolled sources of information.

Treating Reporters Like Spies

While virtually all modern Presidents have expressed concern about "leaks," the remedies and proposed remedies offered by the Reagan and Bush administrations were the most drastic to date. Almost immediately upon taking office, Reagan and his aides began an assault on what they considered dangerous contact with the press, that is, contact outside the control of the issue management apparatus described earlier.

In January, 1981 Reagan approved an executive order which required administration officials from throughout the foreign policy bureaucracy to obtain advanced White House clearance before talking with the press about "national security' concerns. Encouraged by administration hard-liners, Reagan had originally planned to eliminate all background and off-the-record interviews. His more astute media advisors, however, successfully argued against such a move. They realized these were important devices for manipulating the press when controlled properly, and it was up to Gergen to achieve that control. This simply meant that no one outside of Gergen's press office could take a call from the press unless approved. The proposed ban and the possibility of future polygraph tests was intimidation enough. As we will see in a moment, there were further attempts to seal-off uncontrolled access to officials.

Beside limiting reporter's uncontrolled access to officials, issues were also managed by placing tighter restrictions on documents. In 1982 Reagan signed Executive Order 12356, giving administration officials broader authority to withhold information for reasons of "national security." The stricter classification of material not only restricted the press from gaining access to hitherto public documents, it also excluded Congress, government contractors, researchers, and scientists.[71]

Furthermore, documents classified under the presidential order were made exempt from disclosure under the Freedom of Information Act. It even contained a provision allowing for the reclassification of previously declassified documents. In hearings before the House Committee on Government Operations, federal officials who had been called to testify even refused to rule out the possible use of physical force or illegal entry to regain control of previously declassified material.[72]

The executive order also changed the basic classification period from six years to an indefinite period of time, stating only that information shall remain classified "as long as required by national security considerations." Executive Order 12356 attempted to placed the documentary record of federal employees outside the reach of the public, but it was only a beginning.

In 1982 the administration also began a campaign of intimidation against both officials and reporters who strayed outside of the media script. In 1982 Secretary of Defense Weinberger forced more than a score of Defense Department employees to take polygraph tests in an effort to find the source of a leak regarding future American military needs.[73] Then in March, 1983 Reagan issued National Security Directive 84. It permitted the government to review, prior to publication, all written works by former employees. The directive required over 128,000 government employees to sign secrecy agreements which would have, had the directive been successful, subjected them to lifetime censorship.

The directive was, however, met by considerable protest. By

December only a handful of federal employees had signed the secrecy agreements. Of those who had, none were top-level officials.[74] Congress eventually placed a moratorium on its use effective November 22, 1983 to April 16, 1984. By February 1984, Reagan officials were forced to suspend the key provisions of the secrecy agreements and polygraph tests.[75] Though the administration had failed to implement the secrecy agreements, this was only a temporary setback for Reagan officials.

The administration's zeal for secrecy was back in the news by the end of the year when it announced that a space shuttle mission scheduled for launch on January 23, 1985 would be "secret." This latter episode prompted *New York Times* correspondent Hedrick Smith to write "The Reagan administration's efforts to impose tight security on the next mission of the space shuttle reflects both an urge to protect the national security and what some intelligence specialists see as a broader, long-term drive to curb the flow of information on such issues to the public."[76] The extent of the administration's determination was about to be revealed.

After the failure of the national security directive, the administration developed a new strategy. Two months before the directive was scrapped, Under Secretary of Defense Fred Ikle told reporters that the administration was likely to seek tougher penalties against those who leak information to reporters. "The laws are not adequate. . . . We have decided to fight it on all fronts."[77]

The Justice Department opened the attack with the criminal prosecution of a Navy intelligence analyst named Samuel Morison. Morison had sold satellite photographs of a Soviet aircraft carrier under construction to *Jane's Fighting Ships*, a highly respected British publication specializing in military matters. All three of the photographs in question had been previously published. Morison's intention in providing the British publication with the photographs, or so he claimed, was to raise public consciousness of what he perceived to be a greater Soviet threat then had been generally acknowledged.

The Justice department pursued Morison's conviction by pushing for new interpretations of various espionage laws, including the 1917 Espionage Act, the Espionage Act of 1947, and the Communications Intelligence Act of 1950. Simply stated, the Reagan Justice Department wanted to prosecute as "spies" officials, starting with Morison, who made unauthorized disclosures to the press.

The interpretation of the espionage laws sought by the administration was provided by Federal District Judge Joseph H. Young. In ruling against a pretrial defense motion for dismissal of the charges against Morison, Judge Young asserted that even though the case did not fit the mold of a "classic spy scenario," it made little difference: "The danger to the United States is just as great when this information is released to the press as when it is released to an agent of a foreign government." Morison was eventually convicted and sentenced to two years in prison.

The Supreme Court contributed to the government's expanding capacity to control information when on October 17, 1988 it failed to set aside Morison's criminal conviction.

What are the consequences of the Morison case? A legal brief filed by most of the major news organizations, including *The New York Times*, stated that adoption of the prosecution's interpretation of the espionage laws would "affect, and perhaps dramatically alter, the way in which government officials deal with the press, the way in which the press gathers and reports the news, and the way in which the public learns about its government."[78] Morton H. Halperin, then with the American Civil Liberties Union, and a former member of the National Security Council under Henry Kissinger's stewardship, concluded that the Morison conviction constituted the creation of an official secrets act.

> Any government employee who gives any classified information to any newspaper will have broken the law and any newspaper that publishes it will also have broken the law. The statute as interpreted would prevent much of current public debate on national security issues.[79]

The use or threatened use of espionage laws was probably rather exceptional. The more immediate objective was to intimidate the news media and the uncontrolled sources upon whom they relied in investigative reporting. Threatening government workers with espionage laws was merely on the far end of a continuum of threats employed to halt uncontrolled news contact.

A less extreme practice was to simply fire violators of the veil of official secrecy. In 1986, the Reagan administration fired Assistant Undersecretary of Defense Michael Pillsbury for, as it was alleged, disclosing to reporters the administration's plans to give advanced Stinger missiles to the American-backed rebels in Angola and Afghanistan. These are the missiles later used to shoot down, among other aircraft, civilian airliners.

In other instances even more "passive" violations of secrecy led to dismissal. Following the war with Iraq, the Bush administration and Pentagon persistently suppressed discussion of total Iraqi war-related deaths, "directing analysts and military officers not to provide estimates or professional judgments."[80] In 1992 a Census Bureau demographer was fired for including widely published estimates of Iraqi war-related deaths in her official calculation of the total population of Iraq (158,000 dead, including 118,000 civilian war-related deaths). The population estimate were calculated for the Census Bureau's "World Population 1992" handbook, an unclassified document generally available to the public. She had provided these population estimates, including the Iraqi death toll estimates, to an inquiring reporter. Soon afterward, two of her supervisors removed her copy of the report, rewrote it, and claimed the total Iraqi civilian casualties actually stood at five thousand.[81] A former intelligence officer was quoted by *The Post* as saying "I think Beth (the Census Bureau demographer) is collateral damage in the government campaign to avoid discussing the question of Iraqi casualties."

Government officials outside the media management loop were not the only targets of official wrath. The Reagan and Bush administrations also took aim at the journalists who received the information. Initially this came in the form of verbal attacks on the patriotism of the press, as we discussed earlier in the Bonner case.

Secretary of State George Shultz, for instance, said in 1983, "it seems as though the reporters are always against us and so they're always seeking to report something that's going to screw things up." In 1985 Secretary of Defense Casper Weinberger asserted that by publishing details of the secret space shuttle mission, *The Washington Post* had given "aid and comfort to the enemy," language suggesting treason. Reagan's science advisor, George Keyworth, 2nd said in February of 1985 that "the press is trying to tear down America" and "seems to be drawn from a relatively narrow fringe element on the far left in our society."[82] But the campaign to silence uncontrolled press coverage soon took on an even more ominous tone.

In May, 1986 the administration convinced *The Washington Post* to pull on article it was preparing on the secrets of underwater eavesdropping. Robert Pelton, a former employee of the National Security Agency, had been convicted of selling this information to the Russians. Since the Russians already had the information contained in the article, and probably more, *The Post* did not believe national security would be put at risk. *The Post* even submitted several versions of the article to government officials. None were approved. Though *The Post* eventually relented and suppressed the main substance of the story, the episode did not die.[83]

William J. Casey, director of the Central Intelligence Agency, began making threatening telephone calls to news agencies, and even met with *Washington Post* executive editor Ben Bradlee to warn him of possible prosecution under the espionage laws regarding the underwater eavesdropping matter. He also met with Deputy Attorney General D. Lowell Jensen, the man in charge of the Morison case. Casey wanted the *Post, The Washington Times, The New York Times, Time,* and *Newsweek* prosecuted under the espionage statutes for having printed details of intelligence gathering operations. A few days later, on May 19, 1983, Casey asked the Justice Department to consider prosecution of the National Broadcasting Corporation (NBC) for having broadcast a report based on the same information *The Post* had obtained.

On all fronts, the administration seemed to be turning up the heat in the effort to intimidate the news media. As one respected journalist told Mark Hertsgaard, the administration was "moving to expand the bridgehead that it won . . . by successfully squelching a *Washington Post* article. . ." Casey and the rest of the top administration officials were trying to create a sense of menace when it came to reporting on anything remotely connected with "national security."

Soon there was a new twist on the threats. Casey told the *Washington Journalism Review* that "we need to get better control over that whole process" by enacting legislation that would explicitly ban the "misuse of classified information." That is exactly what came next. In 1986 the administration submitted legislation to Congress which expanded the definition of a spy to include journalists who receive unauthorized leaks.[84] The administration's proposed legislation increased the penalty for such activity to "death by firing squad" for those convicted.

The legislation would have also permitted the government to decide—after the fact—whether documents that have already been released to the media could lead to "grave risk of substantial danger to the national security." Under these provisions a reporter who writes about nearly any national defense or foreign policy issue based upon such documentation could theoretically face rather severe penalties.

Though the legislation was unsuccessful, the legislative campaign against leaks continued into the Bush administration. In August, 1989, some fifteen bills were under consideration in the House and Senate regarding the transmission of secrets to any third party, foreign agent or news reporter.[85] The Bush administration even favored legislation which would have made it a crime to disclose *nonsecret* information.[86] Even in the form of proposed legislation, these measure were sure to have a chilling effect. And that was the intent. Such draconian measures by the Reagan and Bush administrations most likely caused more than one reporter or news organization to think twice about pushing too hard on leaked stories. In light of these measures, it really is little wonder that a foreign journal broke the arms to Iran for hostages story.

Paying the Price for the Freedom of Information Act

The United States government estimated it created just under seven million official secrets in 1990, though no one could say for sure due to government secrecy.[87] The Information Security Oversight Office reported that this figure actually represented a significant reduction from the zenith of government secrecy in 1985 when the Reagan administration produced fifteen million secrets.[88] According to James Bamford, the National Security Agency alone produces from 50 to 100 million classified documents a year.[89] The exact figure is difficult to establish. Another estimate puts the total amount at forty tons of material *per day*.[90]

One of the principle means of chipping away at this mountain of classified material is the Freedom of information Act. The 1966 Freedom of Information Act (FOIA) was intended to provide the public with greater access to information concerning what their government was doing and why it was being done. This intention was seriously undermined by an amendment passed in 1986. The expressed purpose of the amendment was to aid academic and journalistic research by exempting it from costly search, review and copying fees. It went into effect in April 1987. The rationale was that the changes would allow for greater public access to government controlled information. The result, however, has been quite the reverse.

The amendment gave agency bureaucrats editorial discretion over the material under its control when assigning fee waivers.[91] Anyone who is a "representative of the news media" is, indeed, qualified for the fee waiver. But a requester must also meet a second standard: Discloser of the requested information must be "likely to contribute significantly to public understanding of the operations or activities of the government and is not primarily in the commercial interest of the requester."[92] Furthermore, the guidelines state that the "Bare assertions by requesters that they are 'researchers' or 'have plans to author a book' are insufficient evidence that a contribution to understanding by the general public will ultimately result from a disclosure." This language placed agency and department officials in the position of determining scholarly potential or newsworthiness of all requests.[93] A few examples indicate that agency officials were not reluctant to exercising that discretion.

The managing editor of the Addison County, Vermont, *Independent* was denied a fee waiver by the Central Intelligence Agency when he requested information regarding CIA recruiting activities on the campus of Middlebury College, one of Addison County's biggest employers. The *Independent*, a small paper published twice weekly, had at the time about 7,500 paid subscribers. The CIA responded as follows:

> Although you are an editor of the Addison Press (sic), the information you seek does not meet the regulatory requirement of current event interest to the general public. Therefore, you will be responsible for search, review and reproduction fees.[94]

Due to the *Independent*'s small size and meager operating budget, the search was canceled.

Researchers have fared no better under the new guidelines. For instance, a University of California, Irvine, professor found it impossible to obtain information held by the FBI and CIA regarding ex-Beatle John Lennon.[95] Lennon had been the subject of FBI and CIA scrutiny since the late 1960s. The agencies in question would say only that to release such information would jeopardize national security. In court, the FBI went so far as to argue that even explaining why releasing then 14-year-old documents on a dead rock star would jeopardize national security would itself jeopardize national security.

This is the real crux of the problem regarding the FOIA. Discretion of what can and cannot be released is almost entirely in the hands of officials who represent agencies with an interest in disclosing as little as possible. Unless one has the financial resources to use the court system when a FOIA request is denied, discretion is in the hands of those agencies. Even if requesting organizations have the financial backing to pay for searches and possible court costs, searches may take months, even years, with no guarantee that any information will make it past the hurdle of national security.

There is even evidence that documents which have been released may not be authentic or free from tampering. In 1992, congressional investigators of the SP-100 nuclear space reactor found a two-page set of instructions issued by NASA on how to handle FOIA requests. According to Congressman Howard Wolpe (D-Mich.), the NASA document instructed its employees to rewrite or destroy documents so as to, quoting from the instructions, "minimize adverse impact" and to mix up documents and camouflage handwriting so as to make the significance of such documents "less meaningful." Finally, the document instructed employees to take steps to "enhance the utility" of various FOIA exemptions.[96]

The effectiveness of the Freedom of Information Act was reduced even further when Ronald Reagan signed an executive order—just two days prior to the end of his presidency—which gave him the power to deny access to any Reagan administration era document that he feels "might impair" national security, law enforcement or the "deliberate processes of the executive branch."[97] Whether it is the result of this executive order or changes to the Freedom of Information Act, it is usually the case that only a minuscule portion of the documentation is ever released.

Attacks on journalists and their sources who stray outside of the controlled environment established by Gergen, Deaver, Baker, and others, in combination with the weakening of the Freedom of

Information Act, made critical reporting exceedingly difficult for news organizations, even those of *The New York Times'* stature. Conservative fiscal organizations like the *Times*, operating in a hostile political environment, were better off playing it safe. Simply take the line of the day, find a Democrat, if possible, willing to comment on it and call it a day. If the restraints of commercialism and the efforts of the administration were not enough to convince an editor that this was the wisest course of action, administration allies in some of the very countries most likely to see gross violations of human rights and terrorism also had an interest in placing restraints on the issue content in the news. In places like El Salvador, reporters who did not toe-the-line were threatened with death, not prison sentences. Many were actually killed. This is the final form of flak.

Deadly Flak

While not a factor in reporting in the United States itself, violence or the threat of violence is an ever-present reality for reporters in some parts of the world. This must be taken into account when trying to understand the relative weight given to political violence stories.

In 1987 the Committee to Protect Journalists documented nearly six hundred incidents of press abuse taking place in seventy-five countries around the world.[98] Twenty-six journalist were killed. The year before the Committee recorded fifteen killings, fifty-six assaults, and 190 arrests or kidnappings[99] And in 1992 there were fifty journalists killed, ninety in jail and a total of nearly two thousand attacks directed at journalists.[100]

At times the killings seemed to be without motive, such as the killing of ABC correspondent Bill Stewart by a Somoza National Guardsman in 1979. But all too often the killings were deliberate. For example, in El Salvador, during the 1982 Constituency Assembly elections, four Dutch journalists were shot to death at close range by the Salvadoran Treasury police. According to the 1993 United Nations Truth Commission report on El Salvador, after police officials interrogated the journalists, they killed them in an ambush. This had been ordered by a senior Salvadoran military officer in Chalatenango province.[101]

At first Salvadoran authorities claimed the newsmen had been caught in a cross fire, a story that soon lost all credibility. The bodies of the journalists were put on display at the morgue while much of the international press corp, in town that week for the elections, were marched through to view the bodies. The display was shocking. The Dutch had not just been shot. Their partially-clothed bodies revealed horribly mutilated genitals and other signs of torture. In the words of one American reporter interviewed in the film documentary "In the Name of Democracy," "Everyone left there (the morgue) as white as a sheet. And those who had made contact with the guerrillas, canceled them and got on the next plane out of town."

During the 1989 Salvadoran presidential elections, three journalists were once again killed in separate incidents, all by the Salvadoran military. *Reuters* photographer Roberto Navas was shot in the back as the motorcycle he was a passenger on was waved through a military checkpoint. Mauricio Pineda, a soundman for a Salvadoran television station, was killed after the van in which he was riding was raked by soldier's automatic weapons fire. The van was clearly marked "PRENSA."

The third victim was once again a Dutch cameraman, Cornel Lagrouw. He and several other journalists were caught in a cross fire after Salvadoran troops moved in to retake a village held by guerrillas. After Lagrouw was hit, his friends, including two American journalists, tried to take him to the nearest hospital. While driving back toward San Salvador, a Salvadoran army helicopter began firing its machine guns at the car, once again clearly marked as a press vehicle. They were forced to take cover in the home of a Salvadoran peasant family while Lagrouw bled to death in the car.[102]

Summary

The intent of this chapter has been to specify the mechanisms used in the exercise of political power. The news, including news of political violence, is the product of economic and political forces. While the corporate commercial interests of modern news organizations fail to lend themselves to hard-hitting, adversarial journalism, a variety of mechanisms have been used in recent years to raise the costs of reporting outside the scripted press releases of line of the day meetings.

This still falls short of a fully controlled news system, such as is found in totalitarian countries without even nominal freedom of the press. Investigative journalists in the United States are still relatively free to report critical, informative stories. In the next chapter, we are interested in examining what may occur when uncontrolled news does make its way into the mainstream press.

Notes

1. Mark Hertsgaard, *On Bended Knee: The Press and the Reagan Presidency* (New York: Farrar Straus Giroux, 1988).

2. Todd Gitlin, *The Whole World Is Watching: The Making and Unmaking of the New Left* (Berkeley: University of California Press, 1980), pp. 249-250.

3. For examples of those who tend to emphasize the role of journalists and their personal behavior or ideology, see Linda Lichter, Robert S. Lichter, and Stanley Rothman, "The Once and Future Journalists," *Washington Journalism Review*, December 1982; Edith Efron, *The News Twisters* (Los Angeles: Nash, 1971); Parenti, Michael, *Inventing Reality: The Politics of the Mass Media* (New York: St. Martin's Press, 1986).

For explanations which tend to emphasize organizational factors, see Warren Breed, "Newspaper 'Opinion Leaders' and the Processes of Socialization," *Journalism Quarterly* 32, Summer 1955, pp. 277-84; Edward Jay Epstein, *News From Nowhere* (New York: Vintage, 1973); Leon Sigal, *Reporters and Officials: The Organization and Politics of News Making* (Lexington, Mass.: Heath, 1973).

4. See Timothy Crouse, *The Boys on the Bus* (New York: Random House, 1973); Michael Massing, "When More is Less: Notes on the Globetrotting, Singleminded Crisis Chasers," *Columbia Journalism Review*, July/August, 1989; John J. Fialka, *Hotel Warriors: Covering the Gulf War* (Baltimore: Published by the Woodrow Wilson Center Press, distributed by the Johns Hopkins University Press, 1991).

5. Gaye Tuchman, "Objectivity as Strategic Ritual," *American Journal of Sociology* 77, January 1972, pp. 660-79; *The TV Establishment: Programming for Power and Profit* (Englewood Cliffs, N.J.: Prentice-Hall); *Making News* (New York: The Free Press, 1978); see also Harvey L. Molotch and Marilyn Lester, "News as Purposive Behavior," *American Sociological Review* 39, 1974, pp. 101-112; "Accidental News: The Great Oil Spill," *American Journal of Sociology* 81, 1975, pp. 235-60; Allan Rachlin, *News as Hegemonic Reality: American Political Culture and Framing of News Accounts* (New York: Praeger, 1988).

6. Quoted by Gitlin, *Whole World*, p. 251.

7. Ibid., p. 251.

8. Ben H. Bagdikian, "Missing From the News," *The Progressive*, August 1989, p. 32.

9. Ben H. Bagdikian, "The Lords of the Global Village," *The Nation*, June 12, 1989, p. 805.

10. Ben H. Bagdikian, *The Media Monopoly*, 2nd edition (Boston: Beacon Press, 1987) pp. 28-29.

11. Parenti, *Inventing Reality*, p. 43.

12. In addition to Bagdikian's work in this area, see Eric Barnouw, *The Sponsor* (Oxford: Oxford University Press, 1978); James D. Squires, *Read All About It: The Corporate Takeover of America's Newspapers* (New York: Times Books, 1993).

13. Doug Underwood, "When MBAs Rule the Newsroom," *Columbia Journalism Review*, March/April 1988; see also Bagdikian, ch. 6.

14. Underwood, "When MBAs Rule the Newsroom," p. 24.

15. Ibid., p. 25.

16. Squires, *Read All About It*, p. 78

17. My description of the formation of the Associated Press and it consequences relies heavily on Bennett, *News*, p. 122.

18. Herman and Chomsky, *Manufacturing Consent*, p. 22.

19. Quoted in Parenti, *Inventing Reality*, pp. 52-53.

20. Ibid., p. 30.

21. Danial Hallin, *The Uncensored War: the Media in Vietnam* (Berkeley: University of California Press, 1989).

22. Paul Fussell, *Wartime: Understanding and Behavior in the Second World War* (Oxford: Oxford University Press, 1989).

23. Underwood, "When MBAs Rule the Newsroom," p. 27. See also Squires, *Read All About It*, pp. 46-48, 66, 76.

24. Quoted in Hertsgaard, *On Bended Knee*, p. 200.

25. See James F. Larson, *Television's Window on the World: International Affairs Coverage on the U.S. Networks* (Norwood, New Jersey: Ablex Publishing Corporation, 1984); Mort Rosenblum, *Coups and Earthquakes: Reporting the World to America* (New York: Harper Colophon Books, 1979); Roger Wallis and Stanley Baran, *The Known World of Broadcast News: International News and the Electronic Media* (London: Routledge, 1990).

26. William A. Dorman and Steven Livingston, "News and Historical Content: The Establishing Phase of the Persian Gulf Policy Debate," *Conflicting Images* (tentative title) W. Lance Bennett and David Paletz eds., (Chicago: University of Chicago Press, 1993).

27. Gergen, of course, joined the Clinton administration in June, 1993.

28. Hertsgaard, *On Bended Knee*, p. 33.

29. John Anthony Maltese, *Spin Control: The White House Office of Communications and the Management of Presidential News* (Chapel Hill: The University of North Carolina Press, 1992) p. 183.

30. Ibid., p. 214.

31. Hertsgaard, *On Bended Knee*, p. 6.

32. Maltese, *Spin Control*, p. 186.

33. Hertsgaard, *On Bended Knee*, pp. 34-35.

34. Ibid., p. 48.

35. Ibid., p. 49.

36. Ibid., p. 49.

37. Maltese, *Spin Control*, p. 185.

38. Hertsgaard, *On Bended Knee*, p. 36.

39. Ibid., p. 29.

40. Jack J. Honomichl, "How Reagan Took America's Pulse: 'The Great Communicator' was a Great Listener of Survey Results," *Advertising Age*, January 23, 1989, p. 1.

41. Ibid., p. 25.

42. Emphasis added.

43. Maltese, *Spin Control*, p. 185.

44. Hertsgaard, *On Bended Knee*, p. 159.

45. Ibid., p. 49.

46. Robert Parry and Peter Kornbluh, "Iran-Contra's Untold Story," *Foreign Policy* 72, Fall 1988, pp. 3-30. See also Stephen Engelberg, "U.S. Propaganda Effort on Latin Policy Reported," *The New York Times*, September 14, 1988, p. A20.

47. Parry and Kornbluh, "Iran-Contra's Untold Story,", p. 5.

48. Ibid., pp. 5-6.

49. Ibid., p. 7.

50. Ibid., p. 17.

51. Ibid., P. 17.

52. There has been remarkable degree of continuity in media management from administration to administration. Many of the practices of the Reagan administration were also found in the Nixon administration. And Bush, though with variations, continued the practices of the Reagan administration. Regarding the Clinton administration, *New York Times* White House correspondent Richard L. Berke told me, "The Clinton administration has closely studied what the Reagan administration did in its media management. They are putting into practice many of the same features: the line-of-the-day-meetings, all of it" (The George Washington University, "National Center for Communications Studies" forum, March 10, 1993). This was before Gergen signed on.

53. Ibid., pp. 40-41.

54 Herman and Chomsky, *Manufacturing Consent*, p. 23.

55. Ibid., p. 23.

56. Hertsgaard, *On Bended Knee*, p. 52.

57. Teicher emphasized that his reference to Richard Haas was only hypothetical and that he did not wish to imply that Haas was or is in any way duplicitous. "In fact," said Teicher, "Haas is one of the more forthright members of the foreign policy establishment."

58. Interviewed in Washington, D.C., April 1, 1992.

59. Hertsgaard, *On Bended Knee*, p. 59.

60. Ibid., p. 59.

61. Mike Hoyt, "The Mozote Massacre: It Was the Reporter's Word Against the 2overnment's," *Columbia Journalism Review*, January/February, 1993, p. 33.

62. Hoyt, "The Mozote Massacre," p. 33.

63. Ibid., p. 197.

64. Bonner's training is in law, not journalism.

65. Michael Massing, "About-face on El Salvador," *Columbia Journalism Review*, November/December 1983.

66 Hertsgaard, *On Bended Knee*, p. 196.

67. Tim Golden, "Salvador Skeletons Confirm Reports of Massacre in 1981," *The New York Times*, October 22, 1992, p. 1.

68. Hoyt, The Mozote Massacre," p. 33.

69. CBS, "60 Minutes," March 14, 1993.

70. Hertsgaard, *On Bended Knee*, p. 72.

71. Robert Pear, "Information Curbs Assailed By Panel," *The New York Times*, August 10, 1982, p. A13.

72. Ibid.

73. Hedrick Smith, A Public Call for Secrecy," *The New York Times*, December 20, 1984, p. A1.

74. Stuart Taylor, Jr., "Reagan Censorship Pact Remains Unsigned by Most Government Officials," *The New York Times*, December 16, 1983, p. A27.

75. Leslie Maitland Werner, "Aide Says Reagan Shifts on Secrecy," *The New York Times*, February 15, 1984, p. A1; see also Stuart Taylor, Jr., "Secrecy Proposals: Risks Weighed Against Gains," *The New York Times*, February 20, 1984, p. A13; Frank Snepp, "Protecting Rights of All Privy to U.S. Secrets," *The New York Times*, February 22, 1984.

77. Hedrick Smith, "A Public Call for Secrecy," p. A1.

77. Ibid.

78. Gerald M. Boyd, "President Defends Rights to Protect Against Leaks," *The New York Times*, April 10, 1986, p. A15.

79. Stuart Taylor, Jr., "Spy Laws Ruled to Apply to Disclosures to Press," *The New York Times*, March 15, 1985, p. A15.

80. Barton Gellman, "Census Worker Who Calculated '91 Iraqi Death Toll Is Told She Will Be Fired," *The Washington Post*, p. A6.

81. Ibid.

82. Stuart Taylor, Jr., "Administration Seeks a Stronger Lock on 'Classified' Files," *The New York Times*, March 24, 1985, p. E5.

83. Danial Schorr, "The Administration's 'Unofficial Secrets Act'," *The New York Times*, August 3, 1986, p. E23.

84. Martin Garbus, *Traitors and Heroes: A Lawyer's Memoir* (New York: Antheneum, 1987), pp. 236-254.

85. Search by Congressional Research Services, August, 1989.

86. Leslie Harris, "Now the Bush Team Wants to Make It a Crime to Reveal Non-Secrets," *The Los Angeles Times*, April 27, 1989, Part II, p. 7.

87. Unsigned, "In '90, U.S. Kept Lid on 6.8 Million Secrets," *Salt Lake City Tribune*, April 3, 1991.

88. According to the Information Security Oversight Office, these figures largely held steady for 1991 (5,868,689 official secrets) and 1992 (6,349,532 official secrets). Telephone interview, March 17, 1993.

89. James Bamford, *The Puzzle Palace: A Report on America's Most Secret Agency* (Boston: Houghton Mifflin, 1982).

90. Steven Emerson and Cristina Del Sesto, *Terrorist: The Inside Story of the Highest-Ranking Iraqi Terrorist Ever to Defect to the West* (New York: Villard Books, 1991), p. 100.

91. James Popkins, "Running the New 'Improved' FOIA Obstacle Course," *Columbia Journalism Review*, July/August 1989, pp. 45-48.

92. Ibid., p. 47.

93. Unsigned, "Educators Assail U.S. Curbs on Access to Data," *The New York Times*, September 14, 1988, p. B9.

94. Popkins, "Running the New 'Improved' FOIA Obstacle Course," p. 46.

95. Jon Wiener, "John Lennon Versus the F.B.I.," *The New Republic*, May 2, 1983, pp. 19-23.

96. The document was entitled "Suggestions for Anticipating Requests Under FOIA." Telephone interview with representative of the National Security Archive, March 24, 1993. See also *The Washington Post*, "NASA Accused of Seeking to Hide Controversial Data," February 28, 1992.

97. *U.S. News and World Report*, August 28/Sept. 4, 1989.

98. The Committee to Protect Journalists was established in 1981 by reporters and editors in response to the violent deaths of several reporters covering Central America. One of the functions of the Committee is to collect and publish strictly verified information regarding instances of harassment, threats, detainment, and assassination of journalists while trying to report the news.

99. Committee for the Protection of Journalists (CPJ) Annual Report, 1988.

100. CPJ Annual Report, 1993.

101. Tim Golden, "U.N. Report Urges Sweeping Changes in Salvadoran Army," *The New York Times*, March 16, 1993, p. 12.

102. Massing, "About-face on El Salvador."

6

Press Treatment of Alleged U.S. Ties to Salvadoran State Terrorism

The public deserves to be reassured about operations of the U.S. government abroad, which have been brought into question as a result of repeated allegations about U.S. government involvement with Salvadoran individuals and groups associated with death squads and other forms of political violence.[1]

—"Recent Political Violence in El Salvador,"
Senate Select Committee on Intelligence

D'Aubuisson thrived because American leaders who feared a communist takeover in El Salvador deliberately turned a blind eye to the use of state-sanctioned terrorism against Marxist guerrillas, their supporters and suspected sympathizers.[2]

—Douglas Farah

Despite the commercial pressures and official management of the news media, news in the United States is not a fully controlled propaganda system. Unmanaged content regarding terrorism and other matters can and does slip into the news. An example would be the presentation of evidence which indicated the United States or its proxies conducted terrorist operations on a regular, sustained basis. The purpose of this chapter is to explore what happened when this occurred.

In previous chapters we have seen examples of American official reluctance to acknowledge the association with terrorism of strategic allies when to do so hindered policy objectives. This was true regarding the Iraqi government, the UNITA rebels in Angola, and Afghan rebel association with terrorist violence. In at least the latter two instances, the press simply ignored U.S.-backed rebel terrorism. But what happens when information which is harmful to the legitimacy of major American government institutions becomes available to reporters? The mythology of the adversarial press would argue that such information would be published unaltered. Journalists, after all, are after "all the news that's fit to print."

An alternative perspective is presented here. A number of scholars have noted that controversy in the news is often restrained.[3] In this view, the relationship between the news media and government officials and institutions is, indeed, marked by adversarialism and controversy—but a limited adversarialism. It is limited in several ways.

In most cases, overly controversial issue interpretations and information will simply be ignored, as we saw in the cases of American-sponsored violence in Angola and Afghanistan, and in the case of Iraq's sponsorship of terrorism throughout the 1980s. Perhaps one of the best examples of this comes from the mainstream media's disregard of the Iran-Contra story prior to Attorney General Meese's press conference. As one commentator remarked, "While some investigative reporters had been burrowing away at contra stories over the past few years, other journalist were regularly overlooking hot tips on U.S.-rebel ties."[4]

Another alternative is to transform the terminology used in the news story. Subtle shifts of meaning can be achieved through relatively minor linguistic alternatives. Here again, an example is found in the aftermath of Iran-Contragate. Questions of how a scandal of this magnitude could have arisen began to focus on President Reagan himself. Was he intellectually fit to be president? Questions concerning Reagan's mental acuity, a sensitive question in relation to a popular president, were transformed into questions regarding his "management style."[5] We saw another instance of this in the last chapter. When Afghan rebels bombed three hotels, a movie theater, and the Kabul airport, the guerrillas were said to be conducting "urban warfare" rather than terrorism.[6]

Another method of regaining control of a story is to encourage personalization of its plot. Critical news—news of all kinds—tends to focus on the personal flaws of individual actors, rather than on sustained institutional processes or dysfunction. Watergate and "Iran-Contragate" offer two examples.

In each case, the national press was confronted with fundamental questions regarding the compatibility of the national security apparatus that had evolved since World War II and democratic institutions and practices. In each case the press evaded these questions in favor of others which focused instead on the personal culpability of Nixon and Reagan and others who were most visible in each episode. Watergate came to be understood as merely a reflection of Nixon's paranoid personality while Iran-Contragate was understood to reflect Reagan's lax "management style." Little attention was paid to institutional flaws which invited two presidents to use the national security apparatus in ways which lead to two major constitutional crisis within a generation.

There is a tendency on the part of mainstream press to present stories which have the potential to be seriously injurious to the credibility of official institutions in ways which more closely conform to the standard assumptions regarding U.S. government conduct. This is not a result of conspiracy but of ideology. It is to suggest that many journalists share with their government counterparts in the news production enterprise a set of basic assumptions about the bounds of social and political normalcy. In the face of anomalous news, news which violates the shared assumptions regarding the moral intent of American conduct, particularly in international affairs, many *journalists and editors will tend to refashion the story in ways which conform to their assumptions and expectations.* The resulting *repair work,* to use Gaye Tuchman's term, includes recasting the story in more familiar terms, or rewriting it in such a way so as to dull the critical edge of the events reported.

According to Danial Hallin, issues in the news can be thought of as occupying concentric circles creating three regions of controversy, each regulated by different journalistic standards and shared assumptions. At the center, within the sphere of consensus, journalists "do not feel compelled either to present opposing views or to remain disinterested observers. On the contrary, the journalist's role is to serve as an advocate or celebrant of consensus values." It is within this sphere that one is able to locate what Herb Gans referred to as "enduring values in the news."[7] Gans placed these consensus values into eight clusters, ranging from ethnocentrism, particularly in war coverage, to Keiloresque glorification of small-town America, to a prominent display of red-blooded respect for individualism.

Ethnocentrism is particularly important with regards to news coverage of war and, by extension, terrorism. As Gans pointed out, the news media described the North Vietnamese and the National Liberation Front as the enemy, "as if they were the declared enemy of the news media, too." American casualty reports were often personalized, while the casualties on the other side were simply described as "the communist death toll."

Similarly, Noam Chomsky argued that American journalists operate within conceptual boundaries established by assumptions concerning America's role in the world. He also offered the example of American news coverage of Vietnam. Shared assumptions precluded journalists from describing United States military involvement in South Vietnam as an "invasion." Rather, the United States was "defending freedom" by, among other activities, establishing and maintaining a series of unpopular, brutal, and corrupt regimes.[8]

At the other extreme of Hallin's metaphor is the sphere of deviance. In instances were the United States confronts deviant ideologies or practices, such as Communism or "terrorism," journalists do not feel bound by considerations of impartiality. As Hallin put it, the sphere of deviance is "the realm of those political actors and views which journalists and the political mainstream of the society reject as unworthy of being heard." Taken together, the sphere of consensus and the sphere of deviance offer a black and white world of 'our' truth versus 'their' disinformation, 'our' freedom and the freedom we seek for others versus 'their' totalitarianism, and so forth.

It is within the middle region of Hallin's schema that journalists practice "objective" and impartial journalism. "The limits of this sphere are defined primarily by the two party system—by the parameters of debate between and within the Democratic and Republican parties—as well as by the decision-making process within the bureaucracies of the executive branch."

In short, controversy is limited to the confines of official debate, as noted earlier. The closer the issue is to a consensus issue, the more likely it will be that objectivity involves a straight recitation of official statements. "Farther out, as the news deals with issues on which consensus is weaker, the principle of balance is increasingly emphasized."[9] Of course, as this limited balance becomes more prominent, so too does criticism of policy.

Shared basic assumptions such as these are sometimes called "paradigms."[10] During normal operation, a paradigm may become circular, self-referencing knowledge based on the systematic exclusion or discrediting of radical challenges. This is perhaps what Herman has in mind with what he calls "marginalization" or the systematic restriction of opposition views in the news.[11]

One of the basic assumptions in the news media's reporting of American foreign policy has been that in its struggle against enemies, the United States never condones terrorism and physical and psychological torture. In the world of mainstream journalism, the United States only *counters* and never *sponsors* terrorism. These are instead the predilections of our worst enemies: Libya, Iran, and sometimes Syria and Iraq. If such assumption were present, and if they are a part of a shared paradigm between most journalists and officials responsible for most news, we would expect to see stories to the contrary generally ignored, transformed, or personalized. Presented below is a case study of such information and how it was handled in various press outlets.

Death Squad Stories

On February 3, 1989, Vice President Dan Quayle delivered a warning to Salvadoran political and military commanders: If Salvadoran security forces did not demonstrate greater commitment to human rights, further United States aid would be jeopardized.[12] Quayle called on the Salvadorans to bring to justice those responsible for human rights abuses.

For those who followed Salvadoran politics, Quayle's warnings, coming as they did just prior to a Salvadoran presidential election, seemed remarkably familiar. In December 1983 then Vice President George Bush traveled to El Salvador to issue the same warning his Vice President would reiterate six years—and thousands of deaths—later.

At the time of Bush's visit to El Salvador, death squad stories had appeared and continued to appear in a variety of news outlets from December 1982 to May 1984. Most of these stories illustrated the paradigmatically correct assumptions found in the mainstream news media regarding the United States and terrorism. They would be placed in what Hallin referred to as the "sphere of legitimate controversy." Also found was a *Progressive* magazine article and the publicity surrounding it. This coverage represented a serious challenge to the paradigmatically correct storyline regarding the United States and its relationship with Salvadoran death squads. A repair process was evident in a third group of articles, comprised of a *Christian Science Monitor* story and its various reprints in other newspapers around the country.

The Policy Objectives

As with other regions of the world, news out of El Salvador had to be managed as best as possible to support desired administration policy. Upon her return from El Salvador in February 1983, Jeane Kirkpatrick told President Reagan and the American news media that unless the United States was willing to substantially increase military aid to El Salvador, it—along with all of Central America—would come under the control of Communist regimes. Reagan began making public statements to the effect that if Congress did not come through with at least double the 1982 military aid level of $82 million, Mexico would ultimately come under attack.[13]

The major stumbling block to this aid, however, was the nagging suspicion of Salvadoran security forces complicity in death squad atrocities, responsible for the murder and disappearance of tens of thousands of people. If the administration was going to get the aid it requested, something had to be done about the death squads. As a Salvadoran tourist official put it after the systematic slaughter of 35,000 civilians by death squads in just three years, El Salvador had an "image problem."

The administration responded with a high level publicity campaign that focused on administration officials going to El Salvador demanding the elimination of the death squads. Beginning with a report of Vice

President Bush's visit to El Salvador, *The New York Times* began a period of extensive coverage of the death squad issue. Seventeen articles in all appeared between December 16, 1983 and March 23, 1984.[14]

These articles framed the death squad issue in quite specific ways: First, the death squads were the result of the deviant activities of individuals and did not reflect Salvadoran or American government agendas. It was, in other words, highly personalized, focusing as it did on the personal culpability of individual Salvadoran military officers operating on their own accord. Secondly, the United States was doing everything it could to pressure the Salvadoran government and military to take action to curb death squad violence. Third, there was no institutional link between the United States government, at any level, at any time, and the terrorism of the death squads.

Stories in this first phase also offered explanations as to the origins of the death squads, how they were said to select their victims, and what remedies were taken to curb their violence.

Death Squad Origins and Operations

Stories containing explanations as to the origins of the death squads appeared in *The Los Angeles Times* on December 18 and 19, 1983 and in *The New York Times* on March 3, 1984. The consistent pattern found in these stories was that the death squads were the result of deviant actions by individuals working outside the framework of governmental institutions, though the individuals involved may also happen to have held positions with the Salvadoran government or military.

. According to *The Los Angeles Times* of December 19, 1983, El Salvadoran death squads were the handiwork of Roberto d'Aubuisson and modeled after the assassination campaigns in Argentina in the 1970s. "The Salvadoran effort was conceived of four years ago by hard-line military officers and businessmen who banded together in the chaos . . . following the 1979 coup." The entire middle third of this 102 paragraph article was devoted to a description of the political turmoil in El Salvador in 1979. The story related the contentions of Roberto d'Aubuisson's critics who said "he was hired outright by the wealthy Salvadoran exiles."[15]

According to *The Los Angeles Times*, in the autumn of 1980 a contingent of Argentines arrived in El Salvador. They were a part of a "floating network of radical anti-communists" who stayed in the country for two months. In that time, it is reported, the Argentines organized the Salvadoran businessmen and their companions into "vigilante groups." "It began as a Ku Klux Klan-style brotherhood of businessmen and proprietors of restaurants, transit companies, hotels, and even . . . a funeral parlor."

The New York Times stories differed considerably from *The Los Angeles Times* on details of death squads origins. *The New York Times* story was based on information provided by an anonymous source who was said to be a former high ranking Salvadoran military officer.[16] It was later disclosed that the anonymous Salvadoran source was Roberto Eulalio Santibanez, a former army colonel and head of El Salvador's intelligence agency.[17]

According to *The Times*, the death squads were created by leading Salvadoran military officers, though again apparently working on their own initiative. Defense Minister Jose Guillermo Garcia and his then deputy, Colonel Nicolas Caranza were alarmed by the alliance between reformist military officers and "leftists" following the October 1979 coup. *The Times* quoted its then anonymous source as saying:

> Garcia and Carranza gave him their most suitable men in each part of the country for his squads," . . . "The goals were to make it seem that the revolutionary junta was incapable of governing, to create chaos so they could push Majano out.[18]

Money to operate the death squads was said to came from wealthy Salvadoran exiles living in Guatemala and Miami.

As with *The Los Angeles Times*, *The New York Times* accounting described d'Aubuisson as the principal organizer of the death squads. *The Times* stated "The man who organized and continues to direct the death squads is Roberto d'Aubuisson, a former army officer."

Instead of Argentines, however, *New York Times* articles stated that Guatemalans instructed the Salvadoran right-wing on how to create and operate death squads. *The Times* related how d'Aubuisson traveled extensively between Guatemala and El Salvador in 1979 and 1980. While in Guatemala, d'Aubuisson met with ultra-rightist leaders who instructed him on the techniques of death squad organization and operation, according to *The Times*.

As with origin stories, allegations regarding the day-to-day operation of the death squads focused their attention on a handful of individuals. *The New York Times* expanded on *The Los Angeles Times* list: "The former military officer said he had direct knowledge of the participation of Mr. d'Aubuisson, General Garcia, and Colonel Caranza in the process of selecting death squad victims." Both papers indicated that suspected involvement in "communist" activities, or any apparent sympathies with the rebels, or even personal grievances constituted sufficient reason for the death squads to target a victim.

Colonel Santibanez's credibility was shaken a few weeks later when it was learned he had been promised $50,000 and actually paid nearly

$30,000 by a group critical of Reagan administration Central America policies.[19]

As for the role of the United States government in all of this, *The Times* reminded the reader that: "In recent months the Administration has made new appeals to Salvadoran leaders to press for an end to death squad activity." The Bush and Shultz trips were described next.

Like American Vice Presidents in El Salvador, mainstream media accounts of the origins and operations of Salvadoran death squads kept reappearing. In August, 1988, *The Washington Post* ran a two part page-one series on the origins and operations of Salvadoran death squads.[20] As was true of *The Los Angeles Times* and *The New York Times* accounts of some five years earlier, *The Washington Post* claimed to present the definitive account of the origins of the death squads.

According to *The Post*, the death squads were the creation of a dentist named Hector Antonio Regaldo, with the backing of the Salvadoran hierarchy. Regaldo organized one of the first death squads in the early 1970s *as a boy scout troop*. Later, Regaldo, working as d'Aubuisson's assistant, organized an ARENA (d'Aubuisson's political party) security apparatus. This apparatus operated out of the national assembly building, though it was not considered a part of the official Salvadoran security establishment. It doubled as a death squad.

The sources for these allegations were two former death squad members, only one of whom was named. According to these sources, victims were selected by Regaldo in meetings at the assembly building. In the one instance where the United States was mentioned at all in *The Post* account, it was said the death squad activity reflected the "frailty of El Salvador's U.S.-backed democratic process."[21] The United States is once again depicted in its paradigmatically correct role as backer of democracy and non-violent political processes.

In summary of the origin and operations stories found in *The New York Times*, *The Los Angeles Times*, and *Washington Post*, the death squads are the result of the actions of a handful of men working on their own initiative. The death squads did not have an institutional history beyond the efforts of d'Aubuisson's and a handful of other Salvadoran officers in 1979 and 80. It just so happens, it would seem, that individuals said to be behind the death squads also held important positions in Salvadoran military or security forces.

To associate the United States with the forces of democracy in El Salvador, as *The Post* did, is reassuring and in keeping with the oft-expressed values of U.S. foreign policy. Death squad remedy and reassurance stories such as this were pervasive. These stories emphasized the role of United States government official in pressuring the Salvadorans to "clean-up the death squads."

Reassurance Stories

The reassurance stories came in the form of American officials "taking care of things," such as in December 1983, when Vice President George Bush flew to El Salvador to pressure Salvadoran and military officials to do something to stop the "activities of right wing death squads." The reported intent of Bush's trip was repeated in nearly all of the subsequent stories in this initial group of twenty articles. *The Los Angeles Times* reported on December 16, 1983 that "The Salvadoran armed forces, in an apparent response to an American ultimatum (delivered by Bush) . . . publicly vowed Thursday to eradicate the right wing death squads." Two weeks later an anonymous State Department official interviewed by *The New York Times* remarked that "El Salvador appears to be carrying out its pledge to curb the "activities" of right wing death squads. One should note that *The New York Times'* standard reference to Salvadoran death squad murder was "death squad activities."

Bush's visit was followed by Secretary of State Shultz's eight hour visit on January 31, 1984, just two months prior to Kirkpatrick's dire warning concerning communist victory in Central America. *The New York Times* quoted Shultz as saying the Salvadorans had made "considerable progress in recent months in curbing right wing death squad activities and improving its human rights record." Shultz was also reported to be happy with the Salvadoran response to American demands that certain members of the security forces be reassigned. This fit well with the themes of the origin and operation stories that understood the death squads to be the result of deviant individuals in El Salvador. Shultz was quoted in a February 1, 1984 *New York Times* article as follows: "Not all the names (were reassigned), but a goodly portion. Its basically a pretty good record, a very good record."[22] But just to make sure one understood the values for which the United States stood, Shultz was also quoted as saying at a luncheon, with d'Aubuisson in attendance, the following: "Death squads and terror have no place in a democracy, and I mince no words in saying it here or anywhere else." Other officials, such as Ambassador Thomas Pickering, were also said to be pressuring Salvadoran officials to eradicate the death squads.

In summary, in remedy stories the United States was understood to be a restorer of social order and justice. This same storyline was evident in the 1988 *Post* articles. Secondly, the death squads did not have an official institutional history, except perhaps the boy scouts. They were merely the products of deviant individuals.

Anomalous News

The objective here is not to attempt to prove the greater truthfulness of any one account of the origins and operations of Salvadoran state terrorism. It is likely that elements of all of the stories are based, at least to some degree, in fact. For instance, it is entirely possible that d'Aubuisson was given instruction on the finer points of death squad operation by both the Guatemalans and the Argentines. And according to the 1993 "Truth Commission" report issued by the United Nations, d'Aubuisson was indeed deeply involved in Salvadoran right-wing terror.[23] Among most observers of Salvadoran politics, this was never in doubt. What I do want to show, however, is that *some* versions of the death squads origins and operations—but particularly origins—were more acceptable to the mainstream press than were others. The relative unacceptability of the version I am about to present had little to do with concerns of sloppy journalism, made-up sources, or any other potential violation of standard journalism norms. Instead, the only violation was that the next version of Salvadoran terrorism violated the bounds of thinkable thought regarding the conduct of the United States in the world.

The Progressive's Version of the Salvadoran Death Squad Story

There is variability in what can and does become news in the United States. The lengths to which the Reagan and Bush administrations went to control the news indicated this as well as anything. Yet as W. Lance Bennett and his colleagues have noted: "There must be times when ambiguous or problematic stories slip through the reporting gates and invite interpretations that, if left unchallenged, would raise questions about who or what in the world is normal, credible, and authentic."[24]

The publication of Allan Nairn's account of Salvadoran terrorism in *The Progressive* offers one example. Nairn is a respected freelance journalist who has written about human rights and Third World issues for *The New Republic* and *The New Yorker*, among other publications. In *The Progressive*'s version of the Salvadoran terrorism story, Nairn clearly identified his sources, mostly high ranking Salvadoran and American officials and former officials. This was something *The New York Times* and *The Los Angeles Times* generally failed to do, though generally out of concern for the well-being of their sources. The problem with the use of anonymous sources, among many, was the issue of credibility. This was evident in United Nations Ambassador Jeane Kirkpatrick's response to the reported ties of d'Aubuisson to the death squads: "I think it is nondefinitive and it involves anonymous informers and that sort of thing."[25]

Nairn interviewed mostly named sources, including Colonel Nicolas Caranza and then director of the Salvadoran Treasury Police, Colonel Blandon, Salvadoran army chief of staff. He also interviewed the American CIA station chief at the American Embassy at the time of the establishment of the institutional base of the Salvadoran death squads, ORDEN and the Salvadoran Security Agency (ANSESAL).

These sources candidly stated a number of claims, some quite extraordinary. For instance, Colonel Caranza claimed that the security forces had good relations with the American embassy in El Salvador. The embassy had even promised training and equipment for interrogation at a time when such equipment would have been against American law. Caranza said he was confident that despite the ban, the security forces would receive the equipment. There were, he said, "other ways, by lets say friends with some members of the embassy. . . . I don't know if it would be wise to put this out for the knowledge of the American people." This was an astonishing insinuation of Contragate-like activity some three full years before the story broke.

Nairn's most prominent and important source was General Jose Alberto "Chele" Medrano, a self-proclaimed CIA agent from the early 1960s. He was the founder of ORDEN, an anti-communist para-military organization, and ANSESAL, an intelligence organization, both developed in the 1960s. In Medrano's words, ORDEN's purpose was to "indoctrinate the peasants regarding the advantages of the democratic system and the disadvantages of the communist system."

ORDEN and ANSESAL were also *the institutional structure upon which the death squads were built and maintained.* ORDEN, in its pursuit of "communists," gathered information on individuals deemed suspicious. "You discovered communists by the way he talks. Generally, he speaks against Yankee imperialism, he speaks against the oligarchy, he speaks against military men. We can spot them easily." In the next paragraph Medrano succinctly described the slaughter of tens of thousands of people, often because they said the wrong words to the wrong people: "In this revolutionary war, the enemy comes from the people. They don't have the rights of Geneva. They are traitors to the country. What can the troops do? When they find them, they kill them."

Medrano made it clear that these organizations and their "activities" were not homegrown or the result of the efforts of a handful of renegade Salvadoran officers in the early 1980s. He stated that "ORDEN and ANSESAL grew out of the State Department, the CIA, the Green Berets, and the Agency for International Development "during the time of Kennedy." The United States even sent Medrano on a three month tour in Vietnam where he studied "every aspect of warfare." Upon his return from Vietnam, Medrano was sent ten Green Beret soldiers by 8th Special Forces commander, Colonel Arthur Simons. The Green Beret helped plan the structure and ideology of ORDEN. At its peak ORDEN had 100,000 members.

Additionally, the CIA provided intelligence information on Salvadorans working and studying abroad. Information on suspected "subversives" was widely shared by the Americans and the Salvadorans. Additionally, the Agency for International Development's Public Safety Office established communications networks used to identify targets. The CIA supplied Salvadoran security forces with the names and location of political dissidents who were then often assassinated by the death squad—security forces. In short, Nairn's article detailed a long, close relationship between the security forces, death squads, and numerous United States government institutions.

The point I am making is not that Nairn was solely correct and the earlier *New York Times* and *Los Angeles Times* articles were necessarily wrong. The point concerns how the respective stories were framed. Unlike the earlier articles, Nairn's article placed the Salvadoran institutional structures that relied on the death squads, and whose personnel who came from these "security" agencies, squarely within the context of United States foreign policy since the early 1960s.

The damaging implication of Nairn's report was not just that death squads were an integral part of the Salvadoran security forces and intelligence agencies, *but that these operations were established and maintained by the United States over many years.* In Nairn's words, the U.S. complicity . . . in the work of Salvador's death squads *is not an aberration.* Rather, it represents a basic, bipartisan, institutional commitment on the part of six American administrations to guard Salvador from people who might organize in ways unfriendly to the U.S. regime .[26]

President Kennedy was fascinated with counterinsurgency warfare in the wake of the French experience in Algeria and Southeast Asia, and Castro's victory in Cuba. His response was to launch a revamping and expansion of United States counterinsurgency capabilities. As a 1962 memorandum from Chairman of the Joint Chiefs of Staff, General Lyman Lemnitzer, summarized that effort:

> What the president had in mind was nothing less than a dynamic national strategy: an action program designed to defeat the Communists without recourse to the hazard or the terror of nuclear war; one designed to defeat subversion where it had already erupted and, even more important, to prevent its taking initial root.[27]

Specifically, this "dynamic national strategy" involved the organization of irregular counterinsurgency units throughout Latin America and elsewhere in the Third World where the United States perceived a threat from Communist expansion. In practice, this strategy aligned the United States with the status quo, no matter how corrupt and brutal. In Iran, SAVAK, the Shahs brutal paramilitary secret police would eventually be organized. In Central America, paramilitary units such as ORDEN, an acronym which is patterned after the Spanish word for order, were established not only in El Salvador but in Honduras, Guatemala, and Panama.

Michael McClintock has chronicled the formation of American counterinsurgency programs in Latin America.[28] McClintock shows how the United States help organize the paramilitary organizations, such as Medrano's ORDEN, through the military, CIA, and Agency for International Development's Public Safety Program. In Guatemala, the United States, according to McClintock, even compiled the data base for what eventually became a death squad/security force's hit list of suspected subversives. Except for Nairn's account, this was the frame or context ignored or otherwise missed by the various death squad origins stories.

News Repair and the Christian Science Monitor's Version

Repair does not utilize conspiracy. Rather, the operation of shared understandings and expectations of reporters and government officials alike—norms—re-orient stories such as Nairn's back into manageable bounds of thought. Such a repair process revealed itself initially in Dennis Volman's May 8, 1984 *Christian Science Monitor* article "Salvadoran Death Squads, a CIA Connection?" But a repair process more forcefully presented itself in the various reprints of the Volman article appearing in newspapers around the country in following days.

According to the *Monitor*, following the 1979 coup the CIA helped organize the Salvadoran National Intelligence Agency (ANI), an operations oriented counter-intelligence unit. It was still financed by the CIA at the time of the publication of these articles. Later the *Monitor* article pointed out in passing that ANI and the Army general staff departments two and five grew out of the original Salvadoran National Security Agency (ANSESAL). The *Monitor* even noted (in a single sentence) that ANSESAL was established in 1962 with "heavy CIA and US military participation." At the same time, however, with the exception of the one oblique refers to ANSESAL, the institutional ties were limited to CIA personnel operating in El Salvador in the 1980s.

Besides the similarities there were substantial differences, differences which were accentuated in the reprints of the Volman article. This is an important point for it was in the reprints that a more thorough repair process occurred. Among the differences was the impression that US involvement was limited to recent CIA operations. This impression was strengthened by this statement in the *Monitor* article: "On a more general level, the U.S. State Department and its representatives at the embassy are putting increasing pressure on the Salvadoran armed forces to control the bloodshed." This impression was also strengthened by an interview of the author of the *Monitor* article on *National Public Radio*'s "All Things Considered," broadcast May 8, 1984. Volman said the following in response to a question regarding the institutional links of the United States with the death squads:

> I think that perhaps in the last few years we're in a situation where the CIA has had its own little fiefdom in Central America . . . (where they) are pushing policies, at least at the grassroots level, on the ground, much further than people in Washington or other government agencies intend them to go. And I think this is one of the essential problems.

Here again, institutions in Washington were distanced from the terrorism in El Salvador.

There were other differences. Unlike the *Progressive*'s named sources, *The Christian Science Monitor*'s two sources remained anonymous, as were the sources for the earlier *New York Times* and *Los Angeles Times* articles. One of the two *Post* sources from the articles in 1988 also remained anonymous. *The Monitor* described its sources as "two well informed sources, closely connected with the upper-reaches of the Salvadoran military and political power structure." The claim made in the article was that the CIA established counterintelligence units (these would be second generation ANSESAL units) that, in the process of questioning suspected subversives, sometimes kills them. Furthermore, this may be done with the knowledge of their CIA counterparts. The *Monitor* article stated

> Most of the killings, both *Monitor* sources say, result from the torture used to extract intelligence information. People die during torture, they say, or are killed because the torturer leaves marks on the bodies which he realizes could be used to prove what was done to the victims.

There can be little doubt that some portion of the Salvadoran death squad victims died under circumstances as described above. At the same time it must be recalled that tens of thousands of victims had died by 1984. At one point in the year just prior to the *Monitor* article, the victims were averaging one thousand a month. Most of the eyewitness accounts as reported in Amnesty International's *Report on Torture* described young and old alike taken from their homes in the middle of the night and found dead the next day, many if not most with obvious signs of torture.

Yet with the description offered by the *Monitor* it would seem the "security forces" were "death squads" due only to their incompetence as interrogators. This was not in keeping with the more common image of death squads as murderers who stole away with loved ones in the night. With Volman's remarks on *National Public Radio*, and with the article's overall impression that only the Central America field offices of the CIA in the post-1979 coup period were responsible for these ties, the impression was left that American involvement with the death squads was but an aberration from the norm.

This should be compared to Nairn's account. Beside the CIA there was the Agency for International Development, particularly its Public Safety Office, the United States embassy in San Salvador, the State Department, the Green Berets, including specifically named commanders, the Federal Bureau of Investigation, and "six American administrations over a twenty year period of time." With the *Monitor* version of events, United States officialdom, "on the whole," was partially restored to being on the side of that which was good and moral. Responsibility for the death squads was once again restricted to the deviant few. This helped preserve the legitimacy of American officials and institutions by narrowing the scope of controversy.

The repair process intensified once the *Monitor* article reached other mass circulation outlets. A search through available newspapers microfilm turned up several interesting *Monitor* reprints. No newspaper in the sample, some twenty-five publications in all, ran the original without alteration. Many newspapers, such as *The New York Times*, did not run the Volman article; effectively ignoring it.

The standard pattern in alteration, following standard editorial practice, was to substantially cut the *Monitor* article, on average to less than half its original length of forty-three paragraphs. One newspaper cut it to but three paragraphs. In most cases what was cut was the *Monitor*'s outline of the historical and institutional links between the United States and the Salvadoran security and intelligence apparatus, which were already scaled back considerably from Nairn's version. Most of the description of these links appeared after the 22nd paragraph of the original *Monitor* article. This position made it more likely to be cut in the editing process. But what is more interesting and important is the material that was *added* to the *Monitor* story as it was reprinted in various newspapers. By both failing to reprint some portions of the *Monitor* article and adding to it, local editors completed the repair process. The story was brought back into line with mainstream expectations.

Brief descriptions of a few examples will illustrate this. *The Los Angeles Times* ran a four paragraph summary of the *Monitor* article, with one of the four paragraphs being a CIA denial. *The Idaho Statesman* ran a two paragraph summary. *The Oregonian* offered the most complete and unsanitized reprint of the original *Monitor* article. While reorganizing the article and cutting it by about a third, it offered all of the description of tortured deleted by other papers. It did, however, cut all reference to long-term institutional links between the United States and Salvadoran death squads.

The Seattle Times also reprinted a version of the *Monitor* article.[30] Its visual effects were the most striking of all the reprints reviewed. While the *Monitor's* original version did not carry photographs, *The Seattle Times* version added the photograph of an angry looking George Bush along with the caption "A Warning to Salvadorans." The Bush photograph, at the top and center of the article, was prominently displayed.

Also added was a sidebar with the headline "Outrageous, says CIA." It went on to offer the official CIA denial of its involvement with Salvadoran death squads. Later, in 1986 when senior Honduran military officers and former U.S. intelligence officers said CIA operatives were minimally aware of Honduran death squad killings and torture, the Agency used the same language but added "accusations of CIA complicity in Salvadoran death squads had surfaced in 1984 and also were the result of Cuban 'disinformation.'" When asked how U.S. congressional and military sources might have found themselves serving as Cuban propaganda agents, the CIA spokesman declined further comment.[31]

In *The Seattle Times* reprint, the two additions, particularly the contradictory "Warning from Bush" photograph and the CIA denial, are the most prominent features of the reprint. With these additions one is left not knowing whether this is a story about United States complicity in the death squads or a story about the United States pressure to end the death squads, or both. What is clear is that the "paradigmatically correct" storyline of the initial *New York Times* and *Los Angeles Times* articles have been inserted into the otherwise contradictory account offered by *The Christian Science Monitor*. The news was repaired in the sense that the paradigmatically correct storyline had crept back into the story of U.S. institutional ties to Salvadoran terrorism.

To gain the full impact of the transition from Nairn in *The Progressive* to the reprinted *Monitor* article in *The Seattle Times*, one must note the photographs which accompanied Nairn's article. Whereas the Seattle newspaper carried the reassuring photograph of George Bush, Nairn's article was accompanied by Michael Kienitz's photographs of Salvadoran soldiers, guerrillas, and dead peasants. One photograph graphically depicted seven dead peasants, including two women, all said to be guerrillas. A group of smiling soldiers stands over the bodies. One body has its detached arm resting on its torso. The next page carries close-up photographs of the horribly mutilated faces of more death squad victims.

The point here is that the photographs in each version of events reinforced the dominant themes found in each respective article. In Nairn's article the brutality of the death squads was emphasized. In *The Seattle Times* reprint of the *Monitor* article, it was the reintroduction of the reassuring American official and CIA denials that were emphasized. These photographs illustrated—quite literally—the repair process.

The Boston Globe reprinted most of *The Christian Science Monitor* article, though with considerable alteration. Here the technique was deletion, not addition. *The Globe*, for instance, dropped altogether this quote from the *Monitor* article: "How absurd you Americans are, this civilian source remarked bitterly. 'With the one hand you send your vice president here to control the death squads, with the other you participate in them."

When passages from the *Monitor* article were not deleted, they were often sanitized. For example, whereas the original article said the following: "According to the civilian source, the two departments pick victims up and torture them, sometimes to death. The tortures, he says—*usually beatings, burnings, and electric shocks*—are often conducted in the building housing the headquarters of the armed forces general staff in San Salvador," *The Boston Globe* reprint deleted entirely the description of the nature of the torture involved (the emphasized portion of the quote above).

The Atlanta Constitution also ran a truncated version of the original *Monitor* story, cutting the historical background section. But once again what is most interesting is what *The Constitution* added. The CIA denial that had appeared as a sidebar in *The Seattle Times* became the third paragraph in *The Atlanta Constitution* version, as if the CIA denial had headed the original article, too.

Similar deletions and additions were found in all of the *Monitor* reprints examined. With these reprinted *Monitor* articles is seen the subtle and not so subtle re-emergence of the standard, paradigmatically correct storyline found in the earlier *New York Times* and *Los Angeles Times* articles, articles that had emerged out of an administration public relations campaign designed to remove a major stumbling block to further United States military aid to El Salvador. The reader was consistently left with reasons to dismiss any assertion of deep and long-term United States government involvement in the creation and maintenance of Salvadoran state terrorism. The storyline was brought back into manageable limits once it made its way to the reprinted *Monitor* versions.

In 1988, with *The Washington Post*'s version of the death squad origins and operations, all history was forgotten in the name of revealing history. The death squads that killed and systematically tortured thousands had, according to *The Post*, their origins in boy scout troops and not in the cold war history of the American CIA, Office of Public Safety, and Green Berets. Death squads once again were merely the progeny of the perverted minds of individuals working outside government structures, and not as a strategic part of U.S. foreign policy. And once again the United States was understood as the force behind moderation and the "democratic process," not terrorism, brutality and political repression. The news was repaired.

Summary

A number of scholars have argued that mainstream journalists are imbued with the values and world view of those they most often cover: government officials and politicians. Because this is the case, journalists tend to present news from within these "bounds of thinkable thought." This is what happened to the death squad story described above. When the story that went beyond the public relations blitz offered by the administration for press and public consumption, when it began to call into question U.S. government complicity, the story was "repaired."

In the last six chapters evidence has been offered which suggests the way we commonly think about terrorism and the news needs to be re-evaluated. In the "tug of war" that determines news content,[32] it is most often official sources who win. Officials, not terrorist, most often set the news agenda.

Political power so exercised is usually done with policy objectives in mind. What did the Reagan administration hope to achieve by setting the terror news agenda?

Notes

1. Typeset, "Recent Political Violence in El Salvador," Report of the Select Committee on Intelligence, United States Senate, October 5, 1984, p. 8.

2. Douglas Farah, "D'Aubuisson: Death Comes to the Executioner," *The Washington Post*, February 23, 1992, C4.

3. See, for instance, Edward S. Herman, "Diversity in the News: 'Marginal-

izing' the Opposition," *Journal of Communication*, Summer 1985, pp. 135-146; Edward S. Herman, Edward S. and Noam Chomsky, *Manufacturing Consent: The Political Economy of the Mass Media* (New York: Pantheon Books, 1988); W. Lance Bennett, "Marginalizing the Majority: Conditioning Public Opinion to Accept Managerial Democracy" in Michael Margolis and Gary A. Manser, eds. *Manipulating Public Opinion: Essays on Public Opinion as the Dependent Variable* (Pacific Grove, CA,: Brooks-Cole, 1989); W. Lance Bennett, Lynne Gressett, and William Haltom, "Repairing the News: A Case Study of the News Paradigm," *Journal of Communication*, Spring 1985, pp. 50-68; Leon Sigal, *Reporters and Officials: the Organization and Politics of News Making* (Lexington, Mass.: Heath, 1973), particularly pp. 37-45.

4. William Boot, "Iranscam: When the Cheering Stopped: Suddenly all the Great Leader Copy Seemed Embarrassing," *Columbia Journalism Review*, March/April 1987, pp. 25-30.

5. Steven V. Roberts, "The Reagan White House: Reagan Concedes 'Mistake' in Arms-for-Hostages Policy; Takes Blame; Vows Changes," *The New York Times*, March 5, 1987.

6. Unsigned, "Afghan Rebels Say They're Bombing Hotels," *The New York Times*, September 5, 1985, p. 11

7. Herbert Gans, *Deciding What's News: A Case Study of CBS Evening News, NBC Nightly News, Newsweek and Time* (New York: Vintage 1979), p. 42.

8. Noam Chomsky, "Beyond the Bounds of Thinkable Thought," *The Progressive*, October 1985.

9. Hertsgaard, *On Bended Knee*, p. 94.

10. Thomas Kuhn, *The Structure of Scientific Revolutions* (Chicago: University of Chicago Press, 1962).

11. Herman, "Diversity in the News."

12. Lindsey Gruson, "Quayle, in Salvador, Discusses Human Rights," *The New York Times*, February 4, 1989, p. 5.

13. Walter LaFeber, *Inevitable Revolutions: The United States in Central America* (New York: W.W. Norton & Co., 1984).

14. The two *Los Angeles Times* articles were written by Laurie Becklund ("Death Squads: Deadly 'Other War'," December 18, 1983, p. 1 and "Death Squads: 'Over the Edge'," December 19, 1983, p. 5). They were included because they represent a major news effort to get to the truth about the death squads. In the words of *The Los Angeles Times*, "The Times conducted a month-long study to try to make sense of what is routinely described as senseless violence" (December 18, 1983).

15. Roberto d'Aubuisson died of cancer on February 20, 1992.

16. Stephen Kinzer, "Ex-Aide in Salvador Accuses Colleagues on Death Squads," *The New York Times*, March 3, 1984, p. A1.

17. Unsigned, "Contra Officer Tied to Death Squads," *The Chicago Tribune*, March 22, 1985, p. 5, zone C.

18. Ibid.

19. Philip Taubman, "Salvadoran Was Paid for Accusations," *The New York Times*, March 21, 1984, p. A3.

20. Douglas Farah, "Death Squads Began as Scout Troop," *The Washington Post*, August 29, 1988, p.1.

21. Ibid.

22. Philip Taubman, "Shultz Indicates Salvadoran Gains on Human Rights," *The New York Times*, February 1, 1984, p. A1.

23. Guy Gugliotta and Douglas Farah, "12 Years of Tortured Truth on El Salvador," *The Washington Post*, March 21, 1993.

24. W. Lance Bennett, Lynne Gressett, and William Haltom, "Repairing the News."

25. Reuters wire service report, March 2, 1984. Found in Nexis search ("Jeane Kirkpatrick and Salvador! and death squads and anonymous").

26. Emphasis added.

27. Quoted by Aryeh Neier, "State Terror and Popular Resistance in Guatemala; the American Connection," *The Nation*, September 7, 1985.

28. Michael McClintock, *Instruments of Statecraft: U.S. Guerrilla Warfare, Counterinsurgency, and Counterterrorism, 1940–1990* (New York: Pantheon Books, 1992)

29. One editor at *The Progress* even felt the *Monitor* had "ripped them off."

30. Dennis Volman, "CIA Linked to Roots of the Death Squads of El Salvador: Sources Describe U.S. Role," *The Seattle Times*, May 13, 1984, p. A13.

31. Reuters wire service, "CIA Denies it Knew of Murder, Torture and Honduras, February 14, 1986.

32. Todd Gitlin, *The Whole World is Watching: The Making and Unmaking of the New Left* (Berkeley: University of California Press, 1980), p. 251.

7

The Terrorism Spectacle:
Foreign Policy Objectives

I speak of peace while covert enmity under the smile of safety wounds the world.
—Shakespeare, Henry IV, Part II

The Reagan and Bush administrations attempted to create a terrorism spectacle which highlighted the violence of enemies while leaving the violence of strategic allies off-stage and in the dark. While some interpretations of the terrorism issue were "organized into politics," others were "organized out."[1] This was achieved through the control of information and access to the channels of mass communication. The objective in both exclusion and emphasis was the legitimation of policies and leaders.[2] As Edelman has described this dynamic: "If yearning for security and protection create leaders, leaders themselves do more than their share to construct the threats to well-being that keep those aspirations alive."[3]

In many of the examples we have reviewed, there were direct links between the given portrayal of terrorism (or non-terrorism) and the supported policy. To support Iraq in its war against Iran, for instance, required removing Iraq from the State Department's list of terror sponsoring nations. To accomplish this required the Reagan and Bush administrations to ignore continued Iraqi involvement in terrorism throughout the 1980s, right up until August 1990 when the policy toward Iraq changed. Of course, Iraq's behavior had not changed, just the desired policies. Likewise, continued support for UNITA rebels in Angola, the rebels in Afghanistan, or the security forces in El Salvador require the United States government to turn a blind eye to their various forms of involvement in terrorism. As Thomas Buergenthal, member of the United Nations' Salvador Truth Commission said in 1993 about U.S. official knowledge of state terrorism in El Salvador: "In some cases, there is a sense that they didn't want to know."[4] There was a more direct link between not knowing and desired policy.

What I offer in this and the next chapter is an overview of other, less direct policy consequences of the terrorism spectacle. I argue that the terrorism spectacle, as seen in official accounts and the news media, was used by the Reagan administration and conservatives more generally to reverse an array of restrictions placed on foreign security assistance programs to the Third World and domestic security investigations in the United States.

Creating the Terrorism Spectacle

We have seen various forms of evidence which have indicated that the Reagan and Bush administrations played politics with the fight against terrorism. There is even more direct evidence that this was the case. Immediately upon taking office the Reagan administration sought to create a crisis atmosphere regarding terrorism. Crisis is an important component of political spectacle for "Like 'problems,' crisis typically rationalize policies . . ."[5]

To that end, in his first public pronouncement as Secretary of State, Alexander Haig declared that international terrorism would replace human rights as the central foreign policy concern of the United States. On January 26, 1981, he also announced the existence of an "international terrorist network," directed by the Soviets, which he said was responsible for hijackings and bombings around the world.[6] In April, 1981, Anthony Quainton, director of the State Department's Office for Combating Terrorism, told reporters that the Reagan administration was determined to give a "very much greater interest, priority and intensity" to the question of terrorism. This was accomplished in part through the control and distribution of information, in this case a revision of government statistics regarding terrorism.

Revising Terrorism Statistics

Three months after President Reagan's inauguration, the administration announced that statistics on international terrorism were being revised.[7] Carried under the fold in a small, back-page article in *The New York Times*, the significance of the revisions would have been easy to miss. The new numbers would result from a simple change in the definition of terrorism used by the State Department and Central Intelligence Agency to identify and count "terrorist" incidents. Adoption of the new definition approximately doubled the number of incidents counted by the United States in the previous twelve years.

The administration was apparently concerned existing statistics would not substantiate its contention that terrorism was a serious problem, or at least one capable of supporting a host of desired policy goals. Treating the issue as a crisis needed statistics of crisis caliber. As Murray Edelman has noted, problems which are said to originate in the hostile intentions of enemies often cannot be know first hand. They are rather known only through the publicity given them by those with an interest in promoting them as problems.[8]

One could argue that the change in definition was superfluous. After all, as we have seen to this point, just about any definition could be selectively applied by the State Department to create just about any statistics it wanted without fear of critical review by the press. It could also ignore the sponsorship of terrorism by strategic allies such as Saddam Hussein and the government death squads in El Salvador without fear of media scrutiny. But in 1981, before the administration had a chance to try out its new press management apparatus, the most reliable course of action was to change the definition used to do the counting.

Not everyone agreed with the new statistical accounting of terrorism. Much of the resistance came from professional intelligence analysts such as Vincent Cannistraro who understood their job to be intelligence assessment, not policy promotion. Publication of the CIA's annual report on terrorism, normally available in April, was withheld "because of disputes among government agencies as to the nature, extent and gravity of terrorism."[9] An unnamed Senate staff official was quoted in the *Times* article as saying that CIA analysts were being pushed or encouraged to expand the definition of terrorism to include "all acts of violence intended to impact on a wider audience than the victims of the violence." "By that definition," said the staffer, "the shooting of President Reagan by John Hinckley would be a terrorist act."[10]

The revisions went into effect despite the objections, and subsequent documentation reflected the change. Perhaps what is even more interesting than the revision is what happened to knowledge of it in coming years. Within six years of the revision, State Department officials at the Office for Counterterrorism were unaware of it. In a conversation with a key member of the State Department's counterterrorism office I mentioned the revision. "What revision?" was the reply from one of the persons in charge of keeping these statistics. Subsequent inquiry revealed that by 1987, key personnel in the State Department's counterterrorism office were unaware of the definitional and statistical revisions they themselves had created. In fact, the following sentence began to appear in each annual report, changing only enough to accommodate the passing of another year:

No one definition of terrorism has gained universal acceptance. For the purposes of this report, however, we have chosen the definition commonly used by the US Government for the past 21 years, which also is widely accepted and one which we have used in previous reports.[11]

How this claim squared with the statistical revision in 1981 is not clear.

Crisis and the Terrorism Spectacle

In a percipient paragraph in the *Times* article about the revision of terrorism statistics, reporter Charles Mohr suggested that the administration's objectives were clear to anyone who could read between press release lines:

> Some Democratic members and staff officials of Congress said they feared the statistical revisions were motivated by a Reagan administration desire to justify a more rigid foreign policy abroad and might also be cited by conservatives to justify increased surreptitious surveillance of political dissidents at home.[12]

Mohr's sources were correct. Within two years the Federal Bureau of Investigation (FBI) was in the midst of a counterterrorism surveillance operation which took them into the homes, universities, churches, synagogues, and union halls of thousands of Americans. This will be discussed in the next chapter.

Also in the name of counterterrorism, the United States would launch invasions, conduct air strikes, and administer counterterrorism training programs for foreign police officers, some of whom were (and remain) the most brutal in the world. Terrorism was Ronald Reagan's crisis—and policy God-sent. What led Mohr, as well as the Congressmen and staffers he anonymously cited, to their insights?

Mohr's suspicions would have come naturally to anyone with a grasp of history. Democratic and Republican presidents alike have utilized crisis to mobilize public opinion, allowing for otherwise impossible policies. Crisis is as much a product of the language used to depict a situation as it is the product of any discernible features of the situation. "The positioning of Russian missiles in Cuba in 1962," remarked Edelman, "precipitated a 'Cuban Missile Crisis' though the stationing of American missiles as close to the Soviet Union even earlier was not defined as a crisis by either country."[13] As with other social issues, "crisis" typically rationalize policies and sanctify authorities uniquely suited for rectifying the crisis as depicted. "A crisis, like all news developments, is a creation of the political language used to depict it;

the appearance of a crisis is a political act, not a recognition of a fact or of a rare situation."[14]

President Truman's efforts in the years immediately following World War II offers an example. By 1947 the United States had completed the most rapid demilitarization in history.[15] To the emerging cold warriors, however, this was not good news. In January, 1946 Navy Secretary James Forrestal told Truman that he should bring in "the heads of the important news services and the leading newspapers . . . and state to them the seriousness of the present situation (with the Soviet Union) and the need for making the country aware of its implications abroad."[16] In his classic account of post-war American foreign policy, Stephen E. Ambrose stated that the President was inclined to follow Forrestal's advice, but at the same time knew that he would never get the economy-minded Republicans or a war-weary public to support rearmament in the absence of a crisis.[17]

As it would in so many other instances during the cold war, the needed crisis came in the form of a faltering right wing regime. Following the collapse of its war-torn economy in the spring of 1947, Great Britain found it impossible to pursue its traditional imperial aspirations. In Greece they were forced to withdraw military support for the corrupt monarchy they had installed at the end of the war. American cold warriors feared that the void left in Greece by Britain's withdrawal would almost surely be filled by the left, most of whom had been in the resistance fighting the Nazis during the war.

This was the crisis Truman needed. Yet the fundamental problem remained: How could he convince the American public that the United States should be involved in yet another European conflict? As Truman himself remarked in his memoirs, "There was considerable discussion (in a March 7 Cabinet meeting) on the best method to apprise the American people of the issues involved."[18] Senator Arthur Vandenberg, the Republican chairman of the Senate Foreign Relations Committee, had warned Truman that if he wanted Congress and the public to support his emerging policy of containment, and the permanent war mentality that went with it, he would have to, in Vandenberg's words, "scare the hell out of the American people"[19]

On March 12, 1947, before a joint session of Congress, Truman addressed the nation. "I wanted no hedging in this speech," Truman explained. In the speech Truman described the situation in Greece in the harshest of terms. Presented in the transcendental terms of "good versus evil" and "freedom versus democracy," Truman got what he wanted. The American public once again supported a president in a time of crisis. On May 15, 1947, Congress appropriated the first $400 million of the Cold War.[20]

Truman was incredibly successful in his efforts to reverse the isolationist tendencies in American political culture. Counted among his successes was the reintroduction of the selective service, expanded second-term defense budgets, and new airbases around the world. He was able to doubled the number of airgroups and produced a 50 percent increase in the armed forces. As Ambrose concluded, Truman was so successful in "scaring the hell out of the American people," the only critics of his policies to receive attention in the press "were those who thought Truman had not gone far enough in standing up to the Communists."[21]

Truman was not the last president to use crisis to promote policy. Johnson used the Gulf of Tonkin incident—which probably never happened—to win a free hand in the conduct of the war in Vietnam. Likewise, President Carter elevated the American hostage situation in Iran to the level of a crisis. In part this was done to conduct a Rose Garden reelection campaign against his Democratic primary challenger, Senator Ted Kennedy.

President Reagan's crisis would be terrorism. It would serve as the rallying cry for overcoming the modern-day version of American isolationism, the "Vietnam syndrome."

Isolationism Revisited: The Vietnam Syndrome

In the wake of the debacle in Vietnam, the United States suffered what many perceived to be a series of foreign policy setbacks. After the fall of the Shah in Iran, perceived Soviet gains in Angola, Mozambique, Ethiopia, Grenada, and Nicaragua, and the humiliating months of American embassy personnel held hostage, Ronald Reagan came to office intent on making "America stand tall again." The first place he was to "draw the line" on further Communists expansion was El Salvador. But as we saw in chapter six, El Salvador's bloodthirsty right wing created image problems for themselves and their Washington benefactors.

These problems were compounded by the lingering problem of the Vietnam syndrome, American public reluctance to become involved in another Third World conflict. As Michael Klare and Peter Kornbluh remarked, any assertion of imperial will, "was conditioned by the domestic repercussions of America's debacle in Vietnam."[22] Gallup polls consistently demonstrated strong American public opposition to expanding American involvement in Latin America. For instance, a 1983 Gallup survey found that 69 percent of the public opposed the idea of using American combat troops in El Salvador. In another poll taken later that same year, 72 percent of the respondents said they thought El Salvador was very or fairly likely to be "another Vietnam."[23]

The Contra war in Nicaragua was proving just as unpopular. In three polls taken by Gallup between March 1986 and January 1987, 52 percent, 58 percent, and 69 percent of the respondents respectively opposed aid to the Contras.[24] Old cold war themes were simply not working. What was worse, contrary to administration intentions, American involvement in El Salvador was actually raising the specter of Vietnam. As much as the American public disliked Communism, in the wake of Vietnam the public was even more opposed to the use of American military force abroad. As Hertsgaard has remarked, "No matter how insistently Reagan officials raised the specter of a Communist takeover of Central America, they would not be able to overcome this sentiment."[25] Furthermore, the specter of Communism itself no longer seemed to be as fearful as it once had been.

Despite the constant cold war rhetoric sounded by administration after administration, Republican and Democrat alike, public fear of communism and war had diminished precipitously since the onset of the cold war. In March 1948, 73 percent of the respondents to a Gallup survey believed the United States would be at war with the Soviet Union within two decades. Yet this fear of war and aggression did not last. By 1964, 29 percent said they feared "the threat of communism or aggression by a Communists power." By 1974 this figure had dropped to 13 percent. And by 1981 in was down to a mere 8 percent.[26] In a psychological sense, the cold war ended for most Americans long before the more concrete symbols of it were torn down in Europe.

After the Soviet invasion of Afghanistan and Reagan's rhetorical assault on the Soviet Union as the "Evil Empire," there was something of a reversal of these trends. A New York Times/CBS poll in April 1983 found that by a three to two margin the public backed Reagan's view of the Soviet Union as an immediate danger and a growing threat.[27] Yet a *Washington Post* poll taken the very next month found that an overwhelming majority of Americans continued to oppose sending U.S. troops to foreign countries to fight against "Communist aggression."[28] Even though the public agreed with Reagan in principle, standard cold war rhetoric alone was an ineffectual pretext for foreign military intervention. The effectiveness of cold war themes to stimulate support for military intervention had diminished considerably. It became apparent to the administration that cold war rhetoric alone would not reverse the Vietnam syndrome. Something more was needed to "scare the hell out of the American people."

Bolstering the Communist "Evil Empire" Rhetoric

Besides the early skirmishes with Libya, the administration's first real success at overcoming the Vietnam syndrome was the invasion of Grenada. Coming just three days after the marine headquarters bombing in Beirut, the language of counterterrorism played a big part in justifying the Grenada campaign. Reagan first connected events in Grenada and Lebanon with standard plot lines about Communists perfidy. He did so by using language much like that used by Truman some forty years before in describing the situation in Greece. But unlike Truman, Reagan added terrorism to the mix. In his address to the nation on October 27, 1983, Reagan stated:

> The events in Lebanon and Grenada, though oceans apart, are closely related. Not only has Moscow assisted and encouraged the violence in both countries, but it provides direct support through a network of surrogates and terrorists.[29]

This is the contemporary version of the "world-wide Communist conspiracy" thesis of yesteryear. In the same address Reagan also stated

> Two hours ago we released the first photos from Grenada. They included pictures of a warehouse of military equipment, one of three we uncovered so far. This warehouse contained weapons and ammunition stacked almost to the ceiling, enough to supply thousands of terrorists.
> Grenada, we were told, was a friendly island paradise for tourism. Well it wasn't. It was a Soviet-Cuban colony being readied as a major military bastion to export terror and undermine democracy.[30]

The Grenada invasion, of course, coming at a time of high emotion resulting from the bombing of the marine headquarters, was a stunning success for President Reagan, at least when measured in terms of public support. After it became apparent the conflict in Grenada would soon be over, Americans seemed gratified that they could win one against terrorists. The United States was not only containing communism, it was countering terrorism, too.

Language such as this was needed to make the lessons of Grenada more generalizable. To speak of counterterrorism provided the much needed boost for cold war atrophy. By January 1986 a Harris survey found that 72 percent of their respondents endorsed the idea of a warning from leading nations that countries backing terrorism would be invaded. Seventy percent in this survey endorsed a policy that would rely on airstrikes against terrorist camps and headquarters.[31] A similar New York Times/CBS poll taken two weeks later, though finding less support for such radical measures, nevertheless found that 40 percent of those questioned thought there were situations in which force could reduce terrorism.[32]

When the United States actually did conduct airstrikes against targets in Libya just a few months later in April of 1986, 71 percent of those who were surveyed by a Gallup poll approved of the action, while 62 percent thought Reagan "makes wise use of military force." Eighty percent thought that the United States should take further military action should Libya be found to conduct or sponsor terrorist acts in the future. And 64 percent thought that the United States should bomb Iran or Syria should either be found to commit terrorist acts against the United States.[33]

If Americans were reluctant to become involved in a war to contain communism, they were more than ready to make up for it in their eagerness to go to war against officially defined terrorism. Like Truman and others before him, Reagan had found his crisis. But shoring-up public support for a militaristic foreign policy is only the beginning of what Reagan hoped to accomplish with terrorism.

Specific Accomplishments of Counterterrorism

Counterterrorism was simply one facet of a more complex military doctrine introduced during the Reagan years. Know as "low-intensity conflict," (LIC) this new thinking represented a fundamental reorientation of American strategic planning. While de-emphasizing European defense, LIC renewed American commitment to the use of military force as a tool of foreign policy. For LIC strategists the Third World replaced Europe as the principal locus of potential conflict. In the words of former Defense Secretary Casper Weinberger, the United States is in a "long twilight struggle" with guerrillas, assassins, terrorists, subversives and revolutionary movements in the Third World.[34] The collapse of the Soviet Union and Warsaw Pact has reinforced this view.

To meet these newly perceived challenges the Reagan administration and Pentagon planners began strengthening and forging new tools of war to match their new strategies. Most of these efforts were directed toward the Special Operations Forces (SOF) of each branch of the military. SOF budget outlays actually rose faster than the rest of the defense budget during the Reagan years. During fiscal year 1981, SOF unclassified budget stood at $441 million. By FY 1987, it stood at $1.7 billion and was estimated to be $8 billion by 1990.[35] At the same time, SOF active-duty manpower increased by 30 percent to just under 15,000 troops (32,000 counting reservists). By 1990 active duty SOF reach 21,000 (38,000 counting reservists).[36]

In the age of $300 billion defense budgets, these figures may seem modest, and many critics at the time believed that far too much emphasis was still being placed on conventional warfare arms expenditures to the determent of special operations. What must be kept in mind, though, is the functional difference between SOF, on the one hand, and the production and maintenance of nuclear weapons and the defense of Western Europe on the other. Nuclear weapons and maintaining a conventional defense force in Western Europe accounted for most of the $300 billion annual defense budgets during the Reagan years. While the nuclear weapons and conventional European defense forces served as a deterrent to war, SOF were and are intended for actually fighting real wars in the Third World. SOF are active while conventional and nuclear forces are reactive.

The primary function of these units is to serve as military trainers and advisors. SOF and probably the CIA and other elements of the SOF comprise what the Pentagon refers to as Military Training Teams (MTT). The level of CIA involvement in MTT is difficult to estimate. CIA and the Special Forces have operated very closely in the past, particularly in Laos, Cambodia, and Vietnam. It is estimated that the U.S. intelligence budget, which is secret even to the Congressmen who vote on it, had tripled to about $25 billion by 1986.[37] Furthermore, CIA personnel grew from about fourteen thousand in 1980 to over nineteen thousand by 1986. The number of operatives rose from about three hundred in 1979 to over one thousand by 1982.[38]

During the Reagan administration's first term in office, MTT man-week hours abroad rose more than five-fold.[39] According to Stephen Goose, between 1981 and 1984, MTTs operated in over three dozen countries, including Grenada, Honduras, Guatemala, El Salvador, Costa Rica, Colombia, Lebanon, Saudi Arabia, Somalia, Tunisia, Morocco, Liberia, Zaire, the Philippines, and Thailand. The backbone of these training missions was their presumed role in countering terrorism. Countering terrorism in the 1980s replaced counterinsurgency as the primary justification of American military involvement in the Third World. In pursuing this rhetorical shift, American military planners were taking advantage of the greater degree of public support for military actions understood as counterterrorism, as opposed to counterinsurgency directed against Communists guerrillas.

Putting Counterterrorism/Counterinsurgency into Historical Perspective

What counterinsurgency was to the Kennedy administration, counterterrorism was to the Reagan administration. To fully appreciate what the Reagan administration hoped to achieve in focusing media and public attention on terrorism in the 1980s, we must understand what was lost to the President in the reform-minded 1970s. The history of American involvement in security forces training is, to say the least, checkered. As Pat M. Holt, former chief of staff of the Senate Foreign Relations committee put it:

> Twenty-five years ago, counterterrorism was called counterinsurgency, and the Kennedy administration put much emphasis on it. A big part of it—and a big part of what the Reagan administration now wants to do in Central America—was a public safety program for training police. The idea was to make good police forces out of bad ones, to teach police how to interrogate a witness without resorting to torture. . . The trouble was that some foreign police forces took the training courses, gladly accepted the equipment, and kept right on beating people up.[40]

As was discussed in the previous chapter, in an attempt to stem the perceived tide of Communists subversion of the Third World, the Kennedy administration created a counterinsurgency apparatus, including the Office of Public Safety (OPS) housed in the Agency for International Development. By 1968, OPS was staffed by nearly six hundred employees who distributed almost $60 million in aid to police forces in thirty-four countries. They also trained hundreds of foreign security and police officers—the distinction between military and police officers is in most instances unclear—at the International Police Academy (IPA) in the Panama Canal Zone.[41] Between 1962 and 1975, OPS provided over $42 million in equipment and trained some two thousand Latin American police personnel.

One of the primary themes of the American training program was that the police were to be separate from the military and that they were to respect human rights in the conduct of their law enforcement efforts. As we saw in chapter six, these goals were not accomplished in El Salvador—or anywhere else for that matter. By the mid-1970s Congress was beginning to wonder if the police training aid wasn't doing more to contribute to the human rights abuses in many of the United States client states than it was to stop them. Even as early as 1965, Senator Wayne Morse noted that even if OPS goals were laudable,

> these programs are being conducted in countries where we have little or no control (over) the purposes for which they will be used . . . Just what we think we can teach the Dominican police that they did not learn for themselves in Trujillo's days is hard to understand.[42]

Disclosures of OPS aid to the extremely repressive police forces in

Iran (the U.S, helped the Shah create the brutal SAVAK), Uganda, Brazil, and Guatemala created pressure to terminate the training program. In El Salvador, General Medrano's ORDEN—and the death squads—was a creation of this program. In 1971, a Committee on Foreign Relations Staff Memorandum regarding Guatemala and the Dominican Republic noted the mounting political costs of the OPS program: "(T)he United States is politically identified with police terrorism . . . On balance, it seems that AID public safety has cost the United States more in political terms than it has gained in improving Guatemalan police efficiency."[43]

In December 1973, Congress passed an amendment to the Foreign Assistance Act of 1961 which stipulated that foreign-aid funds could no longer be used to assist police forces within the borders of foreign countries. This meant that training of these police forces could continue only in the United States and Panama Canal Zone.

Then in 1974, after additional abuses were disclosed, Congress expanded the 1973 prohibition to include all locations, including the United States. Section 660 of the Foreign Assistance Act stated:

> None of the funds available to carry out this Act . . . shall be used to provide training, or advice, or provide any financial support, for police, prisons, or other law enforcement forces for any foreign government or any program of internal intelligence or surveillance on behalf of any foreign government within the United States or abroad.[44]

Though the language sounded comprehensive, in practice it was not. First of all, section 660 covered only those programs funded under the provisions of the Foreign Assistance Act. Exempt were the International Narcotics Control Program (INC) administered jointly by the Department of State and the Justice Department's Drug Enforcement Agency (DEA). In fact, after Section 660 was enacted, funding for INC programs rose by 600 percent.[45] Much of this increased funding went to fill the void left by the termination of the OPS funding. DEA, in turn, increased its involvement in police training.

Getting around the prohibition on training aid didn't end there. The Pentagon was also exempt from the strictures of Section 660. Its International Military Education and Training program, manned by military training teams and other SOF personnel, trained Third World military officers who were then assigned to police duties.

Despite the porous nature of the restrictions resulting from Section 660, the Reagan administration was intent on its elimination. Beginning in 1983 Reagan began a program of incremental elimination of 660. First, Congress and the administration reached an informal agreement which allowed military police training aid to be transferred to Costa Rica and the Eastern Caribbean. The rationale for the aid was that in each instance the police also functioned as the only military force available. Therefore, the aid was military aid, not police training aid. The so called McCollum amendment to the Foreign Assistance Act (Section 660[c]), sponsored by Rep. Bill McCollum (R-Fla.) and passed in 1985, gave Congress's official approval to the informal agreement.

In 1983 and 1984 Congress and the administration also reached agreement on the establishment of an Economic Support Fund (ESF) for an Administration of Justice Program (AoJ) which, among other things, funded and trained a Special Investigative Unit of the Salvadoran police.[46] Its purpose was to investigate the major cases of human rights violations by elements of the Salvadoran security apparatus. Despite the fact that by 1986, funding for the AoJ program had reached $20 million, no one had been brought to justice for the murder of Archbishop Romero and four American church workers in 1980, or any of the rest of the tens of thousands murdered by right wing death squads comprised of security forces personnel.

At the urging of the administration, Congress also created the Anti-Terrorism Assistance program (ATA) administered by the Department of State. Under the heading of "counterterrorism," the administration was slowly rebuilding that which had been lost to the cold warriors in the reforms of the 1970s. Under the provisions of the Foreign Assistance Act, Section 571, Congress appropriated $2.5 million in FY 1984 and $5 million in 1985 to the ATA program. The Act called for the training and supplying of foreign police forces for the purpose of "deter(ing) terrorist groups from engaging in international terrorist acts such as bombing, kidnapping, assassination, hostage taking and hijacking." Furthermore, according to the language of the Act, such assistance may include training services and

> the provision of equipment and other commodities related to bomb detection and disposal, management of hostage situations, physical security, and other matters relating to the detection, deterrence, and prevention of acts of terrorism, the resolution of terrorist incidents, and the apprehension of those involved in such acts.

Two events in 1985 led to a substantial increase in the level of funding for the ATA program. First there was the ambush of four American marines and nine other civilians, two of whom were Americans, by the Salvadoran guerrillas in the Zona Rosa district of San Salvador. The second was the hijacking of a TWA jet to Beirut and the subsequent killing of an American serviceman. Funding for the ATA, in

fact, doubled to almost $10 million per year in FY 1986-87. The same
level of funding was requested for FY 1988. The program continued to
expand. According to *Patterns of Global Terrorism*, in 1991 alone, "more
than 1,900 police and security personnel from 18 countries received such
training, bringing the total number of persons trained in the program to
more than 12,500 from over 70 countries."[47] The language of counterterrorism had replaced the language of counterinsurgency, the Reagan
administration was recreating the same programs previously administered under OPS, programs that led only to the greater brutality of U.S.
client state security forces.

Besides the establishment of the ATA program, in 1984 the
administration used the Pentagon's MTTs to create and train a
Salvadoran SWAT team, without consulting Congress. Advisors trained
a fifty-man unit called Comando Especial Anti-Terrorismo (CEAT).
According to the State Department, the SWAT teams "would operate
under the direct control of the Salvadoran armed forces chief of staff . . .,
(and) is strictly (an) urban counterterrorism (unit)—hostage or barricade
situations and the like—and is not concerned with routine law
enforcement."[48]

CEAT was deployed on June 2, 1985. Their mission was not to counter terrorism but was rather to break a hospital workers strike which
had been declared illegal by the Salvadoran government. They stormed
the hospital and, according to the human rights monitoring organization Americas Watch, forced doctors and nurses to lie on the floor.
Many were bound hand and foot. One patient died when doctors were
prevented from going to her care. CEAT personnel on this mission also
shot and killed four undercover police officers in an apparent case of
mistaken identity.[49]

Administration efforts to use terrorism as a means of reversing the
restrictions of the 1970s didn't end there. After failing in 1985 to have
passed an antiterrorism package that would have essentially repealed
Section 660, the administration announced in October 1985 that it was
going to "reprogram" approximately $4.5 million in unexpended mili-
tary and ATA monies for the purpose of training and supplying Salvadoran police forces. In notifying Congress, the State Department said
it was trying to prevent another Zona Rosa type attack by strengthening
the counterterrorism capabilities of the security forces. Some two thousand members of the Salvadoran security forces were eventually trained
under the program. A second and third reprogramming request provided an additional $6.7 and $7.3 million for 1987. In other words, in
1987, contrary to the restrictions of Section 660, approximately $18.5
million was provide El Salvador, a country with one of the worst
human rights records in the world. With these funds Salvadoran

security forces purchased, among other items, twelve-gauge shotguns and nine-millimeter pistols.[50]

Additionally, under the provisions of either the AoJ or the ATA programs, police counterterrorism programs have been funded for Guatemala, Honduras, Costa Rica, Uruguay, Peru, Colombia, and several Caribbean nations. Growing public concern about terrorism, a concern partly orchestrated by official media management, was used to justify the implementation of desired solutions, solutions not otherwise possible in the face of public resistance to old-style counterinsurgency.

In revising terrorism statistics in 1981, producing tendentious reports throughout the 1980s, and presumably orchestrating extensive media coverage of only enemy acts of terrorism, the administration set the stage for advancing policy goals made difficult by the Vietnam syndrome. This possibly even included the reversal of the prohibition on assassination.

In 1984 the Pentagon had recommendation that it be allowed to form "hit squads" to assassinate "terrorists." This recommendation was rejected. By April 1989 the Army was once again seeking permission to reverse President Ford's 1976 presidential order barring employees of the United States or "those acting on behalf of the United States government" from engaging in, or "conspire to engage in, assassination." Ford's order was in response to Congressional inquiries which disclosed various CIA assassination attempts on the life of Fidel Castro and others. Americans were also involved in the deaths of Ngo Dinh Diem in Vietnam and Salvador Allende in Chile. Writing in the newsletter *Defense Week*, Major General Hugh Overholt, then the Army's judge advocate general (chief legal officer) argued that using military force against "terrorists" to "protect U.S. citizens or the national security of the United States is a legitimate exercise of the international legal right of self-defense and does not constitute assassination."

The Army also requested permission to target those who posed a "continuing threat" to the United States and not just those who constitute an "actual or imminent threat." "This right of self-defense," wrote the general, "would be appropriate to the attack of terrorist leaders or terrorist infrastructure that through their actions pose a continuing threat to U.S. citizens or the national security of the United States."[51] As late as 1993 the Department of Defense's General Counsel's office would not comment "one way or another" on the disposition of this 1989 proposal.[52]

While preemptive assassinations of terrorists would sound reasonable and prudent in a world without questions regarding what terrorism is and who the terrorists are, we do not live is such a world. In the absence of such black and white clarity, safeguards are needed. No mention is made of what authority would determine who ought to be regarded a terrorist or who constitutes a continuing or even immanent threat. Nor is there mention of Congressional oversight or veto power. There has been, as far as I can determine at this time, no additional public comment on the proposal.

Summary

The 1980s witnessed a resurgence in the types of programs and policies that had been restricted in the previous decade. Originally offered as assistance in the efforts at combating Communist subversion abroad, their reincarnation in the 1980s took the form of counterterrorism. This was made possible not just by the actions of people like Abu Nidal. It was also the consequence of a kind of political power that is expressed in the ability to manage issue content and interpretation through the news media. In the next chapter we will see that similar gains were made by those who felt 1970s era restrictions on domestic police activities were an undue burden in their search for subversives. For the Reagan administration, counterterrorism served as the justification for intensifying domestic political intelligence investigations. We turn to this next.

Notes

1. E. E. Schattschneider, *The Semisoveign People* (Hinsdale, Illinois: The Dryden Press, 1960, 1975 reissue), p. 30.

2. Murray Edelman, *Constructing the Political Spectacle* (Chicago: The University of Chicago Press, 1988), p. 30.

3. Edelman, *Constructing the Political Spectacle*, p. 38.

4. John M. Goshko, "Reagan Administration Accused of Lies on El Salvador," *The Washington Post*, March 17, 1993, p. A25.

5. Edelman, *Constructing the Political Spectacle*, pp. 31-32.

6. Don Oberdorfer, "Haig Calls Terrorism Top Priority," *The Washington Post*, January 27, 1981, p. A1.

7. Charles Mohr, "Data on Terrorism Under U.S. Revision," *The New York Times*, April 24, 1981, p A17.

8. Edelman, *Constructing the Political Spectacle*, p. 30

9. *The New York Times*, "Data on Terrorism Under U.S. Revision," April 24, 1981.

10. Ibid.

11. *Patterns of Global Terrorism: 1989*, p. v.

12. Ibid.

13. Edelman, *Constructing the Political Spectacle*, p. 31.

14. Ibid., p. 31.

15. Stephen E. Ambrose, *Rise to Globalism: American Foreign Policy Since 1938*, 5th edition (New York: Penguin Books, 1988), p. 80.

16. Ibid., p. 80.

17. Ibid., p. 82.

18. Ibid., p. 84.

19. Ibid., p. 87.

20. This same scenario was played out again in 1950. As Ambrose remarked:

In June 1950 he (Truman) badly needed another crisis, one that would allow him to prove to the American people that he and the Democratic Party were not soft on Communism, to extend containment to Asia, . . . and most of all to rearm America and NATO. The whole package envisioned in N.S.C. 68, in short, could be wrapped up and tied with a ribbon by an Asian crisis (Ambrose, *Rise to Globalism*, p. 116).

Truman refused to allow the document to be released for review outside of the administration. He realized that in the absence of a crisis "there was little chance of selling the program to the Congress or the public" (Ambrose, *Rise to Globalism*, p. 115). That crisis came in the form of the outbreak of the Korean war on June 25, 1950. I. F. Stone once remarked that when in the summer of 1951 it appeared peace in Korea was about to break-out, American leaders regarded it "as a kind of diabolic plot against rearmament."

The Truman Administration was concerned that as the military spending came to an end, so too would the healthy economy. There were signs of a stagnating economy in 1947. The nascent cold war provided an answer here, too. A few years later, in 1950, *U.S. News & World Report* straightforwardly summed-up the benefits of the then new cold war:

Government planners figure they have found the magic formula for almost endless (economic) good times. . . . Cold War is the catalyst. Cold War is an automatic pump-primer. Turn the spigot and the public clamors for more arms spending. Turn another, the clamor ceases. . . . Cold War demands, if fully exploited, are almost limitless (Parenti, *Inventing Reality*, p. 147).

The spigot referred to, of course, is cold war rhetoric.

21. Ambrose, *Rise to Globalism*, p. 131.

22. Peter Klare and Peter Kornbluh, eds., *Low Intensity Warfare: Counterinsurgency, Proinsurgency, and Antiterrorism in the Eighties* (New York: Pantheon Books, 1988), p. 8.

23. *Gallup Report*, 1983.

24. *Gallup Report*, 1986.

25. Mark Hertsgaard, *On Bended Knee: The Press and the Reagan Presidency* (New York: Farrar Straus Giroux, 1988), p. 185.

26. Gallup Poll, *The Washington Post*, December 22, 1981; Yankelovich, Skelly, and White Survey, *The New York Times*, January 13, 1982; also *The Washington Post*, September 23, 1981.

27. Leslie H. Gelb, "Poll Finds Doubt Over Responses to Soviet Threat," *The New York Times*, April 15, 1983, p. A1.

28. Barry Sussman, "Spread of Communism Considered Lesser Threat," *The Washington Post*, May 25, 1983, p. 1' and Don Oberdorfer, "Poll Finds a Majority Fears Entanglement in Central America: White House Seeks Accord In Dispute Over Nicaragua," *The Washington Post*, p. 1

29. Hedrick Smith, "Reagan Says Cuba Aimed to Take Grenada; Bastion Reported to Fall; Battle Goes On: President Says Invasion Was 'Just in Time' to Avert Occupation," *The New York Times*, Oct 28, 1983, p. A1.

30. Ibid.

31. David K. Shipler, "Poll Finds Americans Divided on Reply to Terrorism," *The New York Times*, February 9, 1986, p. 14.

32. Ibid.

33. *Gallup Report*, April 1986.

34. *Department of Defense Annual Report*, [DODAR], FY 1988.

35. *DODAR*, FY 1987, p. 53; *DODAR*, FY 1988, p. 296; see also Goose, p. 83.

36. SOF include the Delta Force (which is not officially acknowledged to exist), the Army's Special Forces (otherwise known as the Green Berets), the Rangers, the 160th Army Aviation Battalion (formerly the 160th Aviation Battalion of the 101st Air Assault Battalion), and several psychological operations and civil affairs units. The Navy has the sea-air-land (SEAL) units; the Air Force has the Special Operations Wing; and the marines have the special operations capable marine amphibious units (MUAs). Though the Air Force and Navy also have counterterrorism units (The Navy's SEAL Team 6 is stationed at Dam Neck, Virginia, and the Air Force's Special Operations Squadron 8 is located at Hurlburt Field, Florida (Charles Mohr, "Commando Squad is Trained to Kill With Full 'Surprise, Speed, Success," *The New York Times*, June 21, 1985, p. A9), primary counterterrorism responsibilities have been assigned to the Delta Force stationed at Fort Bragg, North Carolina. Estimates of its size vary. In 1986, *The Wall Street Journal*, citing government sources, said that the Delta Force was comprised of three hundred men (Tim Carrington, "Pentagon Buildup Called Long on Big Weapons, Short on Aid for Special Anti-terrorism Units," *The Wall Street Journal*, June 10, 1986, p. 60). *The St. Louis Post-Dispatch* claimed it has two hundred men (Jon Sawyer, "U.S. Delta Force Yet to See Combat," *The St. Louis Post-Dispatch*, June 17, 1985, p. 9A). *NBC Nightly News* claimed 160 men are in the Delta Force (NBC Nightly News transcripts for January 2, 1985). It is given helicopter support by the Army's Task Force 160 located at Fort Campbell, Kentucky.

The Delta Force has been involved in several incidents that most would agree constituted a terrorist threat or action. The presence of the Delta Force was acknowledged in one of the stories found in the sample analyzed in chapter two—the hijacking of a Venezuelan airliner in July 1984. They are also know to have taken part in the rescue of General James Dozier, held by the Red Brigades in Italy in December 1982. They were also present at the site of or on standby at the kidnapping of Western relief workers in the Sudan in 1983, the confrontation involving the Libyan Embassy in London in 1984, and the hijacking of a Kuwaiti airliner in Iran in December of 1984 (Goose, "Low-Intensity Warfare: The Warriors and Their Weapons" in *Low Intensity Warfare: Counterinsurgency,*

Proinsurgency, and Antiterrorism in the Eighties, Michael T. Klare and Peter Kornbluh, eds., [New York: Pantheon Books, 1988], p. 86.) They were also likely present at several other events over the past ten years, including the Achille Lauro in October 1985.

The Special Forces are organized into four Special Forces Groups (SFG), each has about fourteen hundred men. The 1st SFG is stationed at Ft. Lewis, Washington and was activated in 1984. The 5th is at Ft. Campbell, Kentucky. The 7th is at Ft. Bragg. And the 10th is stationed at Ft. Devens, Massachusetts (with a battalion stationed at Bad Tolz, West Germany). There are also special forces detachments in South Korea believed to be a "stay-behind" unit should ROK and U.S. forces be overrun.

Of these perhaps the Rangers, along with the super-secret Delta Force, are the most dedicated and deadly. Spearheading Reagan's invasion of Grenada and Bush's invasion of Panama, the Rangers served as the first wave of the administration's use of force.

I once had the personal experience of watching Ranger commandos attack a defense perimeter. In 1978 my Pershing missile unit was testing second generation night-vision devises. These lightweight goggles turn pitch-black night into a fairly clear greenish daylight.

I once watched several Rangers inch their way toward my Pershing nuclear missile defense perimeter. For several hours through the night we watched them, unbeknownst to them, crawl through brush, slush and mud in an attempt to simulate the capture of our perimeter. Their movements, despite the harsh conditions, were highly controlled.

37. Stephen Engelberg and Leslie H. Gelb, "Overseeing of C.I.A. by Congress Has Produced Decade of Support," *The New York Times,* July 7, 1986, p. A7.

38. Leslie H. Gelb, "Shift is Reported on C.I.A. Actions: Reagan is Said to Limit Groups Ruling on Covert Moves," *The New York Times,* June 11, 1984, p. A1.

39. From 1,161 in 1980 to about 5,787 in 1984. *DISAM Journal,* Vol. 7, No. 2 Winter 1984-85; Goose, fn. 17.

40. Pat M. Holt, "Proper Skepticism About U.S. Counterterrorism Aid," *The Christian Science Monitor,* December 4, 1985, p. 26.

41. Jim Lobe and Anne Manuel, *Police Aid and Political Will: U.S. Policy in El Salvador and Honduras (1962-1987)* (Washington: Washington Office on Latin America, 1987), p. 6.

42. U.S. Congress, Committee on Appropriations, Foreign Assistance and Related Agencies, Hearing Before the Committee on Appropriations, 88th Congress, 2nd Session, Oct 17, 1965, p. 72.

43. "Guatemala and the Dominican Republic," Staff Memorandum, Committee on Foreign Relations, U.S. senate, December 30, 1971.

44. It is interesting to note that the reasoning behind Congress's action was not based upon moral or ethical considerations. Rather, Congress seemed to be more concerned about public relations. Section 660 of the Act goes on to say that:

U.S. participation in the highly sensitive area of public safety and police training unavoidably invites criticism from persons who seek to identify the United States with every act of local police brutality or oppression of any kind in which this program operates.

45. Lobe and Manuel, p. 16.

46. This Unit was in the news in the United States when one of its officers came to Miami to interrogate the only witness to the December 1989 murder of six Jesuit priests in San Salvador. It was reported that the officer and the FBI threatened and harassed the witness in an attempt to get her to recant her testimony. She had described how uniformed members of the Salvadoran military carried out the murders.

47. p. iv.

48. Lobe and Manuel, *Police Aid and Political Will*, p. 23.

49. Shirley Christian, "Salvador Troops Raid Struck Hospitals," *New York Times*, June 3, 1985, p. A3.

50. Lobe and Manuel, *Police Aid and Political Will*, p. 28.

51. Regarding the hit squad proposal, see Leslie H. Gelb, "Administration Debating Antiterrorism Measures," *The New York Times*," April 1, 1987. Regarding Gen. Overholt's proposal, see Mark Thompson, "Army Seeks OK to Kill Terrorists," *The Seattle Times*, April 11, 1989, p. 1.

52. Telephone interview, Department of Defense General Counsel, March 18, 1993.

8

The Terrorism Spectacle:
Domestic Policy Objectives

Perhaps it is a universal truth that the loss of liberty at home is to be charged to provisions against danger, real or pretended, from abroad.
—Letter to Jefferson from Madison,
May 13, 1798

It is axiomatic that individual liberties are secondary to the requirements of internal security and internal civil order.
—*Mandate for Leadership:
Policy Management in a Conservative Administration*

Just as the Reagan administration used the terrorism spectacle as a wedge to reopen foreign policy options formally closed to it, it also used the terrorism spectacle as a rationale for the conduct of otherwise problematic policy options here at home; specifically, domestic intelligence investigations of political opposition groups. In the previous chapter, *New York Times* reporter Charles Mohr indicated the administration's intentions in revising terrorism statistics were clear. The new numbers could be used to justify increased surreptitious surveillance of political dissidents at home as well as military intervention abroad.

A campaign against terrorists in the wake of the 1979-80 Iran hostage crisis was an almost sure-fire way to offset the setbacks experienced by the intelligence community in the 1970s.

Reining in the FBI

The 1970s were difficult years for the American intelligence community. Public and congressional confidence was shaken by one revelation of misconduct after another. A complete review of the decades of intelligent community abuses at home would require far more space than is available here.[1] It is worth noting, however, that every intelligence agency—the Central Intelligence Agency, the Federal Bureau of Investigation, the super-secret National Security Agency, and Military Intelligence—had at least one known domestic surveillance program in the 1950s, 60s, and early 70s. Even the Internal Revenue Service became involved in the search for and harassment of political enemies. On the basis of what had been made public by 1976, one critic charged that the intelligence agencies wielded a "frightening degree of secret, sometimes illegal, and often uncontrollable power." They were, in short, a "corrupt force in American society."[2]

A review of the code names of the numerous operations, all directed at domestic political groups and individuals, reveals the scope of the invasion of privacy: The CIA ran operations CHAOS, SETTER, MERRIMAC, and RESISTANCE; beginning in the 1950s the FBI conducted operations COINTELLPRO, VIDEM, and STUDEN; Military Intelligence ran CABLE SPLICER and GARDEN PLOT; the National Security Agency conducted MINARET and SHAMROCK; while the Internal Revenue Service ran LEPRECHAUN and the Special Services Staff.[3]

The scope of these various inquiries was substantial. At the time of Senate hearings chaired by Senator Frank Church (1975-76), it was revealed the FBI office in Washington, D.C. alone had more than 500,000 domestic intelligence files on groups and individuals. Among those now known to have been included in the FBI files were Supreme Court Justices Felix Frankfurter and William O. Douglas, Dr. Martin Luther King, Dr. Benjamin Spock, Garry Wills, Bertolt Brecht, and John Lennon. Novelist John Steinbeck was watched for thirty years. The Bureau even dispatched agents to the hearings of the Senate Foreign Relations Committee to monitor statements made by Senator Wayne Morse and other Senate critics of the Vietnam war to compare them to the "Communist Party line."[4]

The Bureau conducted electronic surveillance and, when that failed, did black-bag jobs—burglarized—offices and homes. Harassment of dissident political groups and the civil rights movement was common. Prior to his assassination, for example, the FBI attempted to force Martin Luther King to commit suicide by threatening to make public an alleged extra-marital affair.[5]

The Bureau also monitored the mails. One target was a fifteen-year-old high school student who had attempted to write to the Socialist Labor Party for information needed to complete her project for a high school civics class. The Bureau, smelling danger, conducted a "subversive activities" investigation. The local credit bureau and the chief of police were questioned by agents about the student and her parents. Agents even visited her school and told the principal that the student had been placed under investigation due to her contact with the Socialist Worker's Party.[6]

The CIA was also interested in the U.S. mails. In a twenty-year period ending in 1973, the CIA had opened and photographed nearly 250,000 letters, producing a computerized index of 1.5 million names. The IRS also created files. It collected information on more than eleven thousand people and groups. The military kept files on approximately 100,000 civilians.[7]

For decades, the intelligence community had conducted a free-wheeling campaign against tens of thousands of Americans associated with dissident political movements, the civil rights movement and its leaders, and even U.S. Senators and Supreme Court justices. The Church committee concluded that:

> Too many people have been spied upon by too many government agencies and too much information has been collected. The government has often undertaken the secret surveillance of citizens on the basis of their political beliefs, even when those beliefs posed no threat of violence or illegal acts on behalf of a hostile foreign power. . . . Groups and individuals have been harassed and disrupted because of their political views and lifestyles.[8]

In short, speaking out was considered treasonous by the intelligence community. Revelations of intelligence community abuses, both foreign and domestic, led to demands for strict new regulations of the intelligence community. But the Reagan administration would reverse these restrictions with its focus on terrorism at the beginning of the 1980s.

The Backlash

In the wake of the Church committee hearings in the Senate and the Pike committee hearings in the House of Representatives, the American intelligence community was placed under tighter controls after 1975. Several government entities, particularly those associated with domestic intelligence gathering, were either reorganized or eliminated altogether. The Subversive Activities Control Board (SACB) within the executive branch was eliminated. It was one of the agencies that had been charged with ferreting out Communist affiliations of organizations and groups. The Internal Security Division of the Department of Justice was reorganized, becoming a subdivision of the Justice Department's Criminal Division. It had been in charge of prosecution of violations of federal law pertaining to internal security. Many of the government files maintained on private citizens were eliminated. The Attorney General's List of Subversive Organizations, for instance, was eliminated. And the Privacy Act of 1974 forced the U.S. Civil Service Commission to cease using its Security Research Files and Index. It had been in use since 1942 to cross-index information on potentially subversive groups. Prospective federal government employees were no longer interrogated regarding their political loyalties on the standard employment application form.

Changes in Congress were equally sweeping. The House Internal Security Committee (HISC) and the Subcommittee on Internal Security of the Senate Judiciary Committee (SISS) were eliminated. (Describing the history of these two congressional committees, including the witch hunts of the McCarthy years, the Heritage Foundation report laments their elimination, remarking that both had "for many years performed invaluable services in investigating internal security threats . . .")[9]

Most important, and most vexing to conservatives, were the changes in the authorization given the FBI to conduct domestic intelligence investigations. President Ford's reactions to the criticisms of the intelligence agencies were carefully calculated. He attempted to appease the critics while retaining as much latitude as possible for the intelligence community. There would be, for instance, no new sweeping restrictions. In effect, President Ford indicated that:

> value judgments about intelligence activity were relevant to the regulatory effort only insofar as they had been made visible in the law. This was, even in the initial concept, an essentially conservative response to growing public, legislative, and judicial concern about the intelligence agencies.[10]

The most direct expression of this balancing act was Executive Order 11905, United States Foreign Intelligence Activities, issued on February 18, 1976. Pursuant to Executive Order 11905, the "Levi Guidelines," as they came to be known, were formulated by Attorney General Edward H. Levi in the spring of 1976. Two separate sets of guidelines were actually created, one for domestic security operations and another for foreign counterintelligence activities. Of most interest to us are the guidelines for domestic operations.

Of special interest to the Congress and the Attorney General was the level of justification needed before an intrusive domestic intelligence investigation could be initiated. Such investigations include active surveillance such as wiretaps. Specifically, it was questioned whether the new guidelines would employ a strict criminal standard or a looser national security standard.

Under the guidelines eventually adopted, surveillance of domestic groups and individuals could only be done where there was likelihood such groups or individuals were about to use force in violation of the law. This was, in short, much closer to the criminal standard. Authorization for intrusive surveillance was also limited to ninety days, though with the possibility of renewal upon expiration.

The Attorney General told the Church committee at the time that these limitations approached as close as was possible the criminal activities standard desired by the critics of the intelligence community.[11] Many critics, however, felt that Ford's Executive Order and the Attorney General's Guidelines did not go far enough. With a new Democratic administration coming into office, more changes were about to be made.

Subsequent changes made by the Carter administration reinforced and in some instances extended the restrictions placed on the intelligence community. The Foreign Intelligence Surveillance Act was passed in 1978. It required an elaborate review process of all proposed electronic surveillance. If an American citizen was subject to surveillance, a high-level executive official had to certify the information was needed for the national defense. Full approval also required approval of an interagency panel chaired by the Director of the Central Intelligence Agency. If approved there, the proposal had to be sent to the Attorney General. In addition, once approved by the Attorney General, special designated federal district court judges had to approve the proposed electronic surveillance operation. The judge could issue a special one-year warrant when foreign powers were targeted and a ninety-day warrant when U.S. citizens were involved.

Executive Order 12036, issued on January 24, 1978, also enhanced the control and management of the intelligence community. Ford's Executive Order 11905 had allowed the infiltration of domestic organizations within the United States if such organizations were composed primarily of non-U.S. persons and it was reasonably believed to be working on behalf of a foreign power. Carter's Executive Order imposed more restrictive formal regulation and review processes.[12] Covert surveillance at home had, in short, become very difficult.

The Conservative Response

By the end of the 1970s conservative politicians and insiders within the intelligence community were calling for domestic intelligence operations to be unshackled. Critics of Carter's Executive Order believed that the restrictions placed on the counterintelligence divisions of the FBI and CIA severely hampered their ability to ferret out suspected terrorists and Soviet and Cuban spies. Samuel Francis, an analyst for the conservative Heritage Foundation, gave expression to this view in 1980 when he stated that the internal security threat

> is greater (in 1981) than at any time since World War II. . . . Since 1974 there has been a domestic cutback. The House Internal Security Committee has been abolished, the Attorney General's list of subversive organizations is no longer extant, and a great many files on subversives have literally been destroyed. Whenever you have that kind of collapse of internal security operations you are going to have subversive types popping up. You have these people prepared to use violence and conspiratorial methods against the United States.[13]

Francis was the editor of the intelligence portion of the 1981 Heritage Foundation report *Mandate for Leadership: Policy Management in a Conservative Administration*. Written by several anonymous individuals from within the intelligence community and in close collaboration with the Reagan administration, the report laid the intellectual groundwork for future administration policy.

The report reflected the same deep suspicion of nearly all political opposition groups that was evident in the intelligence community prior to the restrictions of the 1970s.[14] Terrorists seemed to be of particular concern to the authors of the report. Because terrorists often emerged as the impatient brethren of otherwise peaceful opposition groups,

> authorities must keep extremist movements under at least moderate surveillance, become familiar with their public positions and members as well as their unstated goals, adherents, and fringe elements, and be prepared to escalate surveillance of whatever groups seem likely to engage in more extreme activities.[15]

To monitor such a broad scope of potential enemies, internal security files should not, the report stated, be "restricted to actual or imminent threats."[16] In other words, the more strict criminal standard should be dropped in favor of the looser national security standard. Who, exactly, might be excluded from surveillance was not clear. Monitoring could at first utilize public records. In other instances, the more serious surveillance "can be carried out by the use of such intelligence techniques as wiretapping, mail covers, informants and, at least occasionally, surreptitious entries."[17]

Measures such as these were necessary, said the report, because terrorists and other types of subversives are difficult to detect:

> (C)lergymen, students, businessmen, entertainers, labor officials, journalists and government workers may engage in subversive activities without

being fully aware of the extent, purpose or control of their activities. Surveillance should also include "radical and new left" groups and "anti-defense and anti-nuclear groups."[18]

The Heritage Foundation report, not surprisingly, also recommended that Attorney General Edward Levi's 1976 guidelines for the Federal Bureau of Investigation (FBI) be amended to provide law enforcement officials greater latitude in domestic political surveillance. It would have appeared to anyone carefully reading this report in 1981 that the Heritage Foundation's authors were declaring war on any and all dissent from official policy. Things amorphously referred to as national security and counterterrorism were placed at the top of the list of priorities. As the Heritage report concluded, "It is axiomatic that individual liberties are secondary to the requirements of internal security and internal civil order."[19] As we will see below, the Reagan administration set priorities along these exact lines.

Rolling Back the Restrictions

To accomplish the unleashing of the intelligence community required a "significant reorientation of public attitudes about intelligence in order to make clear the agencies' important contributions . . . [which] had been obscured—and, indeed, greatly jeopardized—in the era of reform."[20] The revision in terrorism statistics was most certainly a part of the effort to reorient public attitudes. Counterterrorism was the hook upon which the argument for a revitalized intelligence community could be hung. Several columnists and other commentators also came through with a flurry of press reports and columns initiated by conservative critics of, as one of them put it, "the recent orgy of revelations and restraints."[21]

Reagan's proposed revision to Carter's Executive Order 12036 was circulated within the administration in early 1981. When leaked to the press it immediately raised considerable concern for it appeared to be a significant departure from the Carter order. Besides offering a more positive language than was found in Carter's order ("Restrictions on Intelligence Activities," for instance, would become "Conduct of Intelligence Activities"), the oversight role of the Attorney General was downgraded, the requirement to collect information by the least intrusive means was eliminated, restrictions on domestic group infiltration was relaxed, the definition of "United States person" was narrowed, the President's role in approving the most intrusive surveillance techniques was eliminated, and the CIA would in some circumstances be allowed to engage in electronic surveillance within the United States.[22]

Disclosure of these proposed changes put the new administration on the defensive. Presidential counselor Edwin Meese attempted to assuage public concern by indicating that the final version of the order would not substantially change the role and function of the CIA. But at the same time he reiterated that the purpose of the policy review was to improve the nation's ability to fight terrorism. John Shattuck of the American Civil Liberties Union noted that Meese's remarks provided little comfort to those who feared that "a new talisman, 'terrorism,' may come to center stage in Washington," one which offered justification for the unleashing of the intelligence community.[23]

On December 4, 1981, President Reagan issued Executive Order 12333. For our purposes, the central feature of Executive Order 12333 was the deemphasis on the protection of constitutional liberties. This constituted a significant departure from Carter's 1978 order. Specifically, though intelligence agencies were to give full consideration of spheres of individual rights that might be infringed upon by intelligence activities, there was no requirement to preserve these rights.

There would, for instance, no longer be the presumption of the preeminence of individual rights when in conflict with intelligence gathering needs in combating terrorism, as tenuous as that presumption may have been before. Whereas the Carter administration had declared the primacy of established constitutional principles confining governmental powers, the Reagan administration sought once again to balance constitutional liberties with intelligence needs almost entirely predicated upon counterterrorism.

The Attorney General's New Guidelines

On March 7, 1983, Attorney General William French Smith released two sets of guidelines for domestic investigations. First, The Attorney General's Guidelines on General Crimes, Racketeering Enterprise and Domestic Security/Terrorism Investigations (henceforth referred to as Domestic Security Guidelines) provide guidance for all investigations by the FBI of crimes and crime-related activities. All investigations under the Domestic Security Guidelines had to meet a strict criminal standard based on a "factual threshold"—an indication of criminal wrongdoing. The employed factual standard was whether one was "engaging in a political enterprise for the purpose of furthering political or social goals . . . (using) force or violence and a violation of the criminal laws of the United States."[24] Though broad, the guideline required the FBI to establish a criminal connection to the persons or person under investigation.

The second set of guidelines were even more ambiguous. Entitled "The Attorney General Guidelines for FBI Foreign Intelligence Collection and Foreign Counterintelligence Investigations" (henceforth referred to as the FCI Guidelines), they covered "all foreign intelligence, foreign counterintelligence, foreign intelligence support activities, and intelligence investigations of international terrorism conducted by the FBI pursuant to Executive Order 12333."[25]

The FCI Guidelines remain partially classified. What is known about them is that they are "national security" investigations with some type of foreign connection. *No criminal standard applies*, unlike the rather loose criminal standard used with the Domestic Security Guidelines. There are, in short, no provisions for the protection of constitutional rights. In fact, the FCI Guidelines even give conditional authorization to infiltrate groups "that will influence rights protected by the First Amendment," for example through assuming a leadership role in an organization.[26]

Furthermore, in the absence of the "enterprise" standard found in the Domestic Security Guidelines, FCI Guidelines allow the FBI to investigate entire political organizations, even if most of its members are not suspected of being involved in international terrorism. The FCI Guidelines define a terrorist as "an individual or group that knowingly engages in international terrorism or activities in preparation thereof, or knowingly aids or abets any person engaged in such activities."[27]

In short, without the slightest solid indication of criminal wrongdoing, the FCI Guidelines allow the FBI to conduct wholesale investigations of entire organizations. As Gary Stern concluded, the "problem with having separate and lower standards for international terrorism investigations under the FCI Guidelines is that it allows the FBI to target United States persons who may be engaged only in First Amendment activities."[28]

"Supporting foreign terrorists," is a rather ambiguous standard, to say the least. In light of the construction of terrorism in the news—and in public consciousness—it is no standard at all. All that is required is the designation of an adversary as a terrorist in public documentation and the line-of-the-day meetings. Anyone who questions U.S. policy in connection with that adversary could be culpable of supporting foreign terrorists. Domestic opposition groups are placed in the position of being mere fronts for international terrorists. This is exactly what occurred.

CISPES and the Search for Enemies

Rumors of surveillance by government agents had been floating around the Central America activists community since at least 1981, though the FBI had always denied involvement. This remained true until January, 1988 when the Bureau was forced to release about a third of its headquarters files on one particular activist group in response to a Freedom of Information Act lawsuit brought by the Center for Constitutional Rights. Though riddled with deletions, these documents and subsequent investigations indicate that once again the FBI was involved in politically motivated surveillance of First Amendment activity, this time in the name of counterterrorism.[29]

The Committee in Solidarity with the People of El Salvador (CISPES) expressed its support for the "opposition movement in El Salvador (the Democratic Revolutionary Front [FDR] and the Farabundo Marti Front for National Liberation [FMLN] . . . [and] attempts to educate the U.S. public regarding the situation in El Salvador . . ."[30] This statement placed CISPES, along with hundreds of other organizations throughout the United States, in direct opposition to the policies of the Reagan administration.

On March 30, 1983 the FBI began a counterterrorism investigation of CISPES under the provisions of the FCI Guidelines. The Washington, D.C. office of the FBI directed eleven field offices to begin investigating

> the involvement of individuals and the CISPES organization in international terrorism as it affects the El Salvadoran government, and (authorizes) the collection of foreign intelligence and counterintelligence information as it relates to the international terrorism aspects of this investigation .[31]

This, however, was not the first investigation of CISPES by the FBI. In September, 1981 the FBI opened a criminal investigation of CISPES to determine whether it was in violation of the Foreign Agents Registration Act (FARA). By February 23, 1982, the FBI concluded "there was no specific evidence indicating CISPES was acting on behalf of, or at the direction of a foreign power or group."[32] Thirteen months later, the FBI began its second investigation, but this time under looser—and classified—FCI standards which require no indication of criminal behavior.

The preliminary basis for opening the FCI investigation of CISPES rested upon two points: First, a statement in one of CISPES's own publications that it "provides international support for the opposition movement in El Salvador."[33] and, second, the terrorist designation of the FMLN/FDR by the FBI.

Besides relying on the unsubstantiated terrorism charge against the FDR/FMLN and the statement of support for those organizations found in CISPES publications, the FBI relied on another source: Frank Varelli.

A Salvadoran nationalist and the son of a former Salvadoran interior minister and national police chief, Varelli was a paid informant for the FBI. According to an Interim Report produced by the FBI's Criminal Investigative Division, Counterterrorism Section, Varelli told the FBI that CISPES was supplying the FMLN with military aid, "forwarded through Mexico for ultimate use by the guerrilla forces in El Salvador."[34] Varelli had infiltrated CISPES's Dallas office in early 1983. The Interim Report further stated that the investigation of CISPES

> was predicated primarily upon information furnished by Mr. Varelli that the activities of CISPES were being directed by the FDR and the FMLN, giving reason to believe that certain members of CISPES were or may have been engaged in international terrorism, or knowingly aiding or abetting those engaged in terrorist activities, specifically the FMLN.[35]

Once the CISPES investigation became public the FBI and Varelli parted company. The Bureau claimed Varelli had lied to them; Varelli said the FBI urged him to fabricate information which would support the U.S. government claim that CISPES was supporting terrorism.

It is clear from documents obtained by the Center for Constitutional Rights that the FBI's probe of the domestic opposition movement to Reagan administration policies in Central America actually went well beyond the infiltration of a single "terrorist" organization. Like political surveillance of the past, the FBI conducted a broad sweep against ideological opponents. It is known, for instance, that the FBI kept files on at least 2,375 individuals and 1,330 groups. The investigation involved all fifty-nine FBI field offices and created 178 spin-off investigations.[37] One document listed 138 suspect groups somehow connected to CISPES. Included on the list were Oxfam America Inc., the American Civil Liberties Union, the American Federation of Teachers, Amnesty International, the Southern Christian Leadership Conference, the Catholic Maryknoll Sisters of America, and at least one chapter of the United Auto Workers Union.[37] Furthermore, the techniques used were anything but restrained.

In Houston, agents recorded car license plate numbers of all vehicles near an anti-war demonstration. The list was distributed to five field offices. Most field offices took photographs of demonstrators and circulated them to other federal agencies. The Detroit office was particularly prolific in this regard. Agents in Mobile, Alabama even monitored radio talk programs. And a document from the Denver field office indicated the FBI either secured the address book of an opponent to U.S. Central America policy or had somehow copied addresses and telephone numbers from it. In at least one instance the Bureau wiretapped an opponent of administration policy.[38] On April 8, 1983, just nine days after the start of the FCI investigation, the San Juan field office was so eager to do a good job it suggested to Washington that it be allowed to index or otherwise observe all people of El Salvadoran extraction in Puerto Rico and the U.S. Virgin Islands.

Conservative political organizations were also utilized by the FBI in their investigation of the opponents of U.S. foreign policy objectives in Central America. For instance, the Executive Director of the Virginia Based "Young Americans Foundation," obtained CISPES documents by attending a CISPES chapter meeting.[39] He then sent copies of these documents to Edward J. O'Malley, assistant director of intelligence for the FBI. O'Malley then sent them, classified "Secret," to at least thirty-two listed FBI offices around the country. This was the pattern of FBI conduct. Don Edwards, (D-Calif.) has remarked that "not one criminal act was expressly charged to CISPES, yet through innuendo and guilt by association, CISPES was prosecuted, tried, and found guilty of subversion.[40]

The CISPES investigation was a politically motivated search justified by, as the ACLU spokesperson described potential investigations of this sort back in 1981, the "talisman of terrorism."[41] Nor was it in all instances simply a matter of dispassionately collecting information. The New Orleans field office, for instance, sent a Teletype to FBI headquarters in Washington, D.C. which stated:

> It is imperative at this time to formulate some plan of attack against CISPES and specifically, against individuals, (deletion) who defiantly display their contempt for the U.S. government by making speeches and propagandizing their cause while asking for political asylum. New Orleans is of the opinion that Departments of Justice and State should be consulted to explore the possibility of deporting these individuals or at best denying their re-entry after they leave.[42]

References to "un-American activities" such as this are dispersed throughout the heavily edited documents. Another memo, this time from the Chicago office to Director Webster, rather disdainfully refers to CISPES members as "60's activist types" who "surround themselves in more than one activity or organization which has the look of legitimacy." The subject of another secret memorandum merely discusses an article taken from *The Cincinnati Inquirer*. The article refers to persons and organizations who are "involved in activities contrary to the foreign policy of the United States . . ."[43] This, too, is telling. Merely being on the wrong side of U.S. foreign policy was at the heart of the CISPES "counterterrorism" investigation.

News Repair Revisited

In June, 1984, William Webster, the director of the FBI at the time of the CISPES investigation, sent a secret memo to the Bureau's Jacksonville, Florida office. In the memo Webster praised that office's "aggressiveness in approaching this investigation." It is, said Webster, "appreciated by FBIHQ." He concluded by giving the Jacksonville office "Authority to conduct physical surveillance on the Florida State University campus for the purpose of identifying leaders of CISPES and their activities . . ."[44]

Despite the existence of this memo, Oliver B. Revell, executive assistant director of the FBI and the man directly in charge of the CISPES investigation in Washington, claimed in testimony before the United States Senate that Webster was "removed" from the CISPES investigation. Though Webster knew of its existence, said Revell, he *"did not authorize any of its activities."*[45] Revell further claimed that "The case never rose to the level that it require the Director's approval or review."[46]

The incident was telling and revealed something of a news repair process similar to the one described in chapter six. Once again, journalists from the mainstream news media seemed eager to employ selective memory and deletion of fact (beyond the FBI's deletions of another sort with the FOIA request).

Retrieving History

In April, 1985, Webster told the House Judiciary Subcommittee on Civil and Constitutional Rights, chaired by Don Edwards (D-Calif.), that CISPES and other opponents of Reagan's policies in Central America were not under investigation and that claims to the contrary were "unfounded." When asked by Rep. John Conyers whether "anybody who is a member of CISPES is automatically suspect . . . ," Webster responded as follows: "I think the most important question is whether anybody who is a member of CISPES is subject to being interviewed and the answer is no. We are not keeping track of the membership of CISPES as such."[47] Note that Webster changed Conyers' question. Conyers asked whether CISPES members automatically become a "suspect." Webster changed it to "being interviewed." Webster also added "as such" at the end of the last sentence. Webster's testimony was given less than a year after he had sent the memo to Jacksonville authorizing FBI surveillance on the campus of a major state university and praising that office for its aggressive manner. Revell's claim that Webster and the rest of the FBI hierarchy was unaware of the details of the CISPES investigation may be correct, but serious questions remain.

In February, 1987 Edward's committee held hearings to investigate the possibility that the FBI might in some way have been connected with the break-ins of Central American refugee sanctuary churches and Reagan administration Central America foreign policy opposition group offices. The Center for Constitutional Rights (CCR) and the National Lawyers Guild reported ninety-three break-ins and harassment of opposition members and sanctuary churches by May, 1987.[48] In its testimony before the committee, the CCR and the Fund for Open Information and Accountability testified they had learned of the existence of over thirty volumes of CISPES related materials in the Washington Headquarters and Dallas offices alone.

The CCR had first filed a Freedom of Information Request with the FBI in 1986. When the Bureau did not comply, CCR filed an administrative appeal on the grounds of impermissible delay. That was filed in June, 1987 and was denied. The CCR then filed another appeal, this time with federal district court in Dallas. Before a hearing could be scheduled the FBI contacted CCR to negotiate a release date (December 1, 1987 for headquarters files and March 1, 1988 for the Dallas files). Though an agreement was reached, only about a third of the material was ever released. The Bureau eventually released more than two thousand pages of classified material to the House Subcommittee on Constitutional and Civil Rights.[49]

There were at least two different FBI response strategies to these developments. First, once the CCR analysis of the released files began to receive coverage in the national press, the FBI claimed the investigation was motivated solely because of suspected criminal activity on the part of CISPES. The Bureau issued a statement in January, 1988 which stated:

> The predication for and focus of these investigations is alleged criminal activity rather than the motives and beliefs of those being investigated. The FBI is sensitive to the constitutional rights of the American public and the Bureau has no interest in interfering with the exercise of these rights.[50]

On January 23, 1988 a Justice Department spokesperson, Patrick Korten, told *The Atlanta Constitution* the investigation had a proper criminal predicate. He repeated that assertion on the McNeil/Lehrer News Hour.

After Webster was selected to replace William Casey as director of the CIA, the new FBI chief, William Sessions, also denied the existence of a political motive behind the investigation. "The political motivation, I find none of that in there. The fact that there may be a perception that there is a thrust to the investigation, I would deny that categorically."

The Bureau next pursued a two-track damage control strategy: First, while continuing to insist that the investigation was proper in its inception, Oliver B. Revell claimed it was eventually pulled in improper directions by the deceptions of its chief source, Frank Varelli. On February 24, 1988, Revell, the man in charge of the investigation of CISPES in Washington, told the Senate Intelligence Committee that Varelli had misled investigators and that much of his information was later found to be "blatantly false" or "concocted."

The second track was to portray the investigation as relatively low-key and unimportant, done largely at the initiative of lower-level managers at field office level. It was at this point that Revell claimed Webster had only partial knowledge of the investigation. To bolster the claim that the investigation was motivated by a determination to discover whether CISPES was a terrorist organization, Revell read a statement at the February 24 hearing which implicated the group as such. This was strongly criticized by Rep. Edwards.[51] According to Edwards, Revell claimed that CISPES was "believed to have been established with assistance of" the U.S. Communist Party and the Salvadoran Communist Party. He fails to point out, as Edwards noted, that had such assistance been given, it would not have been illegal. "Instead," said Edwards, "he (Revell) left the impression that it was something sinister."

Revell also pursued a similar tactic in remarking that the FMLN conducted terrorist activities in El Salvador, CISPES supported the FMLN, ergo, "CISPES was somehow connected with these activities." Similarly, it was claimed that the FMLN was "a principal component of the DRU," a Cuban based group. "Thus," said Edwards, "the FBI tied CISPES to Fidel Castro, based on CISPES' support for a group that was affiliated (with) another group that was set up with the involvement of Castro."

Finally, "Guilt by ideological association was stretched to the breaking point," said Edwards, when the Bureau suggested a link between CISPES and bombings that had taken place in Washington, D.C., to quote the Bureau, at "about the same time" a CISPES rally was being held in Washington.

It is interesting to note that even though Congressman Edwards found Revell's assertions outrageous, at least one wire service treated them as news. The lead for the Associated Press dispatch reporting this last assertion reads: "When the FBI infiltrated a group of opponents of President Reagan's Central America policies, it suspected they were behind the still-unsolved November 1983 bombing of the U.S. Capital."[52] The dispatch never mentions the grounds upon which the FBI based its suspicions or Edwards response.

What concerned Edwards the most was the FBI's behavior in its attempt to deflect criticism of its CISPES investigation. Said Edwards,

My concern is that the FBI's response to the widespread criticism of its CISPES investigation was an unprecedented release of defamatory file information, suggesting links to Communists, or terrorist groups. This release of unsupported allegations, few of which involve possible criminal conduct, is a major violation of the key rule for police investigatory files -that none of the information can be published except according to established rules and safeguards.

No press source, as far as can be determined, reported Edward's comments. *The Associated Press,* of course, did report the bombing assertion. *The New York Times* coverage of Revell's testimony was also interesting. Philip Shenon, *The New York Times* reporter covering Revell's testimony in the Senate, referred to the "unusual public hearings of the Senate Intelligence Committee," calling "a rare public session for the usually secretive intelligence Committee."[53] One was left to draw the inference that Shenon was informing the reader that Revell's testimony was a dog and pony show, meant more to deflect public criticism than anything else.

Nevertheless, the imperatives of "objectivity" led Shenon to treat what Revell said in an uncritical fashion. This was most evident in the language used by Shenon. Revell "acknowledged," not claimed, the FBI was mislead by Varelli. Revell "disclosed," again, not claimed—that Webster was uninformed, contrary to documentation available at the time. The reporter was passive as the bureau conducted its campaign to re-establish legitimacy. The stakes for the FBI were high. As Sen. Bill Bradley (D.-N.J.) remarked at Revell's testimony, "The FBI's reputation was on the line."

Symbolic Solutions

After Revell's testimony the Bureau promised an internal investigation. In June, 1988 an anonymous official(s) told Shenon of *The New York Times* that the internal report "recommended disciplinary action against a number of bureau officials . . ."[54] In September, Sessions gave public testimony before the Senate Select Committee on Intelligence. He admitted three points: (1) The investigation should have never been opened in the first place. (2) The spin-off investigations of other organizations opened between 1983 and 1987 should not have occurred. (3) There had been "irregularities" in the investigative techniques used by field agents. He was warmly praised by committee members for his forthrightness.[55]

He also claimed that the major problem in the investigation came in October, 1983. That was when FBI headquarters in Washington expanded what had been to that point a fairly limited inquiry by "alerting bureau offices throughout the country to gather information on Cispes."[56] When Sessions told Congress that six mid-level officials of the Bureau were to be disciplined, someone (Shenon doesn't say who) asked why more senior officials had not been disciplined. Sessions responded that "his review showed that others at the bureau, including Mr. Webster and Oliver B. Revell, had no reasonable way to know of problems with the Cispes investigation." As with alleged CIA involvement with Salvadoran terrorists, the CISPES investigation was reduced to aberrational conduct of field officers.

New York Times reporter Shenon did not point out that it was Revell who had approved transmission of the teletype in the first place. The teletype went to all field offices instructing them to "locate all local CISPES chapters, leaders, members and associates." Why did Shenon fail to point out the discrepancy between Sessions' testimony and the public record? The CCR had given *The New York Times* copies of released documents, including the October directive from Revell to all field offices. Why the *Times* did not pursue the contradictions was difficult to understand.

One possibility was the *Times* reporter simply did not read the released FBI documents and the public testimony given by Webster (and had not been alerted to it by any of the members of Congress). Or perhaps the *Times* reporter succumbed to the imperatives of objective journalism. The testimony given by both Revell and Sessions were dramatic and extraordinary. Giving such testimony in open session indicated an agreement to do so between committee members and the FBI. Why? One can only speculate. What was clear was that given the openness of the meeting and the aura of good feeling between committee members and an FBI director "coming clean," *The New York Times* was not about to indicate that the emperor, or in this case the director, had no clothes.

The leading newspaper in the United States seemed impressed or indifferent. *The New York Times* editorial board had nothing to say of Sessions confessions. *The Washington Post* declared in an editorial on the 20th of September that Sessions' testimony and the FBI investigation of itself was "thorough, credible and generally well received." As far as can be determined, no press source raised the fact that sufficient evidence existed to suggest that Webster and Revell were far more aware and involved in the CISPES investigation than their testimony claimed. With the leadership absolved of responsibility in the public ritual of contrition before Congress, the CISPES episode could be treated as a mere aberration. As was the case with the investigation of U.S. government involvement in Salvadoran death squads, it is inferred field officers merely run operations far more vigorously than their bosses in Washington intended or realized.

The press followed suit by forgetting the CISPES investigations ever occurred. (Of course, referring to it as the "CISPES investigation" subtly limits the apparent gravity of the broad scope of targets engaged by FBI agents.) By the end of 1988, William Sessions would be found on the cover of the national newspaper supplement *Parade*. The cover title is: "The Man Who Would Restore the FBI." The only mention of the CISPES investigation noted that it was concluded to have been overly broad. The whole affair is put aside in this way: He (Sessions) told me (the reporter, Peter Maas) following his CISPES testimony that the Bureau has to work within the constitutional limits. 'It happened,' he said. "It was a failure of standards. New guidelines are being drawn up. I am confident it won't happen again.[57]

By the summer of 1989, *The New York Times* seemed eager to complete the restoration of the FBI and William Sessions, its new director. In one of those generally flattering profile pieces *The Times* does on federal officials, Sessions is portrayed as a skilled administrator. The only mention of the CISPES investigation comes in two brief paragraphs, out of nineteen total:

> Mr. Sessions seemed to tighten his grasp on the leadership of the agency last fall by his skillful handling of the political damage from the Bureau's inquiry into a group that opposed the Reagan administration's policy in Central America. . . Lawmakers praised Mr. Sessions for his candor and willingness to censure six FBI employees for mishandling the investigation . . . [58]

Parade Magazine and *The New York Times* offered assurance that all was once again well with the FBI. At the same time, the investigation of CISPES and scores of associated organizations and hundreds of individuals was well on its way to being forgotten.

Unfortunately, by the fall of 1989 the FBI was back in the business of investigating the Central America peace movement. In Los Angeles, an FBI agent named Caldwell threatened a Salvadoran refugee with deportation if he did not act as an undercover agent for the Bureau in its surveillance of a Los Angeles church providing medical care for El Salvador.[59] Congressman Edwards was said to be demanding a full explanation from Director Sessions.

For anyone with the slightest awareness of the history of political surveillance in this country, reassurances such as those offered by Director Sessions have a hollow ring to them. World War I saw the General Intelligence Division of the Bureau of Intelligence (the precursor to the FBI) supply information that led to the arrest of 6,300 resident aliens and the long-term detention of two thousand without due process of the law.[60] The Slacker Raids of 1918 saw fifty thousand men arrested "without warrants or sufficient probable cause for arrest." When Congress enacted the Espionage Act punishing "disloyal utterances, two thousand persons were prosecuted under the act based largely on information supplied by the Bureau of Investigation. In 1920, agents arrested ten thousand persons believed to be members of various factions of the Communist Party. Just prior to the outbreak of the World War II, domestic political activity of the FBI (constituted as a part of Attorney General Harlan Fiske Stone's efforts to reform the Bureau) once again emerged. It is not much of an overstatement to say that to one degree or another the FBI has been involved in domestic political surveillance since its inception as the Bureau of Investigation. To treat the CISPES investigation as an aberration from the FBI's normal conduct was to fail to recognize history and what it can tell us about today and tomorrow.

Summary

The FBI used their classified counterterrorism FCI Guidelines to conduct investigations of those in opposition to the Reagan administration's policies in Central America. They did so pursuant to Executive Orders issued by President Reagan and guidelines crafted by his attorney general, guidelines that allowed the very sort of surveillance activity once made impossible by 1970s era restrictions. Terrorism became the talisman needed to pursue desired solutions which once again violated the constitutional rights of American citizens.

Notes

1. See Morton H. Halperin, Jerry J. Berman, Robert L. Borosage, and Christine M. Marwick, *The Lawless State: The Crimes of the U.S. Intelligence Agencies* (New York: Penguin Books, 1977); Richard E. Morgan, *Domestic Intelligence: Monitoring Dissent in America* (Austin: University of Texas Press, 1980); John M. Oseth, *Regulating U.S. Intelligence Operations: A Study in Definition of the National Interest* (Lexington, Ky.: The University Press of Kentucky, 1985); Frank J. Donner, *The Age of Surveillance: The Aims and Methods of America's Political Intelligence System* (New York: Vintage Books, 1980).

2. Oseth, *Regulating U.S. Intelligence Operations*, p. 50.

3. Halperin, et al., *The Lawless State*, p. 3.

4. Ibid., p. 119.

5. Ibid., pp. 61-89. In 1993 the *Memphis Commercial Appeal* reported that the military had spied on black Americans for more than 75 years. Not only was

Martin Luther King, Jr. spied upon, but so too was his father and grandfather. In the 1960s, the Pentagon even used U2 spy planes in the process (Unsigned, "Military Spied on King, Other Blacks, Paper Says," *The Washington Post*, March 21, 1993, p. A16).

6. Donner, *The Age of Surveillance:*, fn. p. 129. A similar case arose in 1988 involving a seventeen-year-old student from Newark, New Jersey. Todd Patterson was a sixth-grader at the time his hobby, writing to one hundred and sixty-nine countries for information to include in his homemade encyclopedia, caught the interest of the FBI. The Bureau maintained a top-secret file on him. He had received over fifty damaged pieces of mail, mostly from the Eastern Europe.

7. Halperin, et al., *The Lawless State*, p. 3.

8. Select Committee to Study Governmental Operations with Respect to Intelligence Activities, U.S. Senate, Book II, Intelligence Activities and the Rights of Americans," (94th Congress, 2d Sess., Rep. No. 94-755).

9. Charles L. Heatherly, ed., *Mandate for Leadership: Policy Management in a Conservative Administration* (Washington, D.C.: Heritage Foundation, 1981), p. 936.

10. Oseth, *Regulating U.S. Intelligence Operations*, p. 74.

11. Ibid., p. 100.

12. Ibid., p. 120.

13. Donner, *The Age of Surveillance*, p. ix.

14. See Richard Hofstadter, *The Paranoid Style in American Politics and Other Essays* (London: Cape, 1966).

15. Heatherly, *Mandate for Leadership*, p. 940.

16. Ibid., p. 940.

17. See Donner, *The Age of Surveillance*, p. ix.

18. Ibid., p. ix.

19. Ibid., p. x.

20. Oseth, *Regulating U.S. Intelligence Operations*, p. 148.

21. Judith Miller, *The New York Times*, December 8, 1980; see also Ray Cline, *The New York Times*, December 20, 1979; Charles Mohr, *The New York Times*, September 28, 1980. See also *The New York Times* editorial "Retreat from Intelligence," May 6, 1980.

22. Oseth, *Regulating U.S. Intelligence Operations*, pp. 150-151.

23. Charles Mohr, "A.C.L.U. Says Efforts to Combat Terrorism Hold Threat to Rights," *The New York Times*, May 19, 1981, B11.

24. Gary Stern, *Center for National Security Studies Report Number 111*, June 1988, p. 26. Emphasis added.

25. Ibid., p. 26.

26. FCI Guidelines, 15, section IV a)(2)(Special Techniques: Undisclosed Participation). The director must determine that there is "probable cause" and that the "undisclosed participation is essential to establish, enhance, or maintain cover and the effect on the activities of the organization is incidental."

27. FCI Guidelines, Section II (o), p. 4).

28. Stern, *Center for National Security Studies Report Number 111*, p. 28.

29. See also United States General Accounting Office "Report to the

Chairman, Subcommittee on Civil and Constitutional Rights, Committee on the Judiciary, House of Representatives. *International Terrorism: FBI Investigates Domestic Activities to Identify Terrorists* (GAO/GGD-90-112) September 1990.

30. Quoted by Stern, *Center for National Security Studies Report Number 111*, p. 5.

31. FBI Headquarters File, CISPES, File Number 199-8848-1 (March 30, 1983), p. 6; also quoted by Stern, *Center for National Security Studies Report Number 111*, p. 5 and released by the Center for Constitutional Rights.

32. Stern, *Center for National Security Studies Report Number 111*, p. 5.

33. CISPES-HQ file 199-8848-1

34. U.S. Department of Justice, Federal Bureau of Investigation, "An Interim Public Report on the Committee in Solidarity with the People of El Salvador (CISPES)" FBI, Criminal Investigative Division, Counterterrorism Section, February 22, 1988.

35. p. 4.

36. Unsigned, "Senate Panel Criticizes FBI Probe of Protesters," *The Seattle Times*, July 15, 1989, p. 1.

37. Unsigned, "Surveillance Campaign by FBI Reported: Opponents of Reagan's Central America Policy Targeted by Agency, According to Documents," *The Seattle Times*, January 27, 1988, p. 1.

38. Ibid.

39. It is interesting to speculate on how the FBI and its informants rationalized the apparent contradiction involved in this. On the one hand, the FBI justified the CISPES investigation on the grounds that it was potentially a dangerous terrorist organization. On the other, there is the fact that a complete stranger like Boos was able to walk into a CISPES meeting and freely collect documents that presumably linked them to "left wing terrorists." It wasn't until these documents reached the FBI that they became secret.

40. Congressional Record, H707 March 3, 1988.

41. Charles Mohr, "A.C.L.U. Says Efforts to Combat Terrorism Hold Threat to Rights," *The New York Times*, May 19, 1981, B11.

42. Selected Headquarters CISPES Documents, Center for Constitutional Rights.

43. Selected Headquarters CISPES Documents.

44. Selected Headquarters CISPES Documents.

45. Emphasis added.

46. Philip Shenon, "F.B.I. Admits Informer Misled Inquiry," *The New York Times*, February 24, 1988, p. A21.

47. Hearings Before the Subcommittee on Civil and Constitutional Rights, Series No. 25, April 17, typeset p. 29.

48. "Harassment Update," 8th edition, revised May 1987.

49. Wayne King, "F.B.I. Will Give Panel More Surveillance Files," *The New York Times*, February 6, 1988, p. A10.

50. Unsigned, "Surveillance Campaign by FBI Reported: Opponents of Reagan's Central America Policy Targeted by Agency, According to Documents," *The Seattle Times*, January 27, 1988, p. 1.

51. *Congressional Record,* daily report, March 3, 1988, H 707.

52. Unsigned (AP), Latin-policy Foes Were Suspects in Bombing," *The Seattle Times,* February 14, 1988, p. A16

53. Philip Shenon, "F.B.I. Admits Informer Misled Inquiry," *The New York Times,* February 24, 1988, p. A21.

54. Philip Shenon, "F.B.I. Report Said to Urge Punishment in Surveillance," *The New York Times,* June 14, 1988.

55. Senator David Boren (D.-Okla.) told Sessions, "You have not tried to gloss over mistakes. In fact you've highlighted them." Congressman Edwards said he was "impressed by the depth and detail" of the FBI internal report, though he was still concerned about the possibility of a recurrence of a similar investigation in the absence of stricter guidelines.

56. Philip Shenon, "F.B.I. Chief Disciplines Six for Surveillance Activities," *The New York Times,* September 15, 1988.

57. Peter Maas, "The Man Who Would Restore the FBI," *Parade Magazine,* December 18, 1988.

58. David Johnston, "F.B.I. Chief Is Balancing On Very Slippery Track," *The New York Times,* August 18, 1989, p. A14.

59. National Public Radio, "All Things Considered," April 15, 1990.

60. Halperin, et al., *The Lawless State,* p. 94.

9

Considering Alternatives

By 1980 political conservatives in the United States were alarmed at what they perceived to be a series of serious setbacks in American foreign policy and internal security. Of perhaps greatest concern was public reluctance to support United States involvement in Third World conflicts, what Richard Nixon called "the real war."[1] Not only had Vietnam soured the experience of "fighting for democracy" around the world, Communism had lost its ability to "scare the hell out of the American people" into supporting American military intervention in obscure locations around the world.[2]

To reverse this trend new enemies had to be found. With a stock of frightening images, usually comprised of masked Arabs, Middle East insurgents and select Latin American guerrilla movements, officials were offered a partial solution. If fighting Third War communism no longer resonated in the hearts of the American public, terrorism did.

On the domestic front the outlook was just as bleak when Ronald Reagan came to office in 1981. The FBI and CIA were demoralized after a decade of investigations by Congress, special committees, and investigative journalists. As we saw in the last two chapters, the new administration acted quickly, with the terrorism spectacle playing a central role. Meanwhile, and quite ironically, other desired policies required a silencing, a removal from center stage, of the terrorist activities of strategically important allies such as Saddam Hussein and a variety of Salvadoran officers, among others.

As the CISPES investigation indicates, the terrorist enemies in the United States were largely, though not exclusively, those who disagreed with administration policies in Central America. Protester's lawful exercise of First Amendment free speech rights became the grounds for FBI violations of their Fourth Amendment rights against unlawful search and seizure. The Reagan administration was out to get political dissidents at home while it decried the mistreatment of other dissidents abroad. The language of counterterrorism, like the language of anti-Communism a generation earlier, had tremendous utilitarian value for such purposes. As the Heritage Foundation report noted, anyone—"clergymen, students, businessmen, entertainers, labor officials, journalist and government workers"—may wittingly or unwittingly involve themselves in terrorist subversion. Terrorists were the succubi of the contemporary era, laying in wait to seduce the unwary.

Such a mind-set opened the door once again to wholesale surveillance of Americans who peacefully questioned government policy. The terrorist image, often tinged by racist overtones, was already vividly cast in the minds of many Americans. Wirthlin's survey data, the Friday group meetings, the line-of-the-day and communication group meetings, the Thursday seminars and conference calls, the fawning and flak all would create and embellish the necessary codicillary illusions. The effort began with the quiet statistical revisions in the spring of 1981 and the dropping of Iraq from the terror sponsor list the following year. From there it was simply a matter of news management.

I have argued that the terrorism spectacle was seriously distorted in the news through the exercise of political power. Simply stated, power is the ability to establish an issue agenda conducive to the adoption of desired policy options. News media representations of terrorism reflected the ideological and strategic interests of powerful elite political actors and agents, usually key government officials in the executive branch. Key policy officials took advantage of their position as dominant news sources to create a symbolic environment conducive to the adoption of particular problem definitions and, ergo, particular policy goals.

Political power is held by those who have ready access to the channels of mass communication and who vigorously use that access to shape the news content and meaning. It is often argued that in a sense, terrorists have the upper hand in this matter. By commanding media attention, terrorists exercise illegitimate power. While there are certainly occasions when this is the case, more typically the power to shape perceptions of violent events and their principal actors (both perpetrators and victims) usually rests not with the terrorists but with government officials. Who the terrorists are in the first place is a question largely determined by these officials. Those who have routine access to the mass media, those to whom reporters turn when the dust settles and the shooting stops, have the ability to shape coverage and perceptions.

What are the solutions, then, to the terrorism spectacle?

A Survey of Possible Solutions

There have been two general categories of suggested solutions to the problem of power and issue distortion. First, there are suggestions for relatively modest structural changes to government or to news gathering organizations. The second category of suggestions involve changes in technique and skills for both news organizations and citizens who consume the news. Each will be taken up in turn.

Suggested structural solutions seek to reorganize existing institutions which in some way produce, report, or verify the accuracy of information. While some have focused their attention on creating greater degrees of accountability on the information production side of the equation, usually by creating independent oversight and accounting agencies within government, others have centered on creating news organizations free from the restraints of the market. Each suggestion will be taken up in turn.

Walter Lippmann suggested the creation of what we would today call intelligence and oversight agencies. Such agencies would serve to verify points of fact in democratic debates regarding public policy. In Lippmann's words, they would establish "common versions of unseen events . . ." In their absence "the only image of democracy that would work, even in theory, was one based on isolated communities of people whose political facilities were limited, according to Aristotle's famous maxim, by the range of their vision."[3] The creation of oversight agencies provides what is otherwise missing, information relatively free from the distortion of power politics.

Examples approaching Lippmann's ideal would be the General Accounting Office, the Congressional Budget Office, the Securities and the Exchange Commission, and at least theoretically, the analysis side of the Central Intelligence Agency. What are the benefits of such systems of information verification?

Information which is relatively free from the dictates of power politics is, in Lippmann's view, essential for avoiding poor and even disastrous decisions. "It is no accident," said Lippmann, "that the best diplomatic service in the world is the one in which the divorce between the assembling of knowledge and the control of policy is most perfect."[4] The diplomatic service referred to by Lippmann was the British service.

> During the war in many British embassies and in the British Foreign Office there were nearly always men, permanent officials or else special appointees, who quite successfully discounted the prevailing war mind. They discounted the rigmarole of being pro and con, of having favorite

nationalities, and pet aversions, and undelivered perorations in their bosoms. They left that to the political chiefs.[5]

Lippmann goes on to lament the absence of such a practice in the American foreign service. He would probably be even less pleased with the state of American foreign policy formulation today.

This points to the trouble with Lippmann's solution, one he recognized himself. It is not surprising to find the State Department attempting to use adversity to its advantage. But intelligence and oversight agencies, too, whose job it is to supply accurate representations of reality, tend to lack the autonomy required to fulfill their obligations and are often co-opted by policy makers. Describing this tendency in the case of inflated enemy casualty figures in Vietnam, former State Department official Hodding Carter III noted that:

> The CIA's analysts repeatedly challenged the (army) figures during much of 1967, but when a showdown on the figures arose, the CIA's top brass apparently decided that sticking with the truth made for bad bureaucratic politics, since it put the agency at odds with the President, and they backed away temporarily. The military analysts who knew better decided to play good soldier. The American people knew nothing of this and instead were fed a stream of statements claiming that the enemies ranks were being steadily depleted.[6]

For another example one need only recall the confrontation in the spring of 1981 between the analysts in the CIA and the State Department regarding revisions in the statistics on terrorism. The CIA first resisted the revisions but soon gave in. The number of recorded terrorist incidents, as a result, nearly doubled, creating the appearance of a much more serious terrorist problem than was previously understood to exist. The analysts at the CIA had been co-opted into providing numbers which would justify desired policies instead of doing their assigned job of providing accurate intelligence data. The system was turned on its head. Instead of policy being formulated from intelligence data, intelligence data was formulated to support policy. How are such abuses prevented?

To succeed, noted Lippmann, intelligence and oversight agencies in the government would have to have independence. This, in turn, rests on three points: Independent funding, the insulation of tenure, and ready access to facts.[7] Lippmann suggested funding could be established and protected by use of a trust fund. Tenure of officials would help insure at least some degree of political insulation. Access to all available facts is perhaps the most problematic, and certain to raise objections from the powerful (i.e., those who now manage the facts) but not impossible. Indeed, one of the consequences of the Iran-Contra affair was the creation of an independent CIA inspector general who has total access (in theory, anyway) to all levels of classified information and budgets.

Further internal restructuring such as this would be a positive first step. It would, however, be incomplete without a more active press seeking to hold government accountable. We turn next to the suggestions for restructuring at least a portion of the news media.

Structural Modifications of
News Gathering Organizations

In my view, the fundamental problem with the news as it is gathered today is this: As long as the news media are commercial undertakings, owned and operated by several of the largest corporations in the world, certain things are not likely to happen. First, there will be little incentive to change the current operating standards of the news, no matter how banal, so long as there is the continued creation of profit.

Secondly, there will be little incentive to modify news gathering routines which produce the reliable supply of official press releases, conferences, and interviews which passes for news. The demands of efficiency in production makes it rather unlikely that journalists and their organizations will soon bite the hand that feeds them. Government officials, therefore, will continue to dominate news routines which serve as the wellspring of their power. In the meantime, the public is left wanting for information which would empower them in the political process.

Robert Entman has called the interactive consequences of the commercial press and public ignorance the "dilemma of journalism."

> Because most members of the public know and care relatively little about government, they neither seek nor understand high-quality political reporting and analysis. With limited demand for first-rate journalism, most news organizations cannot afford to supply it, and because they do not supple it, most Americans have no practical source of information necessary to become politically sophisticated. Yet it would take an informed and interested citizenry to create enough demand to support top-flight journalism.[8]

When manipulation is added to the mix, the situation seems even more perplexing. As long as the American public is manipulated and lied to—euphemistically referred to as public diplomacy or disinformation—while they are excluded from the process of government by secret arms deals and covet wars, shouldn't we consider the possibility that it is more rational for them to remain "uninformed"? Would an informed, active citizen be someone who read and even committed to memory the presumably first-rate, sophisticated *New York Times* coverage of political violence when so much of that coverage actually served to disinform?

Edelman has made the provocative argument that apathy may be thought of as a kind of countervailing political power to calculated information campaigns such as the terrorism spectacle.

> Unless their audience is receptive to the depiction of a condition as a problem, leaders and interest groups cannot use it to their advantage. . . At some level of consciousness people doubtless sense that they wield this kind of power to acquiesce in elite definitions of problems or to nullify them by ignoring them.[9]

The ability to ignore the breathless stories in the fall of 1990 concerning the "developing Iraqi ties to terrorism" would have, for instance, served one well in an effort to rationally consider developing policy in the Persian Gulf. As long as the news remains subject to what is at best banal content, and at worst government propaganda campaigns, the best coping strategy for the public might be to ignore media content altogether.

Yet, this is probably too extreme and must be qualified. As Bennett points out, "without critical information it is hard even to imagine (much less demand) participating directly in the political process."[10] Reform, then, does not begin with the apathetic public. Rather, it must begin with a serious reexamination of the values pursued by the government and political elite who usually operate outside the view and control of the public.

It should also be remembered that in those instances when a portion of the public steps outside the propaganda loop, when they have created organizations which published newsletters, held educational forums, peacefully demonstrated, issued press releases of their own, attended churches involved in human rights campaigns, and conducted tours of places which were relatively accessible (such as Central America), other organizations like the Federal Bureau of Investigation actively undermined their efforts. In such a political environment the least costly response—at least in the near term—is what is generally referred to as apathy. Others may call it alienation. How do we extricate ourselves from such a situation?

Obviously the first thing which needs to occur is a new commitment to the idea the United States is a democracy in spirit and not just in form. Groups which disagree with government policy or the status quo should not be immediately labeled with the latest condensation symbol and harassed and investigated out of existence. The history of government subversion of oppositional interest groups, however, does not bode well for the future in this regard. Perhaps we are best to reconsider ways of establishing the news media in this country as a source of what Entman refers to as "accountability news," news which attempts to hold government accountable for its actions rather than news which serves to justify desired policy goals.

To do this we must find ways to build on the pockets of outstanding news presentations found in existing structures. Bill Moyers' excellent Public Broadcasting Service television documentary work has brought sophisticated political analyses to living rooms all across America. The same is generally true of the award winning PBS documentary series "Frontline." Some would place The McNeil/Lehrer News Hour in this group, though that program's proclivity to strict adherence to the political mainstream on nearly all issues has raised concerns with some.[11]

On radio, National Public Radio's "All Things Considered" and "Morning Edition" have offered high quality coverage over the years, though here too there is some indication they have suffered in the face of budget cuts and political attacks during the Reagan and Bush years.[12]

Solid documentary analysis on the commercial networks is not beyond imagination. CBS has produced high quality documentaries in the past, such as "Misunderstanding China" (1972), "The Selling of the Pentagon" (1971), and "Vietnam Deception: The Uncounted Enemy" (1982). There was, however, a price to be paid by CBS for these documentaries, one which makes it unlikely we will see repeats in the near future. Both "The Selling of the Pentagon" and "Vietnam Deception" generated strong criticism from the government, defense contractors, and former officials. In response to the latter documentary, former General William C. Westmoreland, commander of forces in Vietnam at the height of the war, brought a multimillion dollar libel suit against CBS. The documentary presented former intelligence officers who told of pressure from Westmoreland and other officers and officials to manufacture intelligence information which would support the desired policy of extending the war. Though an out of court settlement meant a verdict was never reached in the case, something of a shallow vindication for CBS, the suit cost them millions of dollars in legal fees and years of spent energy. Correspondent Mike Wallace, a codefendent with CBS, later reported suffering from severe depression during the trial, at one point even contemplating suicide. This is a cost with a message to any profit maximizing corporation: Leave the controversial material to someone else.

This points to what Entman offered as the first step to lasting improvements in journalism: "Isolate some outlets from the economic market altogether."[13] NPR and PBS are capable of producing critical, often hard hitting analysis precisely because they do not have to worry about maximizing their audience size, at least not to the same degree commercial news services do.[14]

But even here public television and radio enjoy only an imperfect autonomy. As Entman rightfully pointed out, public broadcasters must remain cordial to politicians, foundations and corporations who, along with audience donations, underwrite their programs.[15] Public broadcasting needs greater insulation from these pressures. Entman suggested the creation of a public broadcasting system funded at levels comparable to a major network (approximately $250 million per year). The funding source would come from government trust funds or other means of producing politically insulated sources of funds.

Such an arrangement may appear fiscally unsound in the age of budget deficits until one notes that a 1990 General Accounting Office audit revealed that the Pentagon maintained a $43 billion slush fund, money it could spend without Congressional authorization. With that amount of money, the Pentagon could keep entire weapons systems afloat for years without the approval of Congress.[16] If national security and the defense of freedom can justify $43 billion defense slush funds, it certainly can justify a greater monetary commitment to a free and independent press.

Bagdikian has also suggested a system of progressive taxation on the advertising industry. He speculated such a tax might save us from a portion of the barrage of advertisements we now endure while serving as a source of revenue.[17] Such a source of revenue could be used to fund the public broadcasting at the levels suggested by Entman.

Yet, as Entman also pointed out, structural changes such as these are not likely to occur at any point in the near future. The powerful advertising and corporate business community, that accounts for most commercial promotion in the United States would quite obviously oppose an expansion of public broadcasting and Bagdikian's suggested tax. Precisely because an independently funded news system, one free from commercial considerations and government news management, would be an independent source of information, it is unlikely officials will authorize such a source of accountability news anytime soon.[18]

Structural changes offer the most hope for addressing the imbalance of power (as issue and news management) which currently exists in

America. At the same time, structural modifications seem the least likely to occur. The trends in government in recent years has been to create greater control of information. As long as national security continues to serve as a shield of unquestioned secrecy, and as long as draconian measures are pursued against reporters and sources that provide unauthorized leaks of official secrets, even the proposed publicly funded news organizations will be met by a wall of silence whenever they step outside the official flow of information. With these limitations in mind, perhaps the best strategy is to refine analytical techniques and skills which allow for skillful decoding of official propaganda.

Refining Decoding Techniques and Skills

The emphasis here is learning to recognize and minimize the impact of managed news and issue content in both its production and consumption phases. Bennett, for instance, offers prescriptions for both consumers of the news and journalists.

Journalists could minimize news management by decreasing their reliance on politicians, government agencies and their spokespersons, all of whom are in the business of offering carefully crafted messages. One readily available source of often expert knowledge which is not tapped due to the restrictions of objectivity are the journalists themselves. Journalist should be allowed to use their own eyes and ears to report the news.[19] Some of the best reporting in recent history has approached this ideal. David Halberstram's dispatches from Vietnam, and those of Christopher Dickey, Ray Bonner, and Alma Guillermoprieto from Central America come to mind.

Greater reporter autonomy would address one of the most injurious consequences of objectivity. One of the results of objectivity is to encourage the reporter to pass along assertions he or she knows to be of dubious validity.[20] They are forced by the operation of objectivity, as it is now understood, to be less intelligent than they really are. Reversing this practice would, argued Bennett, place control of the news story with the journalist, "where it properly belongs, not with the political actors who have an interest in manipulating the story to their own advantage."[21]

There are other changes of style or technique which would benefit the citizen. Journalist should avoid the use of buzzwords and stereotypes such as "Arab terrorist." Likewise, one of the measures news consumers could take is to learn to discount buzzwords when they are used. This is a tall order, one which would require a rather radical change in our education system. This will be discussed in a moment.

At present, the temptation for reporters faced with the task of making sense out of confusion in five hundred words or thirty seconds or less is to rely on condensation symbols that tap themes which are familiar to their reading audience. These themes are often reinforced by political ideology and, sometimes, racism. They simplify the complexity of the world yet destroy any opportunity to create more complete understandings. As a result, the violence of Arabs, like that of Communists, is usually terrorism while allies conduct counterterrorism operations, pacification programs, or are freedom fighters.

Learning to discount loaded phrases like "terrorist" would have its costs. We must never forget there really are terrorists who are the correct objects of public scorn. But precisely because this is the case, the temptation for public officials and other powerful news sources is to use political violence as a kind of political capital. The key to correcting this situation may rest with educators.

Education as a Solution

Once again, Walter Lippmann is the source of the inspiration for this solution. Teachers, said Lippmann, can teach the pupil "the habit of examining the sources of his information," including "The authority given for the statement, (and) the circumstances under which the statement was secured."

Lippmann went on to offer these suggestions for a democratic education in a media age:

> He (the teacher) can teach him the character of censorship, or the idea of privacy, and furnish him with knowledge of past propaganda. He can, by the proper use of history, make him aware of the stereotype, and can educate a habit of introspection and the imagery evoked by printed words. He can, in courses in comparative history and anthropology, produce a life-long realization of the ways codes impose a special pattern upon the imagination. He can teach men to catch themselves making allegories, dramatizing relations, and personifying abstractions.[22]

I think what Lippmann was suggesting was this: Education must provide the student with more than mere emotional reactions to the symbols of the state, whether those symbols are enduring ones such as flags, or more ephemeral ones such as "terrorist," "Communist," "radical," "little Hitler," or whatever serves as the current enemy. We must emphasize the values which lie behind the symbols. For example, the flag must come to stand for, among other things, freedom of expression, not merely a sacred icon to which we perfunctorily pledge our allegiance. Likewise, the symbol "terrorist" which represents the revulsion felt for the murder of innocent people, must be applied to *all who so murder*, even if it is our own government or its proxies who do the killing.

This takes us to what I want to argue must be the guiding principle for journalists and news consumers alike. We must learn to abhor hypocrisy. Michael Walzer, I believe, made a similar point, though in a much different way.

Though the possibilities may seem limitless at first glance, the ability of words to manipulate, said Walzer, is limited.[23] There are shared meanings which exist and must be overcome by either lies or elaborate justifications and mythologies. It is not beyond our capacity, for instance, to share what it means to be cruel. The clearest evidence for this comes from the unchanging character of the lies told by soldiers and statesmen. "They lie in order to justify themselves, and (in so doing) . . . describe for us the lineaments of justice. Wherever we find hypocrisy, we also find moral knowledge."[24]

A moral education would be one which provides the student with the skills to recognize hypocrisy. Reading the paper would become an active exercise of citizenship. Simply learning to independently weigh the importance of a story according to the events it describes rather than by the size of the article or its page placement is an important skill. An important part of a moral education is learning to remember that shooting down a plane full of Afghan or Angolan civilians, or bombing them in their homes, schools and public places is terrorism, too, and not merely a resort to a "new strategy" or "urban warfare." Recognition of official manipulation and hypocrisy which places great value on some lives and none at all on others is possible for both journalists and citizens alike.

I have argued the only other alternative is rife with danger. It is an alternative which has in it the seeds of an Orwellian world where two-plus-two can equal five. In such a world power is all there is and all there can be. It is also a world envisioned by Thomas Hobbes. "Because vices and virtues have uncertain signification," because we cannot know right from wrong, the sovereign alone must affix their meaning. This is true, he claimed,

> For one calleth wisdom, what another calleth fear; and one cruelty what another justice, one prodigality, what another magnanimity . . . etc. And therefore such names can never be true grounds of any ratiocination.[25]

For the person who values democracy and human rights, this is no alternative at all.

Notes

1. Richard M. Nixon, *The Real War* (New York: Warner Books, 1980).

2. Stephen E. Ambrose, *Rise to Globalism: American Foreign Policy Since 1938*, 5th edition, (New York: Penguin Books, 1988), p. 87.

3. Walter Lippmann, Walter, *Public Opinion* (New York: Free Press, 1949), p. 247.

4. Ibid., p. 240.

5. Ibid., p. 240.

6. Lance Bennett, *News: The Politics of Illusion* (New York: Longman, 1988), p. 180.

7. Lippmann, *Public Opinion*, p. 243.

8. Robert Entman, *Democracy Without Citizens: Media and the Decay of American Politics* (New York: Oxford University Press, 1989), p. 17.

9. Edelman, *Constructing the Political Spectacle*, p. 33.

10. Bennett, *News*, p. 177.

11. See Edward Said, *Covering Islam: How the Media and the Experts Determine How We See the Rest of the World* (New York: Pantheon Books, 1981).

12. See Lawrence Zuckerman, "Has Success Spoiled NPR?" *Mother Jones*, June/July 1987, pp. 32-39, 44-45.

13. Entman, *Democracy Without Citizens*, p. 134.

14. Ibid., p. 135.

15. This concern was evident in a statement made by Robert Siegal, news director and co-host of NPR's "All Things Considered":

> I thought it was pretty important for us to get off the self-righteous kick that anyone from the State Department is a crank and that one could safely ignore all their criticisms. I don't believe that. Those are the people whom we get information from every day and they are people whom the reporters cover (Zuckerman, p. 39).

16. Unsigned, "Pentagon Can Spend $43 Billion Without Congress' OK," *The Seattle Times*, March 9, 1990, p. A2.

17. Ben H. Bagdikian, *The Media Monopoly*, 2nd edition (Boston: Beacon Press, 1987), pp. 230-231.

18. "Accountability news" is Robert Entman's term taken from *Democracy Without Citizens*.

19. Bennett, *News*, p. 203.

20. Mark Hertsgaard, *On Bended Knee: The Press and the Reagan Presidency* (New York: Farrar Straus Giroux, 1988), p. 64.

21. Bennett, *News*, p. 204.

22. Lippmann, *Public Opinion*, p. 256.

23. Michael Walzer, *Just and Unjust Wars: A Moral Argument with Historical Illustrations* (New York: Basic Books, Inc, 1977), p. 12).

24. Ibid., p. 19.

25. Richard Schlatter, ed. *Hobbes' Thucydides* (New Brunswick, N.J., 1975), pp. 377-385.

Appendix

This appendix offers additional information regarding the methods and design of the study discussed in Chapter four.

Additional Description of
Chapter Four Research Design

Besides information concerning the placement of the article, the date and page on which it appeared, by-line information, and numbers of paragraphs, information regarding the attributions found in the article were also recorded. Paragraphs had to be used rather than column inches because of the microfilm reproduction process. Different size lens used in the photocopying process produced different photocopy sizes. Attributions are simply the voices in the article. They answer the question: Whose descriptions and issue interpretations are found in this article? Attributions were coded according to their status in relation to several categories. Are the sources U.S. government officials? How many friendly foreign officials are found in the article? How many references are there to other news agencies? How often do generic labels such as "officials said" appear?

"Source" may be the reporter, if only the reporter's language is used without specific reference to some other source. An example would be "Terrorists blew-up a bridge today." This would be coded as a reporter label source. If the sentence read "According to President Reagan, this was a reprehensible terrorist act," this would be coded as a /1/, a U.S. official as source, as would any reference to a government source in connection to the description of the violence. Whether the source was named or anonymous was also noted. Also recorded was information as to who the violent actors were according to the source for the story.

The "actor" is usually the person or group doing the politically violent act. "Action" is the designation given to the actual violence. Possibilities include bombed, shot, hijacked, etc.

The "target" is just that, the target of the violence. It is important to note that at times, as in clashes between groups, actors and targets are one and the same. An example would be "Druse and Phalangist militiamen exchanged gunfire today." This would be recorded as Actor: "Druse and Phalangists." Action: "exchanged gunfire." Target: "each other." It is also important to note that "terrorists" as reported by *The Times* appeared as targets, too. This may occur in instances where rival groups attack one another with one referring to the other as "terrorists," or when governments attack "terrorist."

All sources for each actor, action, and target designation were recorded. If the lead was "Israel said today two Palestinian terrorists . . .," then the actor designation would be "Palestinian terrorist" with Israel as the source. References such as "Israel," or whatever nation, were treated as a government spokesperson reference.

Secondly, frequencies for all attributions were recorded. In other words, when the reporter referred any statement to another person or agency, it was counted. This provides a rough indication of who entered the story in what proportions. It was also noted for all sources and attributions whether they were named or unnamed.

Coding

A second coder was given a 30 day sub-sample of the original 200 day sample to search for initial violence stories. The agreement rate was 98 percent, which is to say that 98 percent of the time the two coders discovered the same initial violence stories. Finding the stories proved difficult only when reported in the "shirttail" of a larger article. This is a term sometimes applied to the last few paragraphs of an article, or anywhere else in the article, which constitutes a break in its primary focus. It is usually prefaced with the word "meanwhile." To insure complete coverage, coders simply had to carefully read all potential articles about political violence. Of the selected dates, 36 of the 200 (18 percent of the sample) did not contain an initial violence story. Only one day was entirely free from some story regarding political violence.

Code Sheet for Initial Stories

Page: 1= Page one
               2= All other pages

Origins: 1= Washington D.C., New York
               2= Friendly Foreign
               3= Non-Friendly Foreign

Wire
Service: 1= *New York Times*
               2= Other

Length: _____ (Paragraph Frequency)

Label: 1= Terrorist
               2= Guerrilla/rebel/insurgent
               3= Security/Military
               4= Hijacker
               5= Interactive (2 and 3 above "battle")
               6= Gunmen/assailant
               7= Other

Action: 1= Car bombing
               2= Bombings of other sorts
               3= Shootings
               4= Hijacking
               5= Kidnapping
               6= Other

Target: 1= Hostile official
               2= Hostile civilian
               3= Hostile military/paramilitary
               4= Hostile property
               5= American official
               6= American civilian
               7= American military
               8= American property
               9= Allied civilian
               10= Allied official
               11= Allied military/paramilitary
               12= Allied property
               13= Non-descript civilian or mix or many types of victims.
               14= Interaction (The target when Label is 5 and Action is 6)
               15= Terrorist

Source: 1= United States Government official
               2= Friendly source/official
               3= Police/security forces

4= Hostile source/official
5= Witness
6= Reporter
7= Other

New York Times Attributions Page 2

_____ FUSO (Frequency of U.S. officials)
_____ FNUSO (Frequency of named U.S. officials)
_____ FFFO (Frequency of friendly foreign officials)
_____ FNFFO (Frequency named friendly foreign officials)
_____ FHFO (Frequency of hostile foreign officials)
_____ FNHFO (Frequency of named hostile foreign officials)
_____ FT (Frequency of "terrorist")
_____ FNT (Frequency of named "terrorist")
_____ FGL (Frequency of generic label)
_____ FNA (Frequency of news agency attributions)
_____ FO (Frequency of other)
_____ FS (Frequency of security official attributions)

Codesheet for Follow-up Stories

Follow-up Coverage?   1= Yes   2=No
        Codesheet for Follow-up Stories

Case Number__ __ __ - __ Num: __ __

Page: 1= Page one
             2= All other pages

Origins: 1= Washington D.C., New York
             2= Friendly Foreign
             3= Non-Friendly Foreign

Wire Service: 1= *New York Times*

Length: _____ (Paragraph Frequency)
             2= Other

Label: 1= Terrorist
             2= Guerrilla/rebel/insurgent
             3= Security/Military
             4= Hijacker
             5= Interactive (2 and 3 above "battle")
             6= Gunmen/assailant
             7= Other

Object of Label Designation: 1= Actor 2= Action

Source: 1= United States Government official
             2= Friendly source/official
             3= Police/security forces
             4= Hostile source/official
             5= Witness
             6= Reporter
             7= Other

(The second page of initial story codesheet was also use for coding of follow-up coverage.)

Each initial story was assigned a case number beginning with the year and followed by a three digit coding number. To account for dates on which no initial coverage of violence was found, a coding number was assigned with the notation "No Direct Story." Dates that produced more than one initial story of violence are indicated by the presence of letters at the end of the code. On several occasions there appears "Coding Error." This indicates that a story collected as an initial report actually was, upon further investigation, not an initial violence story. Rather than re-enumerate all subsequent stories and code sheets, the numbers were simply skipped. The following is a list of all initial violence stories in the sample. Limited space prevents the listing of all follow-up coverage.

81001a	No Direct Stories.
81002a	"Hijacked Pakistani Jet Flies to Syria After a Six-Day Standoff in Kabul, March 9, pp. 1–8.
81003a	"Salvadoran Rebels Reportedly in New Clashes with Army," March 27, p. 5.
81003b	"Terrorists in Brazil Bomb Opposition Newspaper," p. 5.
81003c	"Three Injured in Honduras as Assembly is Bombed," p. 5.
81004a	"U.S. Hostage is Shot on Indonesian Jet at Bangkok Airport," March 30, pp. 1–4.
81004b	"Aide to Khomeini Wounded by 2 Gunmen in South Iran," p. 3.
81004c	"Basque Terrorist Suspect Killed," p. 9.
81005a	"Basque terrorists kill 2 retired officers," April 15, 1981, p. 3.
81006a	"Israeli Jets Attack Targets in Lebanon," April 27, 1981, pp. 1–10.
81007a	"Bolivia Says Occupation of U.S. Refinery has Ended," May 4, 1981, p. 5.
81008a	"Four Guatemalans Slain in Leftist-Rightist Rivalry," May 16, 1981, p. 7.
81009a	"Canadian Jet Has Bomb Scare," May 18, 1981, p. 9.
81009b	"Israeli Army Pulls Arab Suspects in Thirteen Slayings in the Gaza Strip," May 18, 1981, p. 13.
81010a	"Israel Says its Jets Hit Libyan Missiles at Sites in Lebanon," May 29, 1981, pp. 1–10.
81010b	"Lebanese Say Israelis Went Straight for Guerrilla Camps," May 29, 1981, p. 10.
81011a	"Snipers Wound Six in Beirut," June 5, 1981, p. 7.
81012a	"Salvadoran Troops Attack Rebels Dug in Volcano," June 6, 1981, p. 4.
81012b	"Land Mine Kills Spanish Officer," June 6, 1981, p. 8.
81012c	"Shelling in Beirut," June 6, 1981, p. 11.
81013a	"Premier is Wounded," June 29, 1981, pp. 1–7.
81013b	"Major Battle Said to Erupt in Salvadoran Port City," June 29, 1981, p. 4.
81014a	"Paisley Unhurt in Car Attack," July 7, 1981, p. 2.
81015	No Direct Stories, July 5, 1981

81016a	"At Least 10 Indian Die in Hindu-Moslem Melees," July 15, 1981, p. 5.
81016b	"2 Guatemala Policemen Killed in Attack on Bus," July 15, 1981, p. 5.
81016c	"2 Yugoslavs Wounded by Assailant in Brussels," July 15, 1981, p. 5.
81016d	"New Battles Erupt in Ulster as IRA Militant is Mourned," July 15, 1981, p. 7.
81016e	"Freelance Journalist for ABC Radio Slain on a Street in Beirut," July 15, 1981, p. 8.
81017a	"Woman in Kibbutz Killed by Rocket," July 21, 1981, p. 6.
81017b	"Arafat Says PLO Will Fight Back," July 21, 1981, pp. 1–6.
81017c	"Gunmen in Iran Wound a Presidential Candidate," July 21, 1981, p. 5.
81018a	"Israel Links Truce to Deep Pullback by Forces of PLO," July 22, 1981, pp. 1–10.
81018b	"2 Israel forces attack in Lebanon," July 22, 1981, p. 10.
81018c	"Polish Plane is Hijacked to West Berlin," July 22, 1981, p. 5.
81018d	"Bomb in Switzerland Injures 15 People," July 22, 1981, p. 5.
81018e	"Salvador Troops Fly to Honduras," July 22, 1981, p. 8.
81019a	"Palestinian, Linked to Munich Slayings, Wounded in Warsaw," August 6, 1981, p. 4.
81019b	"Guerrilla Radio Says Troops Kill 138 Salvadoran Civilians," August 6, 1981, p. 4.
81019c	"Bombs in Ulster Injure Seven and Block Key Railway," August 6, 1981, p. 6.
81019d	"Fire Set By Extremists Still Burning in Greece," August 6, 1981, p. 6.
81020a	"17 Killed in Lebanon Clash," August 8, 1981, p. 2.
81021a	"Salvadoran Army Opens Drive Against Rebels," October 6, 1981, p. 5.
81022a	"Armenian Group Says it Set Two Bombs in Central Geneva," Oct 5, p. 3.
81022b	"66 Leftist Rebels Executed in Iran," Oct 5, p. 8.
81023a	"Egyptian City is Quiet after Clashes," Oct 10, 1981, pp. 1–17.
81023b	"7 Injured by Bomb Blast in Salvador's High Court," Oct 10, 1981, p. 4.
81023c	"Ulster Explosions Cause Damage but no Injuries," Oct 10, 1981, p. 4.
81023d	No Headline, Oct 10, 1981; p. 4.
81023e	"UN Officer Shot in Lebanon," Oct 10, 1981, p. 5.
81023f	"PLO Aide Killed by Bomb in Rome," Oct 10, 1981, p. 5.
81024a	"One Dies in Blast in London Restaurant," Oct 27, 1981, p. 3.
81024b	"IRA Suspect Seized," Oct 27, 1981, p. 3.
81024c	"Egypt Publishes a Report on Police Battles With 'Moslem Terrorists'," Oct 27, 1981, p. 10.

81025	No Direct Stories, Nov 6.
81026a	"IRA Bomb Explodes at Home of British Aide," Nov 14, p. 4.
81027a	"Bomb Explodes at Rail Station," Nov 17, p. 3.
81028a	"San Juan Area Blacked out by Blasts at Power Stations," Nov 28, p. 8.
81028b	"4 Bombings in Teheran Kill 2 and Wound 15," Nov 28, p. 4.
81028c	"One Killed and 4 Hurt in a Bombing in Belfast," Nov 28, p. 4.
81028d	"Honduran Battle Kills Policemen and Leftists," November 28, p. 4.
82001a	"Iran Executes 6 Bahais, Religious Leaders Say," January 9, p. 7.
82001b	"Beirut Clashes Continue for a Third Day," Jan 9, p. 7.
82002a	"U.S.Army Aide is Slain in Paris Near His Home," Jan 19, pp. 1–8.
82002b	"Ethiopia Says it Crushed Eritrean Secessionists," Jan 19, p. 5.
82002c	"IRA Disrupts Rail Traffic," Jan 19, p. 15.
82003	No Direct Stories, Jan 26.
82004	No Direct Stories, Feb 14.
82005a	"51 Indians are Slain in Guatemala Village," Feb 17, p. 7.
82006a	"Corsican Rebels Set off 19 Bombs in France," Feb 18, p. 7.
82007a	"Rebels in Uganda Attack Barracks," Feb 25, p. 9.
82008a	"Tanzian Jet Hijacked; 2 Reported Killed," Feb 27, p. 4.
82008b	No Headline, Feb 27, p. 5.
82008c	"Turkish Regime Seizes Lawyers and Journalists," Feb 27, p. 5.
82009a	"Top Guatemala Officer is Wounded by Rebels," Feb 28, p. 5.
82009b	"Beirut Car Bomb Kills 8 and Leaves 20 Wounded," Feb 28, p. 5.
82009c	"Rightist Leader in Salvador is Wounded in Attack," Feb 28, p. 7.
82009d	"Hijacked Jetliner Arrives in Briton," Feb 28, p. 8.
82010	No Direct Stories, April 11.
82011	No Direct Stories, May 14.
82012a	"Beirut Bomb Kills 12 at French Embassy," May 25, p. 3.
82012b	"Italian Guerrilla Suspect is Slain by Police," May 25, p. 5.
82013a	"Khomeini Son Away Car When Bullets Hit it in Attack," June 16, p. 18.
82014a	"Bomb Injures Two in Paris," June 20, p. 10.
82014b	"Teacher Slain as West Bank Arabs Clash," June 20, p. 12.
82015a	"Israel Bombards Refugee Camps in West Beirut," June 22, pp. 1–8.
82015b	"18 Are Reported Killed in Guatemala Violence," June 22, p. 5.
82016a	"Israel and Syria Clash on Highway to East of Beirut," June 24, pp. 1–14. (Included due to guerrilla involvement).
82016b	"Israel Says Syria Broke Cease-fire," June 24, p. 15.
82017a	"Israel Guns Shell Palestinian Camps in Civilian Areas," July 6, pp. 1–8.
82018	No Direct Stories, July 7.
82019a	"Six Killed in Attack Ankara Airport," August 8. p. 1.
82020	No Direct Stories, Sept 12.
82021a	"8 Reported Slain," Sept 15, p. 1.

82021b	"4 Spanish Policemen Slain in Basque Ambush," Sept 15, p. 5.
82022a	"Honduran Rebels Free 20 Hostages," Sept 23, p. 9.
82023a	"Guatemalan Raids Bring Fear to Mexican Border," Oct 9, p. 2.
82024	No Direct Stories, Oct 19.
82025	No Direct Stories, Oct 20.
82026a	"Ulster Protestant is Again a Rebel target," Oct 21, p. 3.
82026b	"Toronto Group Says it Set off Factory Blast," Oct 21, p. 5.
82026c	"Rome Bomb Rocks Lebanese Embassy," Oct 21, p. 9.
82027a	"Mozambique Rebels Release 6 Missionaries after Seventy Days," Nov 27, p. 2.
82028a	"Druse Chief Hurt in Beirut Bombing," Dec 2, p. 8.
82029a	"Casualties Mount in Lebanese Strife," Dec 14, p. 3.
83001	No Direct Stories, Jan 3.
83002	Code sheet numbering error.
83003a	"Salvador Abduction Reported," Jan 6.
83004a	"City's Fall Called Blow to El Salvador," Feb 2, pp. 1–4.
83004b	"Vietnamese Burn Cambodian Camp," Feb 2, p. 3.
83004c	"Militiamen Clash in Lebanon," Feb 2, p. 3.
83005a	"Up to 50 Peruvian Rebels are Reported Slain," Feb 21, p. 5.
83005b	"Hijacked Libyan Plane Held at Malta Airport," Feb 21, p. 8.
83006	No Direct Stories, March 13.
83007a	"Nicaragua Reports it Troops Battle Rebels Near Honduras," March 29, p. 10.
83008a	"Bombs Kill 6 in Assam; Clashes in Other States," April 8, p. 5.
83009a	"Colombian Leftists Free a Texaco Executive," April 15, p. 7.
83009b	"Peru Says Its Forces Killed 69 Rebels in six days," April 15, p. 7.
83010a	"Building in Ruins," April 19, pp. 1–12.
83011a	"Vietnam Links Shelling to Moral of Guerrillas," April 23, p. 5.
83012a	"37 Reported Slain in Colombian Battles," May 12, p. 7.
83013a	"South Africa Jets Bomb Mozambique," May 23, pp. 1–9.
83013b	"23 Reported Dead in Lebanon Battle," May 23, p. 8.
83014a	"South Africa Jets Raid Mozambique in Reply to Rebels," May 24, pp. 1–3.
83014b	"Corsican Rebels Set off 43 Bombs in Political Warning to Mitterand," May 24, p. 4.
83015a	"South Africa Hangs 3 Guerrillas; Black Nationalist Vow Revenge," June 10, p. 4.
83015b	"Nicaragua Says Army 'Contained' New Assault," June 10, p. 5.
83016a	"Assailants in Istanbul Kill Two and Wound 27 Near Bazaar," June 17, p. 2.
83016b	"Gunmen Said to Kill 15 in Lebanese Port City," June 17, p. 5.
83017a	"Zimbabwe Says Rebels Destroyed Village," June 18, p. 4.
83018a	"Arafat Loyalists Retreat in Bekaa Under Pressure From Rebel Forces," June 30, p. 6.
83019a	"17 Bahai Reported Hanged in 2 Weeks in an Iranian City," July 3, p. 3.

83019b	"Rightists Kill Two in Salvador to Avenge Slaying," July 3, p. 11.
83020a	"Guatemalan's Sister Kidnapped," July 7, p. 2.
83020b	"Hijacked Iran Jet Leaves Kuwait with 185 Hostages," July 7, p. 4.
83021a	"Peru Authorities Holding 271 in Connection with Bombings," July 24, p. 4.
83022a	"New Fighting Breaks out Between PLO Factions," July 25, p. 7.
83023a	"PLO Rivals Clash in Lebanon Again," Aug 2, pp. 1–5.
83023b	"Angolan Rebels Say 78 Died in Attack on Train," Aug 2, p. 9.
83024a	"A Car Bomb Kills 33 and Wounds 125 in Lebanese Town," Aug 8, pp. 1–3.
83025a	"Rival Palestinian Groups Again Battle in Bekaa," Aug 9, p. 5.
83026a	"Druse and Christians Keep up Their Beirut Battles," Aug 14, p. 7.
83026b	"Two Die in Gun Fights in Ireland," Aug 14, p. 15.
83027a	"Colombia Rebels Abduct an American Rancher," Aug 16, p. 5.
83028a	"Lebanese Attack Druse and PLO in Mountains," Sept 17, pp. 1–4.
83029	No Direct Stories, Sept 30.
83030a	"Pro-Israeli Chief Killed in Lebanon," Oct 7, p. 13.
83031a	"11 Bombings in Corsica," Oct 8, p. 4.
83031b	"Rightists Death Squad Kills 4 in El Salvador," Oct 8, p. 5.
83032a	"Nicaragua Evacuates Port Raid by Rebels," Oct 13, p. 13.
83033	No Direct Stories, Oct 27.
83034a	"Arafat's Soldier's Lose Stronghold; Vow to Fight on," Nov 7, pp. 1–10.
83035a	"Pro-Western Angolan Rebels Say They Downed Plane," Nov 11, p. 5.
83036a	"Israeli Jets Bomb Base of Suspects in Marine Attack," Nov 17, pp. 1–16.
83036b	"Arafat Foes Push into Stronghold," Nov 17, pp. 1–16.
83036c	"Atrocities by Insurgents Reported in Peru," Nov 17, p. 5.
83036d	"Drive on Burma Rebels Near Thailand Reported," Nov 17, p. 5.
83037a	"Kuwait Car Bomb Hits U.S Embassy; Damage Extensive," Dec 12, p. 1.
83037b	"Fighting Erupts Near Beirut, Ending 2-day Lull," Dec 12, p. 6.
84001a	"4 Europeans Killed Ugandan Rebels," Jan 24, p. 5.
84001b	"Israel Says Its Troops Hurt 3 Jordanians by Firing in Error," Jan 24, p. 6.
84002a	"U.S. Woman Killed in Salvador," Jan 27, p. 3.
84003a	"Gemayel's Forces Collapsing; He is Said Israel Pact; Reagan Gives Plan on Marines," February 16, pp. 1–16.
84003b	"Policeman is Killed by Sikhs in Punjab," Feb 16, p. 7.
84003c	"Sudan Guerrillas Report Attack on Nile Steamer," Feb 16, p. 7.
84003d	"U.S. Diplomat Slain by Gunmen on Rome Street," Feb 16, pp. 1–13.
84004	Code sheet numbering error.
84005	No Direct Stories, March 3.
84006a	"Combat Flares in Beirut; 11 Israelis Hurt in Sidon," March 5, p. 6.

84006b	"Israeli Warplanes Strike," March 5, p. 6.
84006c	"6 Arabs Wounded in West Bank When Gunmen Opened Fire on Bus," March 5, p. 6.
84007	No Direct Stories, March 6.
84008a	"Nicaragua Says Honduras Aided 2 Rebel Attacks," March 9, p. 4.
84009a	"5 London Bombs Linked to Libyans," March 11, p. 3.
84009b	"Gunmen Opened Fire on Protestant March in Ulster," March 11, p. 4.
84009c	"25 on French Plane Hurt by Chad Airport Bomb," March 11, p. 7.
84009d	"Fighting Goes On in Beirut Sectors," March 11, p. 12.
84010a	"U.S. Envoy Seized in West Beirut, 3rd American to Vanish in 6 weeks," March 17, pp. 1–4.
84010b	"Plane Bombs the Sudan, Which Accuses Libyans," March 17, p. 4.
84011a	"Despite Cease-Fire, Fighting Still Racks Beirut," March 19, p. 11.
84012a	"Big Battle Clears Streets of Beirut," March 24, p. 5.
84013a	"Naga Insurgents Said to Kill 300 Who Refused to Give Aid," April 12, p. 3.
84013b	"Swaziland Searches for South African Rebels," April 12, p. 5.
84013c	"5 Sri Lanka Rebels are Reported Slain," April 12, p. 5.
84013d	"Pol Pot Forces Say They Wrecked a Town," April 12, p. 5.
84014a	"News of Hijacking Denied to Israelis," April 14, p. 4.
84014b	"3 Killed in Spain; Basques are Suspected," April 14, p. 5.
84015a	"3 Killed as Violence Spreads in 2 Indian States," April 20, p. 5.
84015b	"Eritrean Rebels Claim an Ethiopian Town," April 20, p. 5.
84015c	"Second Bomb Goes Off in Namibia Town Where 2 Americans Died," April 20, p. 7.
84016a	"Hindu Priest Killed in Punjab," April 23, p. 3.
84016b	"Angola Dynamite Blast Reportedly Kills 30," April 23, p. 5.
84016c	No Title, April 23, p. 5.
84016d	"A Success is Reported for Cambodian Rebels," April 23, p. 5.
84016e	"Western Sahara Rebels Said to Kill 63 Moroccans," April 23, p. 5.
84017a	"Fighting in Beirut Closes Crossing as Karami Consults on Cabinet," April 29, p. 3.
84017b	"Turks Shot in Teheran; Armenians Claim Attack," April 29, p. 5.
84018a	"Libyan Exiles Assert 15 Died in Attack," May 10, p. 3.
84018b	"5 Libyans Said to Die in Ethiopian Explosion," May 10, p. 4.
84019a	"Qaddafi Assailant is Reported Killed," May 14, p. 3.
84019b	"Beirut Fighting Raises Weekend Deaths to 19," May 14, p. 5.
84019c	"Sri Lankan Kidnappers Say US Couple is Safe," May 14, p. 5.
84020a	"Laos Rebels Reported to Ambush 40 Troops," May 27, p. 4.
84021	No Direct Stories, June 11.
84022a	"Sudan President Reports Success Against Rebels," July 23, p. 5.
84023a	"Hijacked Plane is Recaptured with US Help," July 31, pp. 1–2.
84023b	"Bombings in Pakistan Laid to Afghanistan," July 31, p. 5.
84023c	"Salvador Rebels Kill at Least 57 in Raids," July 31, p. 8.

84024a	"Israeli Jets Bomb Base of a Guerrilla Faction," Aug 17, p. 4.
84024b	"Blast in Red Sea Damages a Cypriot-Registered Vessel," Aug 17, p. 4.
84025a	"Moslem Group Asserts it is Holding Reporter," Sept 5, p. 6.
84025b	"71 Wounded by Bomb at Ulster Train Station," Sept 5, p. 11.
84025c	"Afghan Rebels Say Their Bombing Hotels," Sept 5, p. 11.
84026a	"American Priest in Sudan is Reported Kidnapped," Sept 13, p. 5.
84027	No Direct Stories, Sept 25.
84028	No Direct Stories, Oct 3.
84029a	"Reported Salvador Killing Raises Concern over Right's Intentions," Oct 24, p. 4.
84029b	"Cambodian Rebel Attack," Oct 24, p. 4.
84029c	"Sudan Rebels Released Kidnapped Missionaries," Oct 24, p. 11.
84030a	"4 Policemen in Chile Killed in Bombing," Nov 3, p. 5.
84031a	"Salvadoran Rebels Attack Town but are Repulsed," Nov 10, pp. 1–4.
84031b	"Zimbabwe Rebels Slain a State Senator," Nov 10, p. 5.
84031c	"Heaviest Fighting Since July Breaks out in Beirut," Nov 10, p. 5.
84032a	"Hijackers Free 39 at Airport in Iran but Still Hold 18," Dec 9, pp. 1–13.
84032b	"Lebanese Army Battles Druse Near Beirut," Dec 9, p. 15.
85001a	"Gunmen Kill Libyan Diplomat on a Rome Street," Jan 14, p. 3.
85002a	"Car Bombings in Lebanon Kill 7; Israeli Jets Raid Palestinian Base," Feb 11, p. 4.
85003a	"Khmer Rouge Bases Reported in Peril," Feb 15, p. 3.
85003B	"Anti-Marcos Group Says it Set Hotel Blaze," Feb 15, p. 5.
85004	Code sheet numbering error.
85005	Code sheet numbering error.
85006a	"French Truce Observer Slain in Lebanon," Feb 21, p. 3.
85006b	"Israelis Raid Village," Feb 21, p. 3.
85007a	"Car Bomb Hits an Israeli Convoy in Southern Lebanon, Killing 12," March 11, pp. 1–8.
85007b	"Philippine Battles Kill 15," March 11, p. 8.
85007c	"Anti-Communist Group Raided by Polish Police," March 11, p. 7.
85007d	"Rebels and Soldiers Skirmish in Turkey," March 11, p. 7.
85008a	"Christian-Moslem Fighting Paralyzes Lebanese Port," March 20, p. 3.
85008b	"2 Bombs in Switzerland Wrecks a Factory," March 20, p. 7.
85009a	"20 Reported Killed in Fighting at Port in Lebanon," April 21, p. 19.
85010a	"Beirut Fighting Goes Into Its 7th Day," May 5, p. 3.
85010b	"24 Die in Attack by Sri Lanka Rebels," May 5, p. 7.
85010c	"3 More People Die in South Africa Violence," May 5, p. 7.
85011a	"Luxembourg is Blacked Out as 2 Blasts Topple Towers," May 9, p. 9.

85012a   "Salvador Guerrillas Kidnap 3 More Mayors," May 14, p. 5.

85012b   "Filipino Soldiers Kill 17 Communist Rebels," May 14, p. 5.

85012c   "3 Bombings are Felt in New Caledonia City," May 14, p. 5.

85012d   "Shops Close in New Delhi in a Strike to Protest Wave of bombings," May 14, p. 11.

85013a   "18 Rebels Reported Slain in Sri Lanka," May 17, p. 3.

85013b   "Bomb Explodes in Peru at Home of US Envoy," May 17, p. 5.

85013c   "Salvadoran Judge Slain," May 17, p. 11.

85014a   "Shiites and PLO Continue Battles," May 22, p. 15.

85015a   "Western Sahara Rebels Said to Have Killed 56," May 28, p. 5.

85016a   "Dragnet by Peru Police Gets 2 Suspects in Lima Blasts," June 9, p. 19.

85017a   "Basque Group Says it Killed 4 in 3 Attacks," June 14, p. 7.

85017b   "10 Killed in Botswana in South African Raid," June 14, p. 7.

85018a   "329 Lost on Air-India Plane After Crash Near Ireland; Bomb is Suspected as Cause," June 24, pp. 1–10.

85018b   "Blast Kills 2 as Cargo is Unloaded From Canadian Airliner in Japan," June 24, pp. 1–11.

85018c   "Nicaragua Reports Clashes with Rebels," June 24, p. 5.

85019a   "Two Blasts Sink Green Peace Ship," July 11, p. 4.

85019b   "Israeli Jets Raid Palestinian Sites," July 11, p. 6.

85019c   "Bordeaux Court Explosion," July 11, p. 6.

85020a   "Lebanese Militias Duel in Beirut and Mountains," July 15, p. 3.

85020b   "Ethiopia Rebels Say They Captured Northern City," July 15, p. 3.

85020c   "Sudanese Troops Fight with Rebels in South," July 15, p. 3.

85021a   "Car Bomber Attacks an Israeli Patrol in Lebanon," Aug 1, p. 4.

85021b   "Gunmen in India Kill MP from Gandi Party," Aug 1, p. 5.

85021c   "Bomb Rocks Damascus, Iranian Agency Reports," Aug 1, p. 5.

85022a   "In South Lebanon, Man Riding a Mule Sets Off Explosion," Aug 7, p. 4.

85023a   "6 Killed as Gunmen Battle in Beirut," Aug 10, p. 2.

85024a   "Car Bombs Kill 29 in Moslem Beirut," Aug 20, pp 1–9.

85024b   "24 are Reported Died in Philippine Battles," Aug 20, p. 5.

85024c   No Title, Aug 20, p. 5.

85025a   "Salvador Rebels Anti-Transport Raids," Aug 23, p. 5.

85026a   "2 Israelis are Victims of West Bank Attacks," Aug 25, p. 11.

85026b   "Bomb Threats on Arab Jets," Aug 25, p. 18.

85027a   "Shiite Gunmen in Beirut Attack Christians in Bus," Aug 28, p. 9.

85028a   "Pretoria Mounts a Raid in Angola on Namibia Rebels," Sept 17, pp. 1–4.

85028b   "24 Lebanese Die in Shelling in Tripoli," Sept 17, p. 7.

85028c   "38 are Hurt in Rome in a Grenade Attack on an Outdoor Cafe," Sept 17, p. 13.

85029   No Direct Stories, Oct 15.

85030a   "Gunfire is Reported in Uganda's Capital," Oct 27, p. 5.

85030b	"20 are Hurt in Clashes in New Caledonia," Oct 27, p. 5.
85031a	"Policeman is Killed in Athens Car-bombing," Nov 27, p. 5.
85031b	"Guerrillas Kill 4 Tamils Who Opposed Violence," Nov 27, p. 5.
85031c	"Truck Driver is Hurt by Mine in South Africa," Nov 27, p. 5.
85031d	"Suicide Bomber Strikes Israeli Post in Lebanon," Nov 27, p. 9.
85032a	"25 Wounded by Bombs at 2 Paris Department Stores," Dec 8, p. 3.
85032b	"2 Policemen Killed in Ulster Attack," Dec 8, p. 13.
85033a	"Land Mine Kill 6 in South Africa," Dec 16, p. 7.
86001a	"Combat Said to Rage in Uganda Capital," Jan 25, p. 3.
86002a	"2 are Killed in Beirut; Leaders Snub Gemayel," Jan 28, p. 3.
86002b	"Uganda Rebels, Tightening Their Grip, said to Seize No.2 City," Jan 28, p. 4.
86002c	"3 are Reported Killed in Protests in Haiti," Jan 28, p. 9.
86002d	"Southern Yemen's Rebels Said to Consolidate Hold," Jan 28, p. 9.
86003a	"Raiding Israelis Fight Guerrillas," Feb 21, p. 3.
86004a	"Italian Aide Shot; Terrorist Killed," Feb 22, p. 3.
86004b	"Israelis Storm Lebanese Shiite Town," Feb 22, p. 3.
86004c	"Embassies of 5 Nations are Bombed in Peru," Feb 22, p. 5.
86005a	"Paris Bookstore Explosion," Feb 28, p. 2.
86005b	"Israelis Attack Villages in Southern Lebanon," Feb 28, p. 3.
86006a	No Direct Stories, March 3.
86007a	"South Africa Police Said to Kill 30, One of Worst Daily Tolls in Year," March 27, pp. 1–16.
86007b	"9 Sikhs Killed by Police in Clash in Punjab State," March 27, p. 5.
86007c	"2 Blasts Rock Phalangists Offices; 10 are Killed and 86 Wounded," March 27, p. 12.
86008a	"Honduran Peasants Confirm Report of a Battle," March 28, pp. 1–4.
86008b	"Nicaragua Reports Success," March 28, p. 4.
86008c	"2 More Blacks Reported Slain by Policemen in South Africa," March 28, p. 2.
86008d	"Bomb Wounds 21 in Melbourne," March 28, p. 3.
86008e	"Rocket Hits Town in Israel, and Its Jets Retaliate," March 28, p. 13.
86009a	"4 Killed as Bomb Rips TWA Plane on Way to Athens," April 3, pp. 1–8.
86009b	"A Police Officer is Shot in New Attacks in Ulster," April 3, p. 7.
86010	No Direct Stories, April 28.
86011a	"Bombing in Sri Lanka Capital Kills 11," May 8, p. 3.
86011b	"Frenchman Kidnapped in Beirut," May 8, p. 4.
86012	No Direct Stories, May 13.
86013a	"Nicaraguan Rebels Ambush Germans and Capture Eight," May 19, p. 3.
86014a	"Heavy Fighting Eases in Beirut; Moslems Bury Dead and Get Food," June 5, p. 4.

86014b   "Sikhs at Golden Temple Kill Guard and Wound 7," June 5, p. 5.

86015a   "Mine 28 on Sri Lanka Bus," July 23, p. 4.

86016a   "South Africa Reports Killing 2 Rebel in Gunfight," July 28, p. 2.

86016b   "A Powerful Blast Hits Beirut Neighborhood," July 28, p. 4.

86017   No Direct Stories, Aug 21.

86018a   "1 Killed, 18 Hurt in Paris Explosion," Sept 9, pp. 1–4.

86018b   "Car Bomb Explosion in Cologne," Sept 9, p. 4.

86018c   "10 Dead in Attack on Philippine Church," Sept 9, p. 7.

86018d   "Moslem Factions Battle in 2 Beirut Suburbs," Sept 9, p. 7.

86019a   "2 Soviet Hijackers are Slain in Shootout," Sept 23, p. 3.

86020a   "Two Cities in Peru Shaken by Bombings," Oct 5, p. 5.

86021a   "Grenade Attack Kills 1, Wounds 65 in Jerusalem," Oct 16, p. 8

86021b   "Sri Lanka Ends 3 Day Drive Against the Tamil Guerrillas," Oct 16, p. 13.

86022a   "2 Bombs Explode at Military Sites in Puerto Rico and 8 Are Disarmed," Oct 29, p. 3.

86022b   "Sikh in Gandi's Party is Killed in Punjab," Oct 29, p. 11.

86022c   "Bomb Rips Offices of Lufthansa in Cologne," Oct 29, p. 11.

86023a   "Paris is Struck by 3 Bomb Blasts," Nov 11, p. 9.

86024a   "Israeli Jets Raid Southern Lebanon," Nov 17, p. 6.

86024b   "Catholic Woman Dies Amidst Ulster Strife," Nov 17, p. 9.

86024c   "IBM Site is Bombed in West Germany," Nov 17, p. 9.

86025a   No Direct Stories, Nov 24.

87001a   "Ex-President of Lebanon Survives Car-Bombing," Jan 8, p. 8.

87001b   "2 Killed in Southern Lebanon," Jan 8, p. 8.

87001c   "2 Reported Killed in Raid by Sri Lankan Army," Jan 8, p. 15.

87002a   "Irish Guerrilla Leader's Wife Slain in Attack on Her Home," Feb 1, p. 6.

87002b   "Salvador Air Raid Reported in Town," Feb 1, p. 11.

87002c   "2 Die in Marseilles Car Blast," Feb 1, p. 11.

87003a   "Afghans Attack Guerrilla Camps; 80 are Killed, Scores Wounded," March 26, p. 8.

87004   No Direct Stories, April 2.

87005   No Direct Stories, April 6.

87006a   "Iranian Reported Seized by Beirut," May 1, p. 3.

87007a   "16 Philippine Soldiers Die in Rebel Ambush," May 5, p. 7.

87008   No Direct Stories, May 20.

87009   No Direct Stories, May 21.

87010   No Direct Stories, June 7.

87011   No Direct Stories, June 14.

87012   No Direct Stories, July 14.

87013a   "291 Tamil Rebels Freed Under Sri Lanka Accord," Aug 9, p. 16.

87014   No Direct Stories, Sept 3.

87015a   "3 Israelis are Killed Fighting Guerrillas in Lebanon's South," Sept 17, p. 13.

87016a	"India Cracks Down on Rebels Defying Truce in Sri Lanka," Oct 10, pp. 1–11.
87016b	"Afghanistan Car Bomb Kills 27," Oct 10, p. 6.
87017	No Direct Stories, Oct 16.
87019a	"Contra Attacks Leave a Message in 5 Towns," Oct 24, pp. 1–4.
87020	No Direct Stories, Oct 26.
87021	No Direct Stories, Nov 16.
87022a	"Israelis Kill 3 in Gaza as Arabs are Exhorted to Protest," Dec 19, p. 3.

References

Alexander, Yonah, "Communications Aspects of International Terrorism," *International Problems*, 16 Spring 1977, pp. 55-60.

———, "Terrorism and the Media in the Middle East" in Y. Alexander and S. M. Finger, eds. *Terrorism: Interdisciplinary Perspectives* (New York: John Jay Press, 1977), pp. 166-208.

———, "Terrorism, The Media and the Police," *Journal of International Affairs*, 32:1, 1978, pp. 101-113.

———, "Terrorism and the Media: Some Considerations" in Y. Alexander, D. Carlton and P. Wilkinson, eds. *Terrorism: Theory and Practice* (Boulder, CO.: Westview Press, 1979), pp. 159-174.

———, "Terrorism and the Mass Media" in D. Carlton and C. Schaerf, (eds.), *Contemporary Terrorism* (London: Macmillan, 1981) pp. 50-65.

Ambrose, Stephen E., *Rise to Globalism: American Foreign Policy Since 1938*, 5th edition, (New York: Penguin Books, 1988).

Amnesty International Report 1980 (London: Amnesty International Publications, 1980).

Atwater, Tony, "Network Evening News Coverage of the TWA Hostage Crisis," *Journalism Quarterly*, 64, 1987, pp. 520-525.

———, "News Format in Network Evening News Coverage of the TWA Hijacking," *Journal of Broadcasting & Electronic Media*, 33, 1989, pp. 293-304.

Bachrach, Peter, *The Theory of Democratic Elitism: A Critique* (London: University of London Press, 1969).

Bachrach, Peter and Morton Baratz, "Decisions and Nondecisions: An Analytical Framework," *American Political Science Review* 57, 1963, pp. 632-42.

———, *Power and Poverty: Theory and Practice* (New York: Oxford University Press, 1970).

Bagdikian, Ben H., *The Media Monopoly*, 2nd edition (Boston: Beacon Press, 1987).

———, "The Lords of the Global Village," *The Nation*, June 12, 1989a, pp. 805-820.

———, "Missing From the News," *The Progressive*, August 1989b, pp. 32-34.

Barnouw, Eric, *The Sponsor* (Oxford: Oxford University Press, 1978).

Bassiouni, M. Cherif, "Problems of Media Coverage of Nonstate-Sponsored Terror-Violence Incidents" in L. Z. Freedman and Yonah Alexander, eds., *Perspectives on Terrorism* (Wilmington, DE.: Scholarly Resources, 1983), pp. 177-200.

Bell, J. Bower, *Transnational Terror*. AEI-Hoover Institute Studies, No. 51 (Stanford, CA.: Hoover Institute Press, 1975).

———, "Terrorist Scripts and Live-Action Spectaclars," *Columbia Journalism Review*, 17, May 1978, pp. 47-50.

Bender, Gerald J., James S. Coleman, and Richard L. Sklar, eds., *African Crisis Areas and U.S. Foreign Policy*, (Berkley: University of California Press, 1985).

———, International Affairs in Africa (New Bury, CA.: Sage Publications, 1987).

Bennett, W. Lance, *News: The Politics of Illusion* (New York: Longman Press, Second Edition, 1988).

———, "Marginalizing the Majority: Conditioning Public Opinion to Accept Managerial Democracy" in Michael Margolis and Gary A. Manser, eds. *Manipulating Public Opinion: Essays on Public Opinion as the Dependent Variable* (Pacific Grove, CA,: Brooks-Cole, 1989).

Bennett, W. Lance, Lynne Gressett, and William Haltom, "Repairing the News: A Case Study of the News Paradigm," *Journal of Communication*, Spring 1985, pp. 50- 68.

Blackstock, Nelson, *Cointelpro: The FBI's Secret War on Political Freedom* (New York: A Pathfinder Book, 1988).

Boot, William, "Iranscam: When the Cheering Stopped: Suddenly all the Great Leader Copy Seemed Embarrassing," *Columbia Journalism Review*, March/April 1987, pp. 25 - 30.

Broadcasting, "Calling for a Code on Terrorist Coverage." July 22, 1985, pp. 36-37.

Breed, Warren, "Newspaper 'Opinion Leaders' and the Processes of Socialization," *Journalism Quarterly* 32, Summer 1955, pp. 277-84.

Catton, W. R., "Militants and the Media: Partners in Terrorism?" *Indiana Law Review*,53:4, 1978, pp. 680-715.

Center for Constitutional Rights-National Lawyer's Guild, "Harassment Update," 8th edition, May 1987.

Chafets, Zeev, "Beirut and the Great Media Cover-up," *Commentary*, 78:3, 1984, pp. 20-29.

Chalfont, Lord, "Political Violence and the Role of the Media: Some Perspectives, *Political Communication and Persuasion*, 1:1, 1980, pp. 79-99.

Chomsky, Noam. "Beyond the Bounds of Thinkable Thought," *The Progressive*, October 1985.

Cobb, Roger W. and Charles Elder, *Participation in American Politics* (Baltimore: Johns Hopkins University Press, 1972).

Cockburn, Alexander, "Getting Opium to the Masses: The Political Economy of Addition," *The Nation*, October 30, 1989.

Committee to Protect Journalists, "Attacks on the Press, 1987: A Worldwide Survey," Annual Reports.

Cox, Robert, "Comments: The Media as a Weapon," *Political Communication and Persuasion* 1:3, 1981 pp. 297-300.

Crelinsten, Ronald D., "Terrorism and the Media: Problems, Solutions, and Counterproblems," *Political Communication and Persuasion* 6, pp. 311-339.

Crouse, Timothy, *The Boys on the Bus* (New York: Randon House, 1973).

Crozier, Brian, *The Rebels: A Study of Post-war Insurrections* (Boston: Beacon Press, 1960).

Dickey, Christopher, *With the Contras: A Reporter in the Wilds of Nicaragua* (New York: Simon & Schuster, 1985).

DISAM Journal, vol 7, no. 2, Winter 1984-85.

Donner, Frank J., *The Age of Surveillance: The Aims and Methods of America's Political Intelligence System* (New York: Vintage Books, 1980).

Dormon, William A. and Mansour Farhang, *The U.S. Press and Iran: Foreign Policy and the Journalism of Deference* (Berkeley: University of California Press, 1987).

Dorman, William A. and Steven Livingston, "News and Historical Content: The Establishing Phase of the Persian Gulf Policy Debate," in *Conflicting Images* (tentative title) W. Lance Bennett and David Paletz, eds., (Chicago: University of Chicago Press, 1993).

Dower, John W., *War Without Mercy: Race and Power in the Pacific War* (New York: Pantheon Books, 1986).

Doyle, E. J., "Propaganda by Deed: The Media Response to Terrorism," *Police Chief*, June 1979, pp. 40-41.

Edelman, Murray, *The Symbolic Uses of Politics* (Urbana: University of Illinois Press, 1964).

———, *Political Language: Words that Succeed and Policies that Fail* (New York: Academic Press, 1977).

———, *Constructing the Political Spectacle* (Chicago: The University of Chicago Press, 1988).

Efron, Edith, *The News Twisters* (Los Angeles: Nash, 1971).

Elkins, Michael, "Caging the Beasts" in B. Netanyahu, ed., *International Terrorism: Challenge and response* (New Brunswick, N.J.: Transaction Books, 1981, pp. 230-234.

Elliot, Philip and Peter Golding, "Mass Communication and Social Change: The Imagery of Development and the Development of Imagery" in Emanuel de Kadt and Gavin Williams, eds. *Sociology and Development* (London: Tavistock, 1974).

Emerson, Steven and Cristina Del Sesto, *Terrorist: The Inside Story of the Highest-Ranking Iraqi Terrorist Ever to Defect to the West* (New York: Villard Books, 1991).

Entman, Robert, *Democracy Without Citizens: Media and the Decay of American Politics* (New York: Oxford University Press, 1989).

Epstein, Edward L., "The Uses of 'Terrorism': A Study of Media Bias," *Stanford Journal of International Studies*, 12, Spring 1977, pp. 67-78.

Epstein, Edward Jay, *News From Nowhere* (New York: Vintage, 1973).

Extra!, The newsletter of FAIR, July/August 1988.

Falk, Richard, *Revolutionaries and Functionaries: The Dual Faces of Terrorism* (New York: E. P. Dutton, 1988).

Farnen, Russell F. "Terrorism and the Mass Media: A Systemic Analysis of a Symbiotic Process," *Terrorism*, Vol. 13, pp. 99-143.

Fishman, Mark, *Manufacturing the News* (Austin: University of Texas Press, 1980).

Fialka, John J., *Hotel Warriors: Covering the Gulf War* (Baltimore: Published by the Woodrow Wilson Center Press, distributed by the Johns Hopkins University Press, 1991).

Fussell, Paul, *Wartime: Understanding and Behavior in the Second World War* (Oxford: Oxford University Press, 1989).

Gallup Report, The (Princeton, N.J.: Annual reports 1981-1988).

Gans, Herbert, *Deciding Whats News: A Case Study of CBS Evening News, NBC Nightly News, Newsweek and Time* (New York: Vintage 1979).

Garbus, Martin, *Traitors and Heroes: A Lawyer's Memoir* (New York: Atheneum, 1987).

Gaventa, John, *Power and Powerlessness: Quiescence and Rebellion in an Appalachian Valley* (Urbana: University of Illinous Press, 1980).

Gerbner, George, *Symbolic Functions of Violence and Terror* (Boston: Terrorism and the News Media Research Project, Emerson College, July 1988).

Gitlin, Todd, *The Whole World is Watching: the Making and Unmaking of the New Left* (Berkeley: University of California Press, 1980).

Goldstein, Carl, "Drags to Riches,"*Far Eastern Economic Review*, March 29, 1990, p. 62-63.

Goose, Stephen D., "Low-Intensity Warfare: The Warriors and Their Weapons" in *Low Intensity Warfare: Counterinsurgency, Proinsurgency, and Antiterrorism in the Eighties*, Michael T. Klare and Peter Kornbluh, eds. (New York: Pantheon Books, 1988).

Grosscup, Beau, *The Explosion of Terrorism* (Far Hills, N.J.: New Horizons Press, 1987).

Hallin, Danial, *The Uncensored War: the Media in Vietnam* (Berkley: University of California Press, 1989).

Halloran. J. D., "Mass Communication: Symptom or Cause of Violence?," *International Social Science Journal*, 30, Fall 1978, pp. 816-833.

Halperin, Morton H., Jerry J. Berman, Robert L. Borosage, and Christine M. Marwick, *The Lawless State: The Crimes of the U.S. Intelligence Agencies* (New York: Penguin Books, 1977).

Hammel, Eric, *The Root: The Marines in Beirut, August 1982-February 1984* (San Diego: Harcourt Brace Jovanovich, Publishers, 1985).

Heatherly, Charles L., ed., *Mandate for Leadership: Policy Management in a Conservative Administration* (Washington, D.C.: Heritage Foundation, 1981).

Herman, Edward S., *The Real Terror Network: Terrorism in Fact and Propaganda* (Boston: South End Press, 1982).

———, "Diversity in the News: 'Marginalizing' the Opposition," *Journal of Communication*, Summer 1985, pp. 135 - 146.

———, "Gatekeeper versus Propaganda Models: A Critical American Perspective" in *Communicating Politics: Mass Communication and the Political Process*, Peter Golding, Graham Murdock, and Philip Schlesinger, eds. (New York: Holmes & Meier, 1986).

Herman, Edward S. and Noam Chomsky, *Manufacturing Consent: The Political Economy of the Mass Media* (New York: Pantheon Books, 1988).

Hertsgaard, Mark, *On Bended Knee: The Press and the Reagan Presidency* (New York: Farrar Straus Giroux, 1988).

Hofstadter, Richard, *The Paranoid Style in American Politics and Other Essays* (London: Cape, 1966).

Holsti, Ole R., *Content Analysis for the Social Sciences and the Humanities* (Reading, Mass.: Addison-Wesley, 1969).

Hoyt, Mike, "The Mozote Massacre: It Was the Reporter's Word Against the Government's," *Columbia Journalism Review*, January/February, 1993, pp. 31-34.

Iyengar, Shanto and Donald R. Kinder, *News That Matters: Television and American Opinion* (Chicago: University of Chicago, 1987).

Jenkins, Brian M., *International Terrorism - A New Mode of Conflict* (Los Angeles: Cresent, 1975).

———, "International Terrorism: Trends and Potentialities," *Journal of International Affairs*, Vol 1, No. 1, 1978.

———, *The Study of Terrorism: Definitional Problems*, RAND P-6563 (Santa Monica, CA.: RAND Corporation, 1980).

———, "The Study of Terrorism: Definitional Problems" in *Behavioral and Quantitative Perspectives on Terrorism*, Yonah Alexander and John M. Gleason, eds. (New York: Pergamon Press, 1981).

Keen, Sam, *Faces of the Enemy: Reflections of the Hostile Imagination* (San Francisco: Harper & Row, 1986).

Kelly, Michael J. and Thomas H. Mitchell, "Transnational Terrorism and the Western Elite Press," *Political Communication and Persuasion*, 1:3, 1981, pp. 269-296.

Klare, Peter and Peter Kornbluh, eds., *Low Intensity Warfare: Counterinsurgency, Proinsurgency, and Antiterrorism in the Eighties* (New York: Pantheon Books, 1988).

———, "War in the Shadows: Myth of the 'Low-Intensity Conflict'," *The Seattle Times*, March 20, 1988.

Krattenmaker and Powe, "Television Violence: First Amendment Principles and Social Science Theory," *Virginia Law Review* 64 <1978>, p. 1123-1134).

Kuhn, Thomas, *The Structure of Scientific Revolutions* (Chicago: University of Chicago Press, 1962).

Lakos, Amos, *International Terrorism: A Bibliography* (Boulder: Westview Press, 1986).

LaFeber, Walter, *Inevitable Revolutions: The United States in Central America* (New York: W.W. Norton & Co., 1984).

Lang, Gladys Engel and Kurt Lang, "Some Persistent Questions on Collective Violence and the News Media," *Journal of Social Issues*, 28, 1972, pp. 93-110.

Larson, James F., *Television's Window on the World: International Affairs Coverage on the U.S. Networks* (Norwood, New Jersey: Ablex Publishing Corporation, 1984).

Laqueur, Walter, *Terrorism* (Boston-Toronto: Little, Brown and Company, 1977).

———, "Reflections on Terrorism," *Foreign Affairs*, Fall 1986, pp. 86-100.

Lazarsfeld, Paul. and R. K. Merton,"Mass Communication, Popular Taste and Organized Social Action." In Lyman Bryson <ed.> *The Communication of Ideas*, l948, p. 95-118.

Lernoux, Penny, *Cry of the People* (New York: Doubleday, 1980). Lichter, Robert S. and Stanley Rothman, "Media and Business Elites," *Public Opinion*, October-November 1981.

Lichter, Linda, Robert S. Lichter, and Stanley Rothman, "The Once and Future Journalists," *Washington Journalism Review*, December 1982.

Livingstone, Neil C., "Mastering the Low Frontier of Conflict," *Defense and Foreign Affairs*, December 1984, pp. 9-11.

———, "Fighting Terrorism and 'Dirty Little Wars'," *Air University Review*, March/April 1984, pp. 4-16.

———, *The Cult of Counterterrorism: The 'Weird World' of Spooks, Counterterrorists, Adventurers, and the Not-Quite Professionals* (Lexington, Mass.: Lexington Books, 1990).

Lippmann, Walter, *Public Opinion* (New York: Free Press, 1949).

Lobe, Jim and Anne Manuel, *Police Aid and Political Will: U.S. Policy in El salvador and Honduras (1962-1987)* (Washington: Washington Office on Latin America, 1987).

Lodge, Juliet, ed., *Terrorism: A Challenge to the State* (New York: St. Martins Press, 1981).

Long, David E., *The Anatomy of Terrorism* (New York: Maxwell Macmillian International, 1990).

Lukes, Steven, *Power: A Radical View* (Macmillian, London, 1974).

———, ed., *Power: Readings in Social and Political Theory* (New York: New York University Press, 1986).

Maltese, John Anthony, *Spin Control: The White House Office of Communications and the Management of Presidential News* (Chapel Hill: The University of North Carolina Press, 1992).

Manheim, Jarol B., *All of the People All of the Time: Strategic Communication and American Politics* (Armonk, New York: M.E. Sharpe, Inc., 1991).

———, *The Evolution of Influence: Strategic Public Diplomacy and American Foreign Policy* (tentative title) (New York: Oxford University Press, forthcoming).

Marighella, Carlos, *Pour La Libe`ration du Bre`sil* (Paris: Editions du Seuil, 1970).

———, *Minimanual of the Urban Guerrilla*, (Chapel Hill, N.C.: Documentary Publications, 1985).

Martin, L. John, "The Media's Role in International Terrorism," *Terrorism*, 8:2, 1985, pp. 127-146.

Massing, Michael, "About-face on El Salvador," *Columbia Journalism Review*, November/December 1983.

———, "When More is Less: Notes on the Globetrotting, Singleminded Crisis Chasers," *Columbia Journalism Review*, July/August, 1989.

May, W. F., "Terrorism as strategy and Ecstasy," *Social Research* 41, 1974, pp. 277-98.

McClinton, Michael, *Instruments of Statecraft: U.S. Guerrilla Warfare, Counterinsurgency, and Counterterrorism, 1940-1990* (New York: Pantheon Books, 1992)

McCombs, Maxwell E. and Donald L. Shaw, "The Agenda-Setting Function of the Press" in *Media Power in Politics*, Doris A. Graber, ed. (Washington, D.C.: Congressional Quarterly Inc., CQ Press, 1984), pp. 63-72.

Miles, Sara, "The Real War: Low-Intensity Conflict in Central America," *NACLA Report*, April/May 1986.

Molotch, Harvey L. and Marilyn Lester, "News as Purposive Behavior," *American Sociological Review* 39, 1974, pp. 101-112.

———, "Accidental News: The Great Oil Spill," *American Journal of Sociology* 81, 1975, pp. 235-60.

Morgan, Richard E., *Domestic Intelligence: Monitoring Dissent in America* (Austin: University of Texas Press, 1980).

Motley, James B., "A Perspective on Low-Intensity Conflict," *Military Review*, January 1985, pp. 2-11.

Nacos, Brigitte, David P. Fan, and John T. Young, "Terrorism and the Print Media: The 1985 TWA Hostage Crisis," *Terrorism*, Vol 12, 1989, pp. 107-115.

Netanyahu, Benjamin, ed., *Terrorism: How the West Can Win* (New York: Farrar, Straus & Giroux, 1986).

Neustadt , Richard E., and Ernest R. May, *Thinking in Time: The Uses of History for Decision Makers.* (New York: The Free Press, 1986).

Newell, Nancy Peabody and Richard S. Newell, *The Struggle for Afghanistan* (Ithaca: Cornell University Press, 1981).

Nieberg, H. L., *Political Violence and Behavioral Process* (New York: St. Martins Press, 1969).

Nixon, Richard M., *The Real War* (New York: Warner Books, 1980).

O'Donnell, Wendy M. and Sarah W. Farnsworth, "Prime Time Hostages: A Case Study of Coverage During Captivity," *Political Communication and Persuasion*, Vol 5, 1988, pp. 237-248.

Oseth, John M., *Regulating U.S. Intelligence Operations: A Study in Definition of the National Interest* (Lexington, Ky.: The University Press of Kentucky, 1985).

O'Sullivan, John, "Media Publicity Causes Terrorism," in *Terrorism*, ed. David L. Bender and Bruno Leone (St. Paul, Minn.: Greenhaven Press, 1986), pp. 68-74.

Paletz, David L. and Robert M. Entman, *Media Power Politics* (Lexington, Mass.: Heath, 1981).

Paletz, David L., Peter A. Fozzard, and John Z. Aynian, "The I.R.A., the Red Brigades, and the F.A.L.N. in the New York Times," *Journal of Communication*, Spring 1982, pp. 162-171.

Parenti, Michael, *Inventing Reality: The Politics of the Mass Media* (New York: St. Martin's Press, 1986).

Parry, Robert and Peter Kornbluh, "Iran-Contra's Untold Story," *Foreign Policy* 72, Fall 1988, pp. 3-30.

Picard, Robert G. and Paul D. Adams, "Characterizations of Acts and Perpetrators of Political Violence in Three Elite U.S. Daily Newspapers," *Political Communication and Persuasion*, Vol. 4, 1987, pp. 1-9.

Prados, John, *President's Secret Wars: CIA and Pentagon Covert Operations From World War II Through Iranscam* (New York: Quill William Morrow, 1986).

Popkins, James, "Running the New 'Improved' FOIA Obstacle Course," *Columbia Journalism Review*, July/August 1989, pp. 45-48.

Ra`anan, Uri, Robert L. Pfaltzgraff, jr., Richard H. Shultz, Ernst Halprin, and Igor Lukes, eds., *Hydra of Carnage: the International Linkages of Terrorism and Other Low-Intensity Operations* (Lexington, Mass.: Lexington Books, 1986).

Rachlin, Allan, *News as Hegemonic Reality: American Political Culture and Framing of News Accounts* (New York: Praeger, 1988).

Rosenblum, Mort, *Coups and Earthquakes: Reporting the World to America* (New York: Harper Colophon Books, 1979).

Said, Edward, *Covering Islam: How the Media and the Experts Determine How We See the Rest of the World* (New York: Pantheon Books, 1981).

Salamon, Lester and Stephan Van Evera, "Fear, Apathy and Discrimination: A Test of Three Explanations of Political Participation," *American Political Science Review*, 67, 1973, pp. 1288-1306.

Schattschneider, E. E., *The Semisoveign People* (Hinsdale, Illinois: The Dryden Press, 1960, 1975 reissue).

Schlatter, Richard, ed. *Hobbes' Thucydides* (New Brunswick, N.J., 1975).

Schlesinger, Philip, Graham Murdock, and Philip Elliot, *Televising 'Terrorism': Political Violence in Popular Culture* (London: Comedia Publishing Group, 1983).

Schmid, Alex P., and Janny F. A. De Graaf, *Insurgent Terrorism and the Western News Media: An Exploratory Analysis with a Dutch Case Study* (Leiden: Center for the Study of Social Conflict, 1980).

———, *Violence as Communication: Insurgent Terrorism and the Western News Media* (Beverly Hills, CA.: Sage, 1982).

Schmid, Alex P., *Political Terrorism: A Research Guide to Concepts, Theories, Data Bases and Literature*, 2nd ed. (Amsterdam: SWIDOC, 1986).

Shultz, Richard, "Conceptualizing Political Terrorism: A Typology," *Journal of International Affairs*, 32, 1979, pp. 7-15.

Sigal, Leon, *Reporters and Officials: the Organization and Politics of News Making* (Lexington, Mass.: Heath, 1973).

Silj, Alessandro, "Case Study II: Italy," in David Carlton and Carlo Schaerf (eds.), *Contemporary Terror: Studies in Sub-state Violence*, (London: MacMillan, 1981).

Stern, Gary, *Center for National Security Studies Report Number 111*, June 1988.

Sterling, Claire, *The Terror Network* (New York: Holt, Rinehart and Winston, 1981).

Steuter, Erin, "Understanding the Media/Terrorism Relationship: An Analysis of Ideology and the News in *Time* Magazine," *Political Communication and Persuasion*, Vol. 7, 1990, pp. 257-278.

Squires, James D. *Read All About It: The Corporate Takeover of America's Newspapers* (New York: Times Books, 1993).

Thornton, T. P., "Terror as a Weapon of Political Agitation" in *Internal War: Problems and Approaches*, Harry Eckstein, ed. (New York: Free Press of Glencoe, 1964).

Timmerman, Kenneth R., *The Death Lobby: How the West Armed Iraq* (Boston: Houghton Mifflin Company, 1991)

Tuchman, Gaye, "Objectivity as Strategic Ritual," *American Journal of Sociology* 77, January 1972, pp. 660-79.

————, *The TV Establishment: Programming for Power and Profit* (Englewood Cliffs, N.J.: Prentice-Hall).

————, *Making News* (New York: The Free Press, 1978).

Underwood, Doug, "When MBAs Rule the Newsroom," *Columbia Journalism Review*, March/April 1988.

United Nations, "Truth Commission Report on El Salvador" (summary), March 15, 1993.

Walzer, Michael, *Just and Unjust Wars: A Moral Argument with Historical Illustrations* (New York: Basic Books, Inc, 1977).

Wallis, Roger and Stanley Baran, *The Known World of Broaccast News: International News and the Electronic Media* (London: Routledge, 1990).

Wardlaw, Grant, *Political Terrorism: Theory, Tactics, and Countermeasures* (New York: Cambridge University Press, 1982).

Weimann, Gabriel, "The Theater of Terror: Effects of Press Coverage," *Journal of Communication*, Winter 1983, pp. 38-45.

Wiener, Jon, "John Lennon Versus the F.B.I.," *The New Republic*, May 2, 1983, pp. 19-23.

Wilkinson, Paul, *Terrorism and the Liberal State* (London: Macmillian, 1977).

Zuckerman, Laurence, "Has Success Spoiled NPR?," *Mother Jones*, June/July 1987, pp. 32-39, 44-45.

Government Publications and Partial List of Documents

Congressional Record, "Daily Report," H 707, March 3, 1988.

Department of Defense Annual Report, Fiscal Year 1988.

FBI Authorization Request for Fiscal Year 1986, Hearings Before the Subcommittee on Civil and Constitutional Rights of the Committee on the Judiciary, House of Representatives, 99th Congress, 1st Session.

Hearings and Final Reports of the Committee on the Judiciary, House of Representatives, 93rd Congress, 2nd Session.

Hearings of the Select Committee on Intelligence, House of Representatives, 94th Congress, 1st Session

Hearings and Final Reports of the Select Committee to Study Governmental Operations with Respect to Intelligence Activities, U.S. Senate, 94th Congress, 1st and 2nd Sessions.

Interim Public Report on the Committee in Solidarity with the People of El Salvador (CISPES), Federal Bureau of Investigation, Criminal Investigative Division, Counterterrorism Section, February 22, 1988.

"International Security Relationships," (p. 87), *Department of Defense Almanac,* September/October, 1987.

National Institute on Drug Abuse Statistics Series: Annual Data, 1987, Series 1, #7.

Patterns of Global Terrorism, (Annual reports, 1982-1991), United States Department of State.

Report to the President by the Commission on CIA Activities within the United States (Washington, D.C.: U.S. Government Printing Office, June 1975).

Report to the Chairman, Subcommittee on Civil and Constitutional Rights, Committee on the Judiciary, House of Representatives. "International Terrorism: FBI Investigates Domestic Activities to Identify Terrorists," (Government Accounting Office, September 1990. GAO-GGD-90-112).

U.S. Army, "U.S. Army Operational Concept for Terrorism Counteraction," TRADOC PAM 525-37, March 19, 1984.

U.S./Air Force, Center for Low-Intensity Conflict (CLIC), Activation Plan, January 29, 1986.

U.S. Army Joint Low-Intensity Conflict Project, Final Report: Vol. I, Analytical Review of Low-Intensity Conflict, and Vol. II, Low-Intensity Conflict Issues and Recommendations, TRADOC, Fort Monroe, Va., August 1, 1986.

Index

About the Book and Author

How terrorism is portrayed by the news media, and thus perceived by the public, is directly linked to government's foreign policy goals. Steven Livingston demonstrates the complex interactions among the press, the public, and political actors in illuminating a policymaking process that relies on image management as one strategy in achieving policy objectives—not just in combating terrorism but also in handling other foreign policy problems.

Steven Livingston is assistant professor of political communication at the National Center for Communication Studies, George Washington University.